SPEAKING
WITH
NATURE

"At this time of global ecological crisis, the Earth is urgently calling to us to be awake and reconnect with her ancient wisdom. *Speaking with Nature* is a beautiful response to that call, helping us to listen to the divine feminine and her ways of knowing, and to the spirit world that is all around us. These stories and practices speak to the real need of the time, relearning how to live in sacred companionship with our magical and mysterious inner and outer Earth."

LLEWELLYN VAUGHAN-LEE, PH.D., SUFI TEACHER AND
COAUTHOR OF *SPIRITUAL ECOLOGY*

"*Speaking with Nature* is potent medicine. Written in collaboration by two deeply wise and intentional women, this book is abundant with practical insights, skill-building, and stories to deepen readers' relationships with themselves (the feminine and the sacred) through nature. I was immediately immersed in its accessible, intimate storytelling style and content and couldn't put it down. Whether you are new to Earth Wisdom or shamanism or an experienced practitioner, this book is sure to delight. I LOVE this book!"

NINA SIMONS, COFOUNDER OF BIONEERS AND EDITOR OF
MOONRISE: THE POWER OF WOMEN LEADING FROM THE HEART

"To talk about the sacred in simple, sincere terms is itself a revolutionary act. What touches me most in this book is the writers' daring. It's their courage at expressing what all of us experience in private, magical moments but often don't dare to repeat to ourselves—let alone anyone else. To discover our own inner nature, and how it's one with the nature outside us, isn't just a sweet and blissful process. It can take us right to the edges of grief or sickness, but that's where the healing lies."

PETER KINGSLEY, AUTHOR OF *REALITY* AND
A STORY WAITING TO PIERCE YOU

"A thoughtful and accessible introduction to Earth-centered spirituality, *Speaking with Nature* starts from the simple act of spending time in nature and follows the spirals of life from that starting point out into the wisdom and wonder of the living cosmos. It's a journey worth taking, and Sandra Ingerman and Llyn Roberts are capable guides."

JOHN MICHAEL GREER, GRAND ARCHDRUID,
ANCIENT ORDER OF DRUIDS IN AMERICA,
AND AUTHOR OF *THE DRUIDRY HANDBOOK*

"Sandra and Llyn provide simple yet profound insights into the sacredness and magic of nature and, in so doing, give us clear guidance as to how we can participate in transforming ourselves, our communities, and the world we live in. Rarely have I felt such resonance with a book."

NICKI SCULLY, AUTHOR OF *POWER ANIMAL MEDITATIONS,*
ALCHEMICAL HEALING, AND *PLANETARY HEALING*

"In *Speaking with Nature,* Sandra and Llyn have given us an opportunity to walk with them through the rain forest and desert as they share their experiences of the beings and environs of Nature, where both inner and outer landscapes are explored. As their stories unfold, an ancient remembrance is awakened. Thank you, Sandra and Llyn, for writing this blessing of a book where we all are invited to come home to ourselves as natural beings."

PAM MONTGOMERY, AUTHOR OF *PLANT SPIRIT MEDICINE*

SPEAKING
WITH
NATURE

Awakening to the
Deep Wisdom of the Earth

SANDRA INGERMAN AND LLYN ROBERTS

Illustrations by Susan Cohen Thompson

Bear & Company
Rochester, Vermont • Toronto, Canada

Bear & Company
One Park Street
Rochester, Vermont 05767
www.BearandCompanyBooks.com

Bear & Company is a division of Inner Traditions International

Library of Congress Cataloging-in-Publication Data
Ingerman, Sandra.
  Speaking with nature : awakening to the deep wisdom of the Earth / Sandra
Ingerman and Llyn Roberts ; illustrations by Susan Cohen Thompson.
    pages cm
  ISBN 978-1-59143-190-9 (pbk.) — ISBN 978-1-59143-772-7 (e-book)
  1. Nature—Religious aspects. 2. Shamanism. I. Roberts, Llyn. II. Title.
  BL65.N35I53 2015
  202'.12—dc23

                                                            2014038608

Printed and bound in the United States by McNaughton & Gunn, Inc.

10 9 8 7 6 5 4 3 2

Text design and layout by Virginia Scott Bowman
This book was typeset in Garamond Premier Pro and Legacy Sans with Trajan
Pro, Gill Sans, and Helvetica Neue used as display typefaces
Artwork by Susan Cohen Thompson

To send correspondence to the author of this book, mail a first-class letter to the
author c/o Inner Traditions • Bear & Company, One Park Street, Rochester, VT
05767, and we will forward the communication, or contact the authors directly at
www.sandraingerman.com and **www.llynroberts.com**.

To all beings in the web of life. May all living beings be loved, honored, and respected.

To all who work together to dream into being a planet filled with love, peace, harmony, equality, abundance, honor, and respect for all.

To the Earth, which is our home, and to earth, air, water, and the sun for giving us all that sustains life.

CONTENTS

INTRODUCTION

In Search of the Wild Deep Feminine

Llyn Roberts

In the spring of 2010 I did a vision quest in eastern Washington state with two wonderful guides, Anne Hayden and Sheila Belanger. I wrote about some of my experiences on that journey in my book, *Shapeshifting into Higher Consciousness* (Moon Books, 2011).

Anyone who's done a vision quest knows the strong call that's put out to spirit and nature and that they respond with insights, visions, and sometimes magical manifestations. After the quest comes the challenge of honoring these gifts, which often means that life has to change.

As I wrote in *Shapeshifting into Higher Consciousness,* a miraculous phenomenon occurred on the solo part of my vision quest when I camped alone for three days in a canyon.

I remember repeatedly uttering, "Life will never be the same." I had no idea at the time how accurate that statement would prove to be.

Within weeks of my vision quest, I took a bad fall and, by the end of 2010, had lost the vision in my right eye. On January 5, 2011, I learned that my optic nerve had been damaged; a blood mass pressed against it.

1

Becoming half-blind seemingly overnight, I saw everything different-ly. All that had been familiar suddenly appeared foreign.

I began having vivid dreams in which the recurring theme was the color turquoise. The color showed up on mundane articles, such as jackets, sweaters, and cars, as well as pools of turquoise water, tur-quoise blankets and shawls, and more. My dreams featured these items in diverse shades of turquoise—some rich, dark hues and others lighter, more aquamarine.

Each dream ended with my staring at the turquoise article, which then faded from my awareness so that only the color remained. Then I would gaze intently at the turquoise color for what seemed forever. That would be the last I remembered of each dream.

I puzzled to make sense of this. When I was a child, sky blue and turquoise had always been my favorite colors, yet dreaming a color over and over was new and perplexing. I felt haunted. Something was trying to get my attention.

During this searching time I asked Mick Dodge, a friend on Whidbey Island, Washington, where I lived, to take me to the Olympic Peninsula for a few days' retreat in the wet, wild lands of the Hoh Rain Forest.

Mick was an unusual man with more earth wisdom than many I've met, despite my years of study with indigenous shamanic cultures. Born in the Hoh at the hands of midwives, Mick's adventures include having lived for extended periods in the wilderness.

The Hoh, indigenous home of tribal people who carry the same name, is the largest temperate rain forest in the world, located in the far northwest corner of the United States. The name Hoh, means "white water," or "fast moving water."

Just a few years prior to this time, when I still lived in the Northeast, I had never heard of the Olympic Peninsula or its mountains, the Hoh River Valley or its rain forest. I, like many, didn't even know the United States had a rain forest.

Now, standing by the pristine glacial waters of the Hoh River, it was as if my dreams played out in front of me. In the water swirled and eddied beautiful shades of color—the turquoise of my nocturnal visions. These lands and waters were calling to me.

One year to the day after learning about my optic nerve, on January 5, 2012, I left behind the life I knew to move to the Hoh Rain Forest with Mick Dodge as my escort.

I didn't plan to escape to the forest with a wild man or to live as a hermit. Such behavior doesn't solve the world's problems or stop the violence that escalates in our streets. Yet we each have a unique purpose, a path we are called to follow. Mick Dodge made it possible for me to live reclusively in the Hoh, to take on the forest name Cedar, to muse deeply with the Earth, and to write about it.

During the first days at my cabin on a private strip of land bordering state and national forests, I had a dream about Sandra Ingerman. In my dream Sandra and I worked happily together on a project. The dream was so pleasant and real that when I awoke from this dream I decided to ask Sandra if she'd like to write a book with me.

Speaking with Nature absorbed me the entire time I lived in the Hoh. The land had called me there seemingly for this purpose. My own part was to muse with the nature beings of the rain forest—a miraculous gift, yet while I was communing with the Earth, I was also able to be a bridge between Mick Dodge and prime-time television, facilitating his series on the National Geographic channel titled, *The Legend of Mick Dodge.*

The Hoh definitely had an agenda. I believe these waters, lands, and nature beings called in the events and people that would help it to be seen, perhaps simply for us to remember, love, and preserve it and all natural places.

I never doubted that the Earth is conscious and my time in the Hoh confirmed it. Those who are open to hearing nature's call can participate in an amazing unfolding—exciting, reassuring, and also humbling. The magic of the wild and the rhythms of nature lead us back to the intelligence and mystery of life. As in ancient indigenous and matriarchal cultures that recognized the mystery and deep feminine nature of the Earth, we are reminded to hold both women and the Earth as sacred.

Despite all we may do these days to reconnect with nature—and with the creative feminine force—we can still feel separate from the deep feminine power of the Earth, which also resides within us. This book offers ways to bridge these gaps and open to our instinctual nature.

The feminine principle is known by many names. She is associated with dreaming and the unconscious and with darkness, the Earth, and its plants and animals. The sacred feminine embodies spirit and mystery. She connects us with power, fertility, and sensuality; with water as well as solitude; with incubation, death, and death's partner—rebirth. Reviver of the dead, nurturer of life and the inner worlds of feeling, sensing, and intuiting, the deep feminine is an alchemical muse.

Sandra and I write in a personal way about the nature beings that have called to us. We share inspired stories of the lands, skies, and waters where we each live, as we also explore the physical traits, habits, and habitats of these and other earthly creatures through the lens of the feminine. Our intent is to open you, the reader, to powerful lessons about living life with grace.

Goddesses from cultures as diverse as the Amazon Rain Forest and Egypt are interwoven within these chapters. Reading this book will open you to their spirit medicine and subtle messages, as well as those of plants, animals, and elements. It offers practices and journeys that can be used at home or anywhere to access feminine qualities of these goddesses and of nature in everyday life—to deepen the power within.

Sandra and I invite you to experience this directly for yourself in the natural world of your own bioregion, whether that's a backyard, a city park, or wilderness. The creative feminine force comes alive through personal experience. These musings encourage a deep sense of belonging with nature and respect for all life, the calling card of the divine woman. Though easy to overlook in modern societies that focus so much on the individual, intimacy with the Earth helps us see ourselves with fresh eyes and relate to our natural environment with more compassion and awareness.

Ultimately it's difficult to separate "feminine" from "masculine" aspects of life; they are all part of the whole. In the same vein the "light" or divine aspects of the feminine, such as beauty and universal love, hold equal value to the instinctual nature in each of us, which includes "shadow" aspects of the human psyche and of nature.

In taking a feminine approach to the writing itself, Sandra and I allowed our understanding of the plants, animals, and landscapes we wrote about to evolve as they spoke to us. We did not make solid interpretations, instead allowing their stories to unfold. We invite you, the reader, to personally explore the land, waters, and nature beings where you live.

The more we tap into the deep wisdom of the Earth and open our hearts to nature's mystery and the life all around us, the healthier our planet and we will be.

As we have written this book intuitively, Sandra and I encourage you to consider the same approach in your reading. For instance, this may not be a book to read cover to cover. You may prefer to scan the chapter headings or simply open the book at random and see what nature being and teachings appear and where they take you. Allowing the living presence of the beings in this book to engage you is likely to enliven the relationship between you and the nature beings in the area where you live. Serendipity will occur.

Shamans the world over teach about mythical and spiritual worlds that parallel the material world. The dreams and "invisible" realities of shamanism are an aspect of the feminine. As you read these essays, we hope you feel encouraged to honor your dreams and intuition, as well as other unseen, subtle, and even forgotten, suppressed, and undervalued ways of being that the feminine often represents.

Dreams have always been a guiding force in my life. My move to the Hoh Valley was precipitated by dreams that became invaluable tracking signs when the idea arose to move to the dark, untamed side of the Hoh River, where local legends say women never last more than two months. If not for my turquoise dreams and the guidance of Mick Dodge, who appeared in my dreams years before we ever met, I would not have had the courage to move to the Hoh. If not for my dream about Sandra, she and I would not have mused and written for two years about the nature beings in our diverse locales.

Many of us are afraid to follow the mysterious trail of our dreams, or we dismiss them, thinking they are just fantasy.

And there are also times we make the error of thinking our dreams are ours alone.

Nature and the Earth are conscious; they speak to us now through our dreams, intuition, and deep longings, along with auspicious happenstance. For those who are willing to participate, nature invites hunches, experiences, and circumstances that will guide us. We don't have to move to the wilderness to do this. The power and intelligence of the Earth is all around and within us, always accessible.

As you engage these writings, allow them to open you to the feminine power of nature where you live. You will learn more about yourself and be inspired to live in greater harmony with the forces all around you.

It's time to heal ourselves as we also transform our relationship with the Earth. Nature is calling us home.

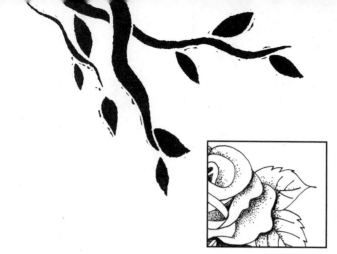

Cultivating a Fertile Inner Landscape

Sandra Ingerman

I was delighted and intrigued when Llyn Roberts invited me to cowrite on the divine feminine, and we had many rich discussions about how we could create a book that would be unique and meaningful to readers. One of the key aspects in bringing back the wisdom of the feminine is reconnecting with nature and with the Earth, which is our home. Since Llyn and I lived in very different kinds of places, we were excited to explore our commonality.

There are trees in Santa Fe and plenty of plant life, but all of nature has to be quite hardy to adapt to the extreme climate of the land, and this is very different from the verdant forest where Llyn was living.

Nature, too, contains many contrasts; among them, both masculine and feminine aspects. Perceiving a need for more balance in the world, we both chose to focus on the feminine aspects, to tell stories of the beauty and power of the feminine. At the same time, we acknowledge the divine masculine that is part of all of nature.

The divine feminine embraces us, holds us in love and support, and teaches us about the power of compassion. The divine feminine also cuts through illusions to where we need to release and surrender. We are part of this great Earth and part of all the cycles of change that go along with being creatures of nature. Many of us have disconnected from nature's cycles and rhythms, but our health and well-being demand that we remember we are one with nature and that we live from that connection.

Much of the physical and emotional illness we experience today comes from being "out of sync" with nature's rhythms. There are a wealth of stories of people regaining their health by simply spending time in nature and reconnecting with the Earth.

At the same time, the environmental challenges we are experiencing are a result of our disconnection from the importance of treating our sustaining Earth with honor and respect.

In indigenous cultures it is understood that everything that exists is alive and has a spirit; that we are joined with the Earth and all of life via our spiritual interconnectedness. We have the capacity to tap into our spiritual nature and communicate with "the spirit that lives in all things" in nature—the land and sea mammals, birds, fish, invertebrates, reptiles, insects, plants, trees, fungi, moss, algae, rocks, crystals, microorganisms, and so on. When referring to the spirit that lives within each aspect of nature, Llyn and I call these aspects "nature beings."

We can also communicate with the elements: earth, air, water, and fire. The elements give and sustain life and need to be honored and respected.

Our process in writing this book was quite interesting. We live in very different places and decided we'd each write essays on nature beings in our local ecosystems. Once we began the process, the nature beings started speaking strongly to both of us, and we moved with the intelligence of the sacred feminine and began writing our essays as we each felt inspired. In a nonlinear, spiraling fashion that reflects cycles and growth in nature, we then began weaving tales and teachings together. This is the style of traditional shamanic cultures, in which stories penetrate deeply beyond the mind in a larger story that connects all life.

All the qualities we write about of the different nature beings are

also contained within all of life; you cannot separate them from the life force. In our stories about nature, we focus on the qualities of the feminine that are part of all life, hoping to invoke your imagination and passion to start your own exploration of the divine feminine and nature as a doorway into life's mysteries and truths.

In my essays there are times I use the plural "we," thus including you, the reader, as part of a global community. Working in community is an aspect of the divine feminine. Moving away from a hierarchical structure to work together as a community allows us to grow and evolve on personal levels and also be in service to all of life. In embracing our unique gifts, talents, and strengths, we become positive change makers.

Although I grew up in Brooklyn, in an urban environment, I always had a deep appreciation of nature. I loved the trees and sang to them each day. I was in awe of the night sky and sang to the moon. As a teenager I walked miles to the ocean and watched as the sun went down and the moon rose. Sometimes I sat on the beach all night just to see the beauty of the rising sun at dawn.

In turn, nature does recognize and see us. I learned this in my thirties, when I was flying from Albuquerque to teach a workshop in Milwaukee. I had a window seat with a beautiful view of the full moon, and as I drifted into a peaceful state, I heard the moon say to me: "Do you remember when you sang to me as I child? I do!"

That special message reminded me that nature is aware of how we honor and respect all that is alive. We all live on this great Earth supported by the same elements of earth, air, water, and the sun, nature beings that share the environment with us.

Nature is intelligent and is a helping spirit that holds the blueprint for all of us for how to live a healthy life. When we awaken from our ordinary state of consciousness, we experience the divine life force that is unseen by our ordinary eyes. A deeper connection with nature is healing, returning passion and enthusiasm for life and taking us back to the magic we knew as kids.

As Llyn and I wrote our essays, memories surfaced of special times in nature. We hope our stories will help you to recall and reflect on your own special memories of your connection with the natural world and inspire you to deepen that connection.

At the end of each essay, you'll find a variety of practices to assist you in creating a deep relationship with the nature beings wherever you live, whether it is an urban or rural environment.

Many of these exercises were inspired by the practice of shamanism, which has been my life and my work since 1980. Shamanism is an ancient universal practice that dates back more than 100,000 years. One of its core teachings is the web of life that connects all living beings. Unless we connect back to this web of life, we experience separation, which creates much of the emotional and physical illness we are seeing today.

Traditional shamanic cultures taught people how to live with honor, respect, and gratitude for nature and for life itself, in harmony with the natural world. All community members were supported in developing and sharing their strengths, talents, and creative gifts that would contribute to the health of the community.

My passion in teaching shamanism has been to help people remember the creative power they were born with, reestablish their connections with the natural world, and honor and respect that which gives us life. I teach them how to create a life filled with meaning and passion and return to the state of awe and wonder we experienced as children. The practice of shamanism teaches that the world we live in is a dream and we must be the dreamers of a good world for all of life, not only for ourselves, but for our descendants. It teaches that everything in our visible world manifested from a word or a thought that was born from our invisible and inner world. Thus, true joy, health, and abundance comes from having a rich inner world and cultivating a fertile inner landscape. As we develop a rich inner landscape, we experience a state of inner peace and are not so thrown off center by all the changes that occur in the outer world. Life is filled with change, and our sense of inner peace cannot be dependent on every change that occurs in the outer world. We must learn how to cooperate with the changes that are part of life and maintain a sense of permanence and deep peace no matter what is happening in our lives.

The practice of shamanism teaches that there is a deeper reality to our visible and tangible world. In those hidden realms are helping spirits who have deep compassion and love for us as we grow, evolve, and navigate our way through life. The helping spirits might appear in the form of an animal, a plant, a tree, or even an insect. There are also mythological beings, the spirit of the elements, and Hidden Folk—nature beings we can't see with the naked eye—that might guide us. As we learn how to move into heightened states of awareness, we can speak to the spirit that lives in all things—even the seemingly inanimate ones, such as rocks and crystals—and to all the nature spirits we have grown to love. There are also helping spirits who appear to us as teachers in human form who might appear as a god or goddess, an ancestral helping spirit, or a legendary figure.

Shamans perform what is called a "shamanic journey" to enter the hidden realms of what some cultures refer to as "the Other World" or "the Dreamtime." There are, however, many ways to travel into the hidden and invisible realms and access the spirits who provide healing and deep spiritual guidance. Nature is one doorway into these realms.

HOW TO
USE THIS BOOK

Spending time in nature will be your doorway into the seen and unseen realms where you can communicate with the nature beings in your surroundings. The exercises we suggest will guide you to a deeper appreciation for the lands, waters, animals, birds, and other beings you live with and in making contact with the helping spirits in nature.

In some instances we will suggest you listen to a drumming track or an audio track that features other shamanic instruments. This shamanic music will put you into a deep meditative state and allow you to let go of life's ordinary thoughts and distractions that prevent you from exploring the hidden realms of nature. For these practices you can also listen to music you find to be uplifting and spiritually expanding. It's best not to use music that includes words, because words might distract from the intention of the exercises. Suggestions for drumming CDs and shamanic music are provided in the About the Authors and Illustrator and Their Work section at the back of the book.

If you have a drum or rattle, you may enjoy drumming or rattling while performing some of the exercises. This will help you to step away from any mind chatter so that you can increase your concentration, find your energetic center, and focus fully on the spiritual practice. You can make a rattle by placing into a container, such as a small glass bottle, pebbles, corn, or seeds. Or you can find two sticks in nature and click them together to provide percussion.

Most important is spending time outside in nature. If you live in a city, find a park where you can walk, observe, feel, and listen to the natural world. At times you may simply lie on the bare ground. Lying on the earth and connecting your heartbeat with the heartbeat of the Earth, as well as moving your body in ways that mimic nature's movements and walking barefoot, when you can, will reestablish a sense of peace, joy, and harmony within you.

When you walk in nature and speak to the spirit of the elements and to other nature beings, the true wisdom comes through a transmission that is beyond rational understanding. This energetic transmission touches a knowing you were born with, of oneness with the Earth, which acts as fertilizer for your growth.

There is no "right" way to perform the practices in this book. We truly mean to inspire you to find your unique ways to reconnect with the natural world and the intelligence of nature.

Shamanism is a practice of direct revelation, which means you have the ability to work directly with the spirit of the Earth and nature beings. As you learn how to enliven your outer and inner senses of sight, hearing, smell, touch, and taste, you will be amazed by how much nature has to share with you. This depth of connection will teach you how to communicate with and respect other life forms that share our Earth and show you how to improve your quality of life. As you open your heart and body to the Earth, intuition naturally unfolds. Over time you will see your own reflection in all of nature.

While writing *Speaking with Nature*, Llyn lived in the Hoh Rain Forest in Washington State, which receives twelve to fourteen feet of rain annually—a lush and rich green plant paradise that is abundant with flowing waters. Sandra lived in the Sangre de Cristo Mountains of Sante Fe, New Mexico, at 7,000 feet in the high desert—a land that experiences times of extreme drought, very cold temperatures in winter, extreme heat in summer, and high winds for much of the year. Just as we found corresponding connections in our own environments, we will lead you into meeting the spirit of the land where you live so you can deepen your connection with the land and gain a better understanding of how to improve the quality of your life.

Sometimes we complemented each other by writing about the same nature being, and at others we wrote about aspects of the landscape that differed. For example, in one chapter Llyn wrote on Glacial Silt and Sandra wrote on Sand.

The animals, too, are different in different environments. In one chapter Llyn wrote on Elk and Sandra wrote on Snake, both of us following our inner guidance.

As you proceed with the material, you might find yourself surprised and, hopefully, delighted to read about the nature beings that called to us. May you be inspired to listen to and honor nature beings that are calling to you where you live, to connect with the elements, and to cultivate your inner garden and a rich inner landscape.

Certain themes embrace a variety of teachings, both the shadow and the light, and there is quite a bit on death, rebirth, and initiation. We share ways of using your creativity to live the life you desire, in harmony with nature. We also explore ways of nurturing yourself, opening to universal love, and meeting your divine self. It is important for all of us to learn how to create and anchor sacred space, as the times in which we live are so filled with change. We share stories that will help you to weave your physical and spiritual life together, supported by the deep wisdom of the Earth.

At the end of the book, you'll find two instructional essays. "How to Work with Omens" teaches how to be observant of omens and signs that appear in nature as you hold the intention of a question or seek guidance. "How to Work with Grief" is designed to support your hurting heart, bruised as it may be from all the death and destruction we witness due to environmental shifts, disasters, and abuse created by unconscious human behavior.

The nature beings we write about reflect the principle of creativity and fertility in the natural world. There is such a depth of ancient wisdom we can embrace and feel as we awaken to the power of nature. But we must go beyond reading and feeding our minds to experiencing with our bodies as well as our inner senses and reconnecting with the power of creation and fertility.

Inhabit the beauty of the seen and unseen worlds of nature. Earth is your home! Nature is speaking to you and calling you home.

1

SNOWY OWL

Snowy Owl

Sandra

As you begin the adventure of this book, close your eyes and take a few long, deep breaths. With each slow exhale leave your ordinary thoughts behind. Allow your imagination to take you to the northern region of the Arctic. You are now in an environment of deep snow and ice. Without the intrusion of power lines, the airwaves are still and silent. There is a deep power in the stillness of Mother Earth.

Look around you and take in the beauty of this snowy terrain. Feel yourself standing on the frozen earth. Although the ground is frozen, the molecules within are in constant movement, as life is always in movement. Take some deep breaths and breathe in the clean, fresh, cold air. Imagine what the air would taste like in your mouth. Feel the air traveling down your throat and into your lungs. Touch the snow and ice with your fingers—feel the coldness and texture. Notice how your heartbeat changes as you connect with the majestic nature of this land. Listen to the silence. Experience a state of wonder as you go farther into a landscape filled with deep mystery.

Notice one of the inhabitants of the Arctic—the Snowy Owl—swooping in for a landing. The powerful presence of the Snowy Owl in nature, or even its image in a photo, is breathtaking.

Delight in the owl's intense beaming yellow eyes and soft, regal feathers. These predominantly white feathers allow Snowy Owl to blend into the frozen landscape of Arctic snow and ice, hidden from both predators and prey.

Fully experience the great beauty and power of Snowy Owl, and when you feel complete take some deep breaths and bring your awareness back into the physical space where you started.

As you will see, Snowy Owl has much to teach us about the feminine and our connection to nature. A nomadic bird, Snowy Owl relocates when the weather changes. In January 2012 rising numbers of Snowy Owls started migrating in mass numbers from the Arctic to many parts of the United States. One leading researcher described the migration as "unbelievable." Another researcher called this the most significant wildlife event in decades.

Owls have been seen in indigenous cultures to be predictive of weather changes, and Snowy Owl is now showing us that as the Earth evolves we, too, must move and flow with the changes.

Snowy Owl blended in with the snow of the Arctic but stands out in contrast in more southerly environments. One message we can interpret from this is that as the Earth changes we need to come out of hiding and be seen. If you found comfort blending in with your surroundings, the goddess energies, the feminine, might now be asking you to stand out and make your strengths known. It is time to share what is bubbling up from deep within you, to show up and be seen and heard.

We can relate the migration of the Snowy Owl to the aspect of the feminine called "Changing Woman" in the Navajo tradition; like the changing seasons, she represents the eternal changes in the cycles

of life. We are one with the Earth, and as part of the Earth, we go through cycles of evolution in our lives and within our bodies.

When we perceive life through the eyes of spirit, versus through our personality and ego, we perceive the beauty and joy in life no matter what the outer circumstances. But when we perceive the world only through the eyes of ego, we can move into a state of suffering and despair. At present the climate is changing to such a degree that mass changes to the Earth are having an impact not just on human life, but on all life. There are changes in the economy, political unrest, and an increase in violence. The weaving of life and the fabric of reality as we know it is unraveling.

Over the years many have been writing about the quickening change in consciousness and evolution. And at the same time, as we embrace the principle of unity and oneness in the web of life, the Earth is also experiencing exponential changes and a death. Death is not an end but rather a transition and rite of passage into something new.

We are all part of a collective dream. As spiritual practitioners we must acknowledge the way the current dream is dissolving and a new consciousness being born that embraces a healthier way of living on the Earth.

Over the years I have taught that when someone is diagnosed with an illness, it is important to perceive her in her divine perfection and light—more than a body and a personality. Who we are beyond the skin is luminous divine light. As we recognize the spiritual nature of a person and see her in her divine light and perfection, we stimulate her inner radiance, which leads to healing. We want to feed the energy of divine perfection that empowers healing rather than feeding the power of the illness. What we give energy to, we give life to. What we feed grows.

Using this same teaching we must focus on perceiving the divine light of the Earth instead of seeing the Earth as toxic and ill. We need to surrender the outcome of the evolutionary process that is in motion. We must cooperate with change rather than resist it.

At the same time it is important to create a path of beauty by envisioning the Earth and all in the web of life embracing such qualities as love, light, balance, harmony, beauty, peace, equality, and abundance. In this way we weave a new strong and vital fabric of reality into being. Holding a vision and dreaming into being the world we wish to live in while surrendering the outcome is a paradox we must learn to dance. You will delve into dreaming practices in the essay on Mushroom.

There is nowhere to escape for safety and comfort except by resting in our spirit and spiritual practices. Our spirit is immortal and is a place within each of us that provides a sense of calm and permanence.

At the same time we must recognize that the Earth is evolving and changing into new landscapes, just as human consciousness is evolving and the landscapes within all of us are changing, too.

Santa Fe is located in the high desert at 7,000 feet, and I live at 7,400 feet. Climate change in the high desert is quite dramatic, and winter and summer storms can create intense changes in the landscape. Witnessing the storms can be frightening but also exhilarating.

My house is on a piece of land where there is a long *arroyo,* or dry riverbed, that can be walked for long distances. It is a favorite place for people to bring their dogs or ride horses. My special treat in this populous area is to walk at midday, when I have the arroyo to myself, and not see a house or person for miles.

When we have major snowstorms or rainfall, it is amazing to watch the changes that occur to the landscape of the arroyo. While I was writing *Speaking with Nature,* we received heavy rain—1.25 inches in less than hour—from a slow-moving thunderstorm. This might not seem like much rain to those living in other parts of the country, but here in the desert it is a major event that causes flash floods. And as the flash floods rage down the arroyo, the landscape changes dramatically.

I have lived on my land for twenty years, and there are times after a storm when I no longer recognize parts of the landscape that have been so familiar to me. It's exciting to take a walk after the rain and see how the arroyo has changed again.

After this particularly heavy rainfall, I had to find new walking paths, as the rain had carved different paths in the sand. The arroyo widened in places and became deep and narrow in others. Bushes had been completely uprooted as the sand beneath them washed away. As I walked I felt such a deep knowing and understanding that the changes to the landscape we live in are a microcosm of what is happening on a planetary level.

The landscape of the Earth is evolving and changing just as it has done throughout time. Land masses have changed over centuries and will continue to do so. There were once land bridges connecting different parts of the Earth where now there is ocean, and water has replaced areas that were once land. Earth changes are in continual motion.

As the Earth keeps changing, we experience a level of destruction that is harsh for the people, animals, and all of life. We watch as homes and lives are lost.

As a collective we must continue to perceive the Earth in her spiritual aspect and divine spiritual light. We must continue to build a strong, beautiful field of spiritual light with all the work we do together. We must learn to perceive, acknowledge, and give gratitude for the beauty and light of life, remembering that with each change new life continues to be born.

Owls live in Santa Fe and often show up in my life as an omen during times of passage and transition. I love owls, and I have come to rely on Owl to acknowledge that I am moving in the right direction.

Many years ago I had a powerful and life-changing teaching that came from Owl. As I traveled around the United States teaching workshops one year, I was surprised and curious when participants gave me gifts that represented Owl. I was gifted with owl statues, owl feathers, and owl fetishes.

Then when I was at home, I received a gift in the mail. I opened the box and it contained an Owl mask.

Obviously the universe was trying to tell me something, so I decided to perform a shamanic journey and ask my trusted guardian spirit why I was getting so many Owl gifts. Why was Owl coming into my life at this time?

My guardian spirit gave me a very interesting response. He told me that Owl not only sees in the dark, but also has a type of radar that I was going to need soon. And then the journey abruptly ended.

Shortly after my journey I was teaching in St. Louis and flew home late Sunday night after the workshop. During the flight all the lights went out in the airplane and the cabin attendants were walking up and down the aisles with flashlights. I was very tired and quite happy in the darkness, as I could close my eyes and drift off to sleep.

Suddenly the captain came on the loudspeaker to announce there was a problem with the electrical system in the airplane. He alerted us that the plane did not have the radar needed to navigate through an approaching thunderstorm. I then remembered the message of my helping spirit, that Owl has a type of radar I would soon need.

We did land safely in Albuquerque, but I was left with teachings that were very important to my growth and evolution. One teaching was that the universe was providing me with help and protection that I would need in the future. In this instance Owl came into my life to act as a guardian spirit for the future event.

There are times when we go through challenging situations and feel very alone, but as we are one with the goddess, Source, and the power of the universe, we are always being supported and protected by the unconditional love from which we were created. We often don't engage our senses deeply enough to notice signs that we are being guided and protected during times of danger.

I also learned that it is important not to give my power away and look to others to interpret my symbols. For example, in descriptions of Owl in most symbology books, radar is not a quality mentioned. I might have missed the life-changing teaching I received during this flight had I looked up the symbology of Owl in a book. I needed to continue to honor my power to receive my own direct revelation.

Are there ways you give your authority away to others? The times we live in demand that we trust our own inner guidance, inner wisdom, and intuition.

Divine radar is guiding the Snowy Owl away from the Arctic so that it might survive and thrive in these changing times. Being connected to the web of life means that we have this same radar guiding us. Snowy Owl encourages us to go within and experience our own internal radar that we may follow the inner knowing of changes we must make in our lives.

The behavior of Snowy Owl can be a model for us. It is a living being that stays centered, silent, and waits patiently for its food. These are important qualities for us to embrace. We must stay centered in the midst of change and learn to stay focused on our vision. By going within the deep inner silence, we access our own inner knowing, which guides us.

And we must be patient. So many of us are impatient and want to see immediate results from our practice. There is a right timing when what we need to know will be revealed. The key is to learn how to trust our intuition. We must disengage from the wealth of outer distractions most of us experience throughout the day and learn how to be still, for all is revealed through the silence.

Birds have an inner sense that tells them when to migrate; they know when the change in seasons is occurring. Similarly, there is a voice within each of us that informs us how to move forward during times of great change. We just need to tune in, listen, and follow our own radar.

We are caretakers of the Earth, a responsibility many of us have neglected. Humans have become very self-absorbed and some have forgotten the preciousness and divine nature of all of life. As we learn to trust our inner wisdom and radar, it is also important to stand strong in community. Community represents the strength of feminine power to create change.

In 2013 flocks of Snowy Owls migrated to New York. No one really knows what led the birds there, but we must trust in the intelligence of nature.

However, the owls were flying near a major airport and could have caused a serious accident if they flew into a plane's engine, so officials made a choice to kill these beautiful creatures to avoid loss of human life.

Public pressure forced an end to the senseless killing of these majestic birds who were following their own flight path, and ways were found to trap and relocate the birds away from the airport.

The feminine teaches us about finding that same collective voice to be caretakers who honor and respect all nature beings. It is time for us to stand out, be seen, and be heard.

🌿 Practices

Nature is intelligent. We are both part of nature and an instrument of nature, so it is important for us to remember how to attune ourselves to our environment.

We can relearn and remember how to feel changes in weather and in the seasons—not just external weather and seasons, but also internal changes in our lives. We are shown signs when it is time to make a change, but often we choose to ignore the inner voice, inner radar, or signs we are being given. We often stay in relationships, jobs, homes, and other life situations when the healthy decision would be to leave.

Spending time in nature teaches us how to read the signs of transition. Nature is our most powerful teacher in this regard. We don't have to look at a calendar to know what the season is, because we can see the changes in wildlife and plant life. We can feel the changes in our bones and smell the change in the air. We can feel a shift in our body as sometimes we feel a need to rest and go inward during certain seasons, whereas other seasons inspire us to be playful, active, and social. We must honor our inner knowing of when to be still or active and when to make changes in our life.

These simple exercises can help you to become more connected to nature:

- 🍃 Take walks in nature. Even in a city there are parks you can visit. The more time you spend in nature, the more you will find yourself aligning with the river of life. In doing this you will feel healthier physically, emotionally, and spiritually.

- 🍃 Take time to walk in silence or sit by a tree or plant that calls to you. Learn how to block out the noise from your mind by taking very deep breaths and imagining yourself traveling within to the core of your being. Feel your roots growing into the earth and your body being fed by the sunlight. Pay attention to what is bubbling up from your deep inner well. Let feelings arise so they can be observed and transformed. Listen to intuitive messages emerging from your inner wisdom.

⟐ As you spend time in nature, notice changes in the animal life you see during different seasons. Do you see different types of birds? Do you hear new bird songs when the seasons change? Observe how the wildlife becomes more active in your area at different times of the year.

⟐ Learn to experience changes in patterns in nature without having to turn to a calendar or the news. Notice the different quality in the fragrance of the air during weather and seasonal changes. Pay attention to the changes in texture, moisture, and fragrance of the soil. You might notice the air tasting different during shifts in the weather and seasons. Watch how the colors of the leaves change on the trees, and observe how the quality of light shifts over the year, and the changing times of sunrise and sunset. Tune in to how your body feels when the seasons change. Notice how one season flows into the next. There is a flow to the cycles and seasons in nature. Awaken from the mass collective trance to live fully in the flow of nature and life.

As you align and attune to the changes and transitions in nature, you will begin to feel these same cycles affecting and changing you. Life is always changing. There are no endings, just transitions leading to new growth and life.

Over time you will become more observant of changes in nature, whether you are in a park or city. As you walk from your car, train, or bus to work or other daily activities, fully open your senses to perceive your ever-changing environment.

We have the same inner radar as migrating birds to assist us in navigating life's transitions with grace and ease. As we learn how to be silent and open all our senses to the signs we are being given, we flow gracefully with the river of life.

Snowy Owl

Llyn

As I read Sandra's opening lines to Snowy Owl, I can smell the crisp Arctic air and envision the barren (to our eyes) tundra terrain of this magnificent bird. I can feel, as if deeply in my bones, the silent flight of Owl.

I had two dreams about Snowy Owl before writing about this nature being. Following these dreams I mused with Owl so intently that I clearly imagined one flying through the forest near my home. I began to speak with this invisible bird that seemed so real to me.

The very next morning an Owl appeared outside my cabin in the Olympic Mountains of the Pacific Northwest. This was the first Owl I had seen since moving to this isolated glacial valley eight months earlier.

The great horned one flew soundlessly out of the woods and settled onto the moss-laden branch of an old-growth maple tree outside my barn. I stood with my bare feet on the earth looking up at the Owl. It was dark under the broad-leafed canopy, and blind as I am in one eye, I was frustrated not to be able to see details of the large bird's body. Squinting didn't help so I decided to sense instead of see it. As I tuned in to the Owl in this way, I had the most exquisite feeling.

This feeling intensified when the bird's head turned clear around on its neck to face me. I could not see its eyes but I felt them. Then, in a soundless flash, expansive wings spread from the tufted body as the bird lifted from the branch and took flight.

After this experience I traveled to an event and returned home to visitors and forgot about Owl. On my second morning back home, I awoke sensing the invisible bird I had mused with following my dreams. Within minutes my forest guide, Mick Dodge, came running into the cabin to say that an Owl was again in the tree. He had neither glimpsed one nor heard an Owl's magical hoot while I was away.

The bird was gone by the time I arrived outside so I went for a walk. Moments down the path, Owl flew out of the forest and alighted on a branch close by me, and a shiver of excitement ran up my spine. The bird and I looked at one another. This time I could clearly see its tufted ears and striped body. My heart opened to this beautiful creature.

That afternoon Owl visited again, flying from tree to tree encircling my visiting colleagues, Marilyn Dexter and DiAnn Baxley, Mick Dodge, and me. We stood together watching the Owl in awe. Each of us spotted the bird for days thereafter and we were awakened by its nightly hoot.

During this time I asked the invisible now-turned-visible Owl, "Dear Owl, why all the dreams and visitations?"

Owl replied the obvious: "I want your attention, of course! I have important things to say!"

Owls of all species have long been symbols of wisdom and the ability to see in the dark. In this regard it is noteworthy that Snowy Owl's yellow eyes are similar in size to a human's eyes. In first spotting the Great Horned Owl, I had to let go of trying to see it with my physical eyes and, instead, soften my gaze and feel it with my heart. Only then did it come into focus.

Owl invites us to open to the feminine principle and seek beyond

words, thoughts, and the linear ways of mind to deeper ways of knowing.

Sandra writes about internal radar. The knowing of the heart—the subtle sense, intuition, or whatever we like to call it—can prepare us for what lies ahead. It can also guide us when we're under duress, such as when change arrives quickly without warning. At such times in my own life, I use a simple mantra that softens my panic and helps me to drop beneath confused thoughts to the creative place of inner knowing: "Relax the mind, touch the earth, and drop into the heart and body."

It is common knowledge now that the human species is at a threshold. Overly rigid rational, linear, materially focused, patriarchal constructs are failing. As the world continues to change all around us, the whisperings of our hearts, the signs we see in daily life, the longings and gut knowing of the body—all related to the sacred feminine—offer guidance we need.

The birds I dreamed about and mused with became as real to me as those I encountered in the physical world. The dreams and the musing appeared to call out to the Owls living in the forest. Or perhaps the Owls of the Hoh Rain Forest called to *me* through the vehicle of my dreams and musing? Or both. Whichever the case, the coinciding of nocturnal and daytime dreaming with Owl sightings demonstrates what indigenous cosmology has been founded on for millennia—that all life is one connected web.

Feminine wisdom ways remind us to consciously engage the web of life by revering the Earth and by recognizing and honoring the signs that show up in our lives, which are reverberations from other aspects of the web.

In addition to tending to signs, some Amazonian tribes upon rising purge what's left in their stomachs from the night before and share their dreams. The messages that appear in dreamtime guide them and shape their daily life dream.

Tending to signs in the environment and in life is second nature among many original and shamanic peoples. Far from the Amazon, in an equally exotic part of the world, indigenous peoples on the Asian steppe display astounding ability using their "moon ears" to decipher the meaning of sounds too faint for most of us to hear. They also read the subtle behaviors of animals as prophecy of what is to come.

Although it may seem the case, this level of enchanted engagement with the world isn't reserved for far-flung lands. Magic is alive and well on our own lands, though largely ignored in modern life, just waiting for us to pierce through illusory veils that cause us to forget life's wonder.

It's time to rediscover wonderment through the eyes of the divine feminine, and the phenomenon of unexplained healings indicates this is happening.

It's not uncommon these days to know of someone whose medical affliction has vanished in a single healing session. I've seen many miracles in my own practice of almost thirty years. Likewise, spontaneous recoveries account for an untold number of allopathic successes. These examples, and discoveries of quantum sciences, confirm what ancient worldviews convey: that our reality is not static, but mutable. The power is here and now.

Just as Great Horned Owls showed up in my backyard, Snowy Owl is showing up in our backyards here in the United States. As Sandra wrote, Snowy Owls migrated south *en masse* at the beginning of 2012. Thousands were spotted across the country. Despite their appetite for tundra lemmings, these dignified Arctic birds are now traveling vast distances from everything that's familiar to hunt other small mammals in lower latitudes.

In our own lives many of us feel we are also reaching beyond everything we know, as we experience major changes in relationship, occupation, health, finances, or in other ways. The personal shifts we undergo seem to reverberate with the global changes we see happening all around us: economic, environmental, and social. Our individual and world terrains—reality as we know it—are being stretched, reshaped, and redefined. Owl's message is that we can find our way through these changes by using our intuition, reading the signs, and cultivating a deep trust in the interconnected web of life.

Owl says, "You must feel your way through these times. Everything you need and seek you will find within yourself."

Owl's eloquent adaptation to change is helped by the fact that it is a comfortably nomadic creature much like our human ancestors, the original people.

There are nomads living in yurts on the Asian steppe today who can pack up everything they own in an hour and be on their way. Few of us can even imagine this. Rich and poor alike, we are steeped in possessions and obligations. Despite this, money and busy-ness have not made us happy because true wealth is found in how we relate to and care for each other and the Earth.

I witnessed a Mayan elder saying that corporations do not hold the power we in the modern world think they do; it is we who wield unshakable power when we align with the Earth. This man lived simply, with little money and few goods, and had been jailed and abused for his allegiance to traditional ways. Despite his troubles he felt happy and rich. The Earth filled this beautiful elder; they shared a bond that could not be shaken.

Similarly, in days of old Tibetan and other spiritual pilgrims lived austerely in caves and traveled by foot on the land. They owned and carried virtually nothing and even relied on patrons to feed them. However, their communion with the Earth brought them and their followers untold rewards from the natural world and mystical realms.

Disregard for nature and contemporary insulated lifestyles cut us off from this natural flow and intelligence of the Earth that barefoot cultures—who also dreamed while lying upon the earth—have known for centuries. Science now confirms that the thousands of sensory nerve receptors in the soles of our feet channel vibrational energy from the earth. Many people claim that opening these connections not only makes us happier, it can heal us. Test this out yourself by walking barefoot, or lying down, upon the earth. Try this when you're feeling out of sorts, such as when you've spent too much time in a shopping mall or on the computer. Commit to thirty minutes of earth contact a day and see how you feel.

The Earth and our own earth-bodies are inseparable. There are spiritual paths that ignore the body and/or view our worldly and earthly human journey merely as a distraction from "higher" states.

In this earthly life there is no Snowy Owl without a nest (this bird is a ground nester), and there is no bird that soars vast distances without a strong body—physical mastery. It is much the same for human beings. We must care for our bodies and also revere our larger nest, the Earth.

Owl's message is that we need to grow strong in our bodies, get sacred and active in our respect for the Earth, and also let her wisdom flow through and guide us. This inspires us to live more simply and with integrity, in accord with all that is shifting now on our planet.

The mass Great White sighting of 2012 that Sandra mentioned is a sign of this shifting. The unprecedented migration reflects changes in our environment, and as Sandra wrote, indigenous cultures have always seen Owls as predictive of weather changes. Native American lore cites the significance of the rare white animals being born during these times, such as white buffalo, but also all white animals. Their color—and unusual migration—tells us we are in the midst of great change.

Why white?

White is related to transcendence, a recurring theme in classical epics. For instance, in the J. R. R. Tolkien trilogy, *The Lord of the Rings,* a grizzly battle unfolds between a wizard, Gandalf the Grey, and a fire demon, the Balrog. Gandalf does finally overcome the fiery monster, and in the process Gandalf the Grey becomes Gandalf the White. He's no longer the wizard he was. In fact, Gandalf's identity is so incinerated by the transformational fires that he barely remembers his name. His higher nature (represented by white) is the sole identity that remains.

We may not be wizards yet we all know what it's like to be forged by life's fire. And similarly to Gandalf's experience, we cannot avoid the heat of change now playing out on the planetary stage. This infiltrates every aspect of the world we know. We *can* use the opportunity to purge mindsets and habits that keep us from living in more wholesome ways. We can retrieve our higher nature.

In an attempt to align with indigenous ways, many healing arts practitioners now use shamanism as a means of fighting bad spirits and warding off dark forces. Some healers smudge and guard incessantly to cast off bad energies. But this fear-based approach is very different from the attitude of powerful people I've worked with in remote parts of the world, where the focus is less on how to protect and more on empowerment and resilience.

Resonant with this the fictional Gandalf the Grey indulges the battle that burns away all but his luminous self. As Gandalf the White he stands radiant, emitting light that casts no shadow. His divine presence is so forceful that enemies naturally fall away.

This perspective is worth considering, as it helps us look at life less dualistically.

Spiritual elders from diverse traditions say we are at a precipice: We can choose to live in more fluid ways, aligned with the Earth and the mystery of life itself, or suffer the consequences. The rare birth of white animals and the unusual migration of Snowy Owls are but signs of a new era yet to fully manifest. The mundane world that we know has never been separate from the divine world we aspire to; now the illusory veils between them are growing thin.

In greeting the fires of change, we invite alchemy and magic. We open to wonderment and to feeling our way through powerful change. The inspired feminine expression calls to each of us.

🌿 Practice

The Great White, or Snowy Owl, invites us to get strong in our bodies and in our care for, and connection with, the Earth. Among its feminine teachings are to follow the signs, trust our inner wisdom and subtle senses, and remember the interconnected web of life.

In addition to what is outlined above, here is a simple practice to help us embrace these deep qualities.

Find a comfortable place to sit or lie down undisturbed. Being in nature is ideal but this can also be done anytime and anywhere.

Take several deep refreshing breaths and relax further with each exhale. Even if you are indoors, feel that you sink into the embrace of Mother Earth with each outbreath.

When you feel relaxed, imagine a meshing of luminous strands, a weaving of sparkling threads of light. Envision or feel this light-weave as clearly as you can. Or simply know this illuminated web is there.

The light web is crafted of pure life force. It links all sentient forms, suffusing and connecting everything material and physical. Life-affirming actions, thoughts, and feelings strengthen our ability to remember this light webbing. At such times we may even sense, see, or feel it. Yet, when we are in a state of separation and fear, we tend to forget this light web. Ultimately the luminous mesh of life force is independent of what we think or do; it is unconditionally always there, never separate from us.

Take time to imagine and feel the light that weaves this living luminous webbing. Drop into your heart and body and make this experience as real as you can. Reach out with your fingertips or palms and feel as if you can gently touch a luminous strand, or several threads of light.

What are the sensations?

Sense that the web reverberates with your touch. As it does the light brightens and glows.

Stay with your experience of this webbing. Again, make it as real as you can. How would you describe the texture or shape? What do you feel?

People often describe the touch of this light fabric as a warm tingling feeling or like the buoyancy you feel in moving your hands and fingers through air or water.

What do you notice?

What do you feel as you gently move your hands through the pulsing web of pure light?

Divine light interconnects and suffuses all life. We are part of this web-work even when we feel angry, lost, or fearful. Our state of mind and emotions do not affect this web-work, yet our state of being can affect whether we will remember and feel our unity with the light. Luminosity is all around and within us, all the time. We just need to open to and remember it.

Feel the loving intention and the indestructible quality of this light—the source from which all life arises and to which all life returns. Bask in power. Feel the goodness.

Take all the time you like.

When you feel complete, take some time to make a gentle transition back to ordinary time and space. As you come fully back, make a silent commitment to remember that this life-web is always with you. Feel it move with you when you walk. Sense it when you go to sleep at night. Know this force is never separate from you, even when you forget about it. Just know this.

And remember to ask the light to help you feel its presence more; invite it to be a conscious part of your everyday life. Open to participating and co-creating with this intelligent and loving force.

2
GLACIAL SILT
AND SAND

Glacial Silt

Llyn

Imagine resting on a large rock at the bank of a surging river. The stone upon which you sit is cold and damp from river spray and mist. A chill bites your fingers and frosty vapors moisten your face. Everything in this verdant pocket whispers "water," including the towering trees that drip with moss and disperse tons of water every day.

As you watch the river flow, tiny vortices materialize in the water, then disappear. Continuously changing tree shadows glide on the river's smooth surface. Its milky sheen continuously morphs from jade to pale aqua. The hazy tint offers a clear indication that glacial peaks feed these fluvial depths.

What you just experienced is part of daily life for me, as I live in a glacial valley in the farthest northwest corner of the United States. The turquoise beauty of the Hoh River drew me to this glacial range rising up from the world's largest temperate rain forest. I learn new things about glaciers, and Silt, every day.

Through thousands of years of slow procession, mountains of ice and snow grind rocky sedimentary layers of earth into clay and fine sand. The heavier fragments settle, but the lighter stone particles either become airborne or travel down the mountain with the glacial melt. Also known as "Glacial Flour," "Rock Flour," or "Stone Dust," the Silt bonds with ice crystals in the frigid waters, giving the river its opaque tint.

I drink glacial waters piped in from an underground spring to my cabin. Not a day passes without my appreciating the nourishing minerals that flow down from the snow-laden peaks.

The world's glaciers are melting faster than they have in centuries. The outpouring from these ice mountains into our waterways has an impact on animal patterns and plant habitat and can initiate climate change. Increased glacial melting warns us to shift how we live on this planet.

Yet nature has its wisdom. Just as drinking mineralized water can benefit human life, scientists tell us that the influx of glacial melt has some cleansing effects for our oceans. Glacial Silt is an amazingly rich restorer of life.

As I reflect on this humble dust ground from stone, I think of the many indigenous groups that use stones in ancient healing rituals. Healers from diverse cultures transmit energy from the earth through stones. In a healing ceremony a shaman may rest stones on the body of his or her client, rub them with vigor against the person's skin, or even click two rocks together in different areas around and near the body. However, it's not necessary to have the stones physically present for people to benefit, as their energy can be felt from a distance. Shamans believe a stone's spirit imbues the person needing healing with strength and power.

Shamans work in different ways. In the Andes shamans pray and make offerings to the spirits of volcanic mountains that loom across

their valley. A shaman may ask a revered rock to help a neighbor get well. Or a healer may "shapeshift" into (embody the energy of) a sacred mountain during a cleansing to transmit its spiritual force to a person who is ill. In this instance the healer may blow through cupped hands into the heart area, then at the forehead, then over the person's crown at the top of the head. The shaman's breath infuses the client with the mountain's positive force.

People who undergo such rituals claim they feel stronger. I have seen many become healed of physical and emotional disease.

Because I drink glacial waters and muse by glacial streams and Rock Flour beds, I am connected with the spirit of these ancient lands and waters. Yet just as the healing force of stones is transmitted through time and space, this softer stone of Silt, which derives from land that's tens of thousands of years old, can benefit us even if we are a world away. We can meditate on Stone Dust for strength, to feel healed by the earth. We can ask the spirit of Glacial Silt and the stones of our own lands for help. We can ask good energy to extend to animals, people, and environments beyond us, just as shamans do with revered rocks and volcanoes.

The particles formed by glacial ice grinding against sedimentary rock are powdery soft, not solid and hard. Unlike the large boulders that water flows over or around, smooth Silt offers no resistance; it surges effortlessly with the river.

This easy flow is a good reminder for us to also stay fluid, to glide with life's currents. But the most intriguing things we learn from Silt are its sacred feminine teachings about power.

Glacial Silt, soft and yielding, has a delicate power, but in glacial pools and rivers, you can't see the fine stone, only a milky tint. Similarly, our strength of spirit may be subtle or concealed.

I witnessed an example of a power that's refined and mysterious like Silt at a recent gathering. During our short time together, one person in the circle dominated the exchange, leaving little room for anyone else to speak. We've all experienced such situations and may also recall times that we ourselves have felt insecure and demanded this kind of attention. In such a situation we lose power, rather than gaining it. But Silt has a quiet power. In this instance a tranquil young woman sat next to the person doing all the talking. I sensed an aura about her; her eyes were warm and wise. When she eventually spoke her words were few, yet they were heartfelt and strong. I later learned I wasn't the only one moved by this woman's gentle manner.

It's probably not difficult to think of someone who is subdued and sincere. This person likely stays out of the limelight and doesn't force personal views. Similarly, Silt stone affirms that power doesn't have to be bold or showy; we can make a large impact without uttering a word.

Once, after sitting with Silt for weeks to learn more about its— and my own—subtle power, Silt spoke to me. It was not the complex teaching I'd been waiting for, but a modest statement:

"I am what I am," said Silt.

"And what is that?" I asked the milky, swirling stone.

Glacial Silt responded, "I am, of course, the physical and spiritual force of stone that flows with water."

I sensed an invitation from Silt to drop the need to be anything but me. I tried to empty myself in the next few minutes and relax.

"Who am I if I completely let go?" I wondered.

The question initially made my mind wild. I was fighting letting go.

I brought my attention back to the river. The swiftly moving water gurgled loudly, and over time the sounds absorbed me. I relaxed and then I knew.

"I am the same. I am the physical and spiritual force of a human—the water I flow with is life."

Energy seemed to rise up through my body in a gentle wave.

"Am I feeling Silt's power?"

I was feeling *my* power.

Just as the reserved girl and the shaman's stones emanate energy, when we rest with who we are, we generate palpable force. Contrary to what many think and teach, we don't have to act in special ways or do, or be, anything but who we really are to attain this.

"Is our power always there?" I asked Silt.

I watched the hazy aqua colors—which I know to be Silt—coalesce in the water and then release in chaotic and unpredictable patterns. Silt's movement was freshly choreographed each moment by the river's ever-changing course. The Glacial Silt was inseparable from the water that swept it along.

Like Silt tossed by the river's currents, we each experience chaos. Every one of us knows times when everything appears inside out or upside down and nothing seems right. At these times we may feel lost, as if we never had intrinsic strength or power. Or we may feel drained of our power, not connected to our subtle spiritual force.

Silt, though indiscernible, is steadfastly one with the water. Just so is our power always there.

There are times when we feel resilient, and then again some of us hide from power. Silt tells us there is nothing to fear in being who we are or in being powerful.

Glacial Silt is a good ally. She helps us nurture quiet fortitude and spiritual strength. She teaches that we can be gentle, soft, and strong—all at the same time.

Whether in the Olympic Mountains of the Pacific Northwest, the Andes, the Alps, or anywhere else on this planet, Glacial Silt is a unique alchemy of land, ice, and water.

The earthy flecks discharged by glacial rubbing are ancient, of an entirely different ecosystem from today's world. Likewise, the pristine waters melt from glacial giants formed close to seventy thousand years ago. The turquoise colors are in the water, not a reflection of the color of the sky.

Once when I was standing by the Hoh River with an old timer born and raised in this area, the wizened man said, "The sky was bluer back then. The glaciers hold that color. It's the blue of a sky from 65,000 years ago that yer lookin' at in these waters."

I remember when I grasped that these waters secretly disperse Silt throughout the entire Hoh River Valley system. The Silt not only flows with meltwater, as I first assumed. Its minerals infiltrate the land, cruising for miles through underground streams and rivers, trickling up delicate root systems, rising up the trunks and branches of trees, and dispersing water into the air through their leaves.

Silt is also spread far and wide through the scat and body remains of animals that consume silt-rich waters and plants and then travel on.

All that live in this valley thrive on the mineral-rich water of Silt.

I saw Glacial Silt for what it is: a delicate, invisible, prolific giver of life. Here in the Hoh Valley in the Olympic Mountains, that life includes the largest elk as well as the largest variety of large trees in the world, such as western red cedar, sitka spruce, and douglas fir.

The feminine wisdom teaching of Glacial Silt is to be who we truly are. It invites a soft, intangible presence that humbly offers a multitude of blessings.

🍂 Practice

We can open to the feminine qualities of Glacial Silt by meditating on it and on the insights shared in the writings above. We can also connect with, and learn from, the gentle, discreet powers of nature where we each live.

For instance, nutrients and minerals are the hidden gentle forces that enrich trees. Root systems, which begin humbly as tender shoots, are the unseen strength supporting trees and gripping the soil so it won't wash away. These elements, combined with the spirit of the tree, manifest a subtle and silent power.

If weather permits, take some quiet time outdoors by your favorite tree on your land, in a nearby park, or in your backyard. If you must stay inside, sit by a window or near an indoor plant or relax and envision a tree.

Sit or lie on the earth by the tree on a natural fiber blanket, or imagine being there. In either case simply be with this nature being.

Let your mind settle. Allow yourself to feel looser and more relaxed with each breath. Invite calm feelings.

When you feel peaceful and centered, tune in to the tree and its surroundings.

Observe everything around you. What natural sounds do you hear? What do you see? What natural scents do you sniff and what sensations arise in your body as you smell these?

What do you notice? What do you feel as you sit or lie by this tree?

Take time to immerse yourself in your senses. Settle fully into each moment.

When you feel ready, look at and appreciate the tree, just as you opened to its environment. Look as this tree as if for the first time.

Take all the time you like recognizing how beautiful this tree is—the trunk and bark, leaves and branches, and its many details.

Next, think on the inner forces that nurture this tree. As you contemplate these, try to sense or feel the tree's hidden power. Detect its gentle invisible force.

How does this feel? How do you recognize it?

Take all the time you like in making the invisible palpable. Close your eyes if it helps to focus. When you clearly sense the tree's subtle hidden force, take a few refreshing breaths.

Now, tune in to the hidden gentle power in yourself.

As nutrients and Silt enrich trees and lands, and as the spirit of the tree radiates from its essence, imagine this same energy within you.

Take time to get to know your own elusive but ever-present force.

What is this like?

As you focus, see if you can detect an inner glow. You may note a warm feeling in your body that rises and radiates out to every part of you, including your hands and feet. Or notice however you experience this subtle spiritual force. Concentrate.

What do you feel? Do you discern a presence in or around you?

What catches your attention?

Take all the time you like. Allow and invite the feelings of your subtle power to grow.

This creative strength is always with you. It is who you are. Yet your invisible power is easier to feel when you slow down and tune in, taking the time to focus on it.

Don't be afraid to open to that fluid, resilient place, drop facades, and be who you are. There is nothing to do and nothing to be. You are the physical and spiritual force of a human. Feel the river of life that flows through you. That gentle potency is you.

Is this familiar? When have you felt it before?

Take all the time you like feeling your own and the tree's soft and strong power. Then thank the tree or plant in whatever words feel right.

If you practice this way regularly, over time the hidden forces of nature and your own spiritual nature will be accessible. It will feel natural. Bring the experience of your subtle power to moments in your daily life, such as when you're in the grocery store, at a business meeting, in a restaurant, or outside walking. Also try to sense it in others; feel it with your spiritual antennae and look for it in their eyes.

Notice when you feel lost to your subtle inner strength. This may be when you feel afraid, sad, angry, or confused. Remember to take some gentle breaths at these times. Let your muscles soften, if only just a bit. Reflect on the subtle strength of Silt to help revive your own strength. Go deeply into those enriching turquoise waters.

If you still can't feel your spiritual power, just be with that. Trust that the force is present amidst the chaos, just as Glacial Silt is inseparable from turbulent waters. To be soft and strong sometimes means we just have to surrender and be with what is. It's humbling to feel out of control—a feeling we all know. Yet Silt reminds us that no matter the turmoil, we never lose our true power; our invincible spirit is there. Just as Silt is invisible—one with the water—nothing can destroy our invisible force. We are that, now and always.

The Silt of mature water mineralizes the land, waters, animals, and us. This watering is the release of ancient consciousness—soil and ice from an entirely different ecosystem.

Likewise we humans are internally rich. If we nurture the tender spiritual strength hidden within, our power will ripen. As we find ways to share that strength, the waters that release now, and the spirits and the Earth, will channel their wisdom through us.

Sand

Sandra

I am transported to the Hoh Forest as I reflect on what Llyn wrote about Glacial Silt. I feel the texture of the Silt as I dip my fingers into the cold river water. I smell the fragrance of the rich and moist earth. I feel my body sitting on the moist earth of the riverbed, and I can feel the coolness traveling to my skin through my jeans. I sink into the earth and into myself in this relaxing, nurturing environment and listen to the comforting sound of the flowing river.

Then my attention and consciousness shift to the Southwest, and the contrast of living in the desert, which is so different from living in the rain forest. As I have already shared in Snowy Owl, my house is situated on a piece of land bordering an arroyo that goes on for miles, where many local residents enjoy jogging and walking.

An arroyo is a dry riverbed. Unlike the cool, moist Glacial Silt of the Hoh River, here the sand is dry and can be dusty. But like silt, Sand is created from crushed rocks. Technically Sand is loose particles of hard, broken rock.

Many years ago a friend gifted me with a fossilized seashell she'd found in the mountains of Santa Fe. In the early Cretaceous Epoch, which started 145 million years ago, parts of New Mexico were

covered by ocean. When you gaze out from any hilltop in Santa Fe today, you can almost envision the land as ocean floor. Eventually, over thousands of years of water flowing and earth lifting, mountains formed where once had been mighty ocean.

As Llyn wrote, there is healing power in stones. There is also healing power in the way that stones are ground by the infinity of time. Rock, Silt, and Sand are great healers and have always been used to cleanse the body not only of dirt, but also of unwanted spiritual energies.

Being a desert dweller I am in awe of the beautiful mountains and rocks that have been carved and sculpted by water and wind over time. The Southwest is known for its stunning natural red rock sculptures. We humans also are carved into who we are by nature, the helping spirits, and universal forces.

In indigenous traditions the spiritual process of being sculpted is considered to be an initiation. Likewise the ego is carved and polished by different life circumstances—or initiations—that reveal our inner light. We experience change, the little deaths of life, and then we are reborn. In each person's lifetime it happens again and again. This is how we mature, grow, and evolve.

We are body, mind, and spirit. When we step away from body and mind, we discover we are luminous beings, not quite as solid as is often taught in our modern Western culture. We are not simply matter and form; we are divine light.

As we go through life we tend to focus on the process of individuation and following social norms. We often forget our spiritual nature and the truth of who we are, but our souls yearn for us to remember. Gradually we suffer loss that wears away at our sense of ego and the belief that we are separate from the Divine. Surviving challenging times ultimately initiates us into a deeper state of oneness.

Thousands of people are drawn to exploring and understanding the teaching of unity consciousness, but before we can experience ourselves as one with all of life, we must drop our attachment to ego and to the state of separation created by the mind. Our souls create situations that insist we allow our sense of separation to be worn away by what life brings for us. We go through a process of surrender to our inner light and our inner knowing; time and experience carve us into beings that allow our true beauty to shine forth.

I have always had a deep relationship with Sand. My nickname is Sandy so I can't help but think of Sand when someone calls my name.

I spent a great deal of time by the ocean before moving to the desert. When I was very young I lived near Coney Island in Brooklyn, and my mother used to take my brother and me to the beach to escape the heat of summer. We sat on the sand under an umbrella and swam in the cool ocean water.

My brother and I built sandcastles for hours at the beach. We used to dig our foundation into the dry sand, then wet the sand just enough to build a castle. I'll always remember the grainy feeling of wetting the sand and molding it in my hand. The final touch was to drench some sand completely and allow it to drip through my fingers, creating decorations on the castle towers. It reminded me of frosting and decorating a cake.

Part of the magic of building sandcastles is to watch as the ocean waves close in on the completed masterpiece, dissolving and dismembering the structure that took so much time and energy to build. There is a certain thrill that comes from watching the ocean melt a sandcastle and wash it back to sea. As each grain of sand fades back into the whole, new waves bring grains of sand back to the beach. The cycle of returning to the eternal and being reborn is repeated again and again.

As a child I did not understand that the ocean was teaching me about the power of change and that all life is impermanent. The ocean teaches that form changes while the essence of form remains eternal. This is the teaching that comes with all of life's initiations.

It is also interesting to observe how children love to be buried in sand. I remember a certain type of indescribable comfort lying in a hole my brother and I dug and being buried in wet, cool sand up to my neck. It felt as if I could lie there for eternity, held in the arms of the Great Mother. Eventually a wave would wash over me, freeing me from the sand and leaving me feeling cleansed and renewed.

In the late 1970s, while studying marine biology at San Francisco State University, I spent most of my time at a beach south of San Francisco studying life in tide pools. I also studied algae and, during the last year of my studies, conducted a research project on hermit crabs. This research and my beach exploration absorbed hours of time each morning. I often got so absorbed in exploring tide pools that I forgot to watch the time or notice that the tide had changed. Many a day I ended up losing my ground when high tide surprised me, and several times I ended up being swept into the ocean, losing all my samples and having to swim back to shore in my winter jacket, clothes, and shoes.

My research project compared an ocean species of hermit crab with a species that lived in the San Mateo mudflats, so each day also brought me to the mudflats. My research partner and I quickly learned the way of the mudflats, as well as an important life lesson.

When walking in mudflats you have to walk quickly and cannot stop. If you stop, you sink into the mud. And I mean really sink into the mud, as you would sink into quicksand. Sometimes only one of us would sink, but there were days where the mud took both of us down, all the way up to our necks. There would be minutes of panic before we regained a sense of the need to move in order to survive and swam out of the mud. We were truly mud women when we emerged—shoes, clothes, hats, coats, and glasses all caked in mud.

This time at the mudflats was during a drought in San Francisco, which meant that all water had been turned off in park restrooms, so we had to drive forty minutes back to San Francisco completely caked in mud. The staff at the marine biology lab got used to our coming in looking like mud monsters and just threw us into the showers, but it took quite a while to get clean.

Walking on wet sand/mud taught me about the power of movement in times of my life when I've felt pulled down by a strong, challenging emotion. Of course there are times in life that require us to be with what is and be still, but there are also times when we are in an initiation process that calls us to keep moving through times of darkness and the unknown. During these times of initiation, we cannot think our way through. Rather it is the strength of our spirit that carries us through.

It is through the movement that we let go of impurities and parts of our personality that don't serve us, so that we can allow in the light of the Divine.

✿ Practice

Take some time to sit in nature. If you live in a city, find a park where you can be undisturbed. Carve out some time in your day when you can relax and sink into the power and beauty of nature.

Find a comfortable place to sit. Take a few deep, cleansing breaths. Feel the earth beneath you. Much of the earth we sit on was rock at some point in time. The ancient quality of the earth reminds us that life is eternal.

Take some deep breaths and smell the fragrance of the earth, trees, and plants around you. Notice the quality of the air and if it is cool or warm, moist or dry.

Look around you and observe how the water and winds of time have carved rock formations where you are. Appreciate their beauty and the power of the elements to carve away what is on the surface so its deep hidden beauty can be revealed. Appreciate how ancient the Earth is.

Take time to reflect on your life. Often we focus on old hurts and don't always allow ourselves to appreciate the fullness of the life cycle of events in our lives. What might have started as a painful experience helped you to grow into a deeper person. What kept you from your intuition and your deep inner wisdom might have been carved away. You have grown into the incredible person you are now. You are different from the person you were before you went through life initiations.

This is evolution. Everything that is alive evolves and grows.

We are sculpted by life just as rock is sculpted by the elements. We embrace the qualities of Silt and Sand that have been ground down through time so that our healing powers and our beauty can glitter with the luminous light that shines through us.

Make a decision to surrender to what life brings for you. Don't be afraid of growth and evolution. The ego fears change, but your soul and spirit will always guide you forward to allow what no longer serves your highest good to literally be ground away from your being.

We cannot operate out of fear and spirit at the same time. We cannot sleep through the initiations that life presents to us. We cannot simply power through with body and mind; we need the strength of spirit.

Feel the excitement of your life adventure in the opportunities life presents to assist you in tapping into your unlimited potential and creative nature.

As an anonymous author has written, "Sand is matter that has been transformed and has almost become liquid and spiritual." Life will transform you in the same way.

3

BLACKBERRY PLANT AND WILD ROSE

Blackberry Plant

Llyn

Close your eyes and imagine the aroma of a freshly baked blackberry pie. Mmmmm. Some cooks let their berry pies cool before serving, but others serve them piping hot right from the oven. How do you enjoy yours? Blackberries also make delicious jam. A lavish spread on a thick slice of buttered grain toast is, to me, a taste of heaven.

I have always been a lover of berries, which grew abundant in the sultry summers of my New England childhood. My own children spent their early years living on a mountain in New Hampshire, so they, too, know the simple joys of picking and eating vine-ripened berries.

Despite its flavorful fruit and the untold medicinal value in its leaves and roots, Blackberry Plant is often seen as a thorny intruder. The dreaded poison ivy I grew up with is seen in the same way, although with a worse reputation because of the bubbly, itchy rash we can get by rubbing our clothes or skin against its oils and no redeeming factor of sweet sustenance.

Regardless of whether we judge a nature being as a benefit or an irritant, nature is intelligent. Prickly boundaries keep unwanted influences out while land restores. "Invasive" Blackberry and poison ivy grow where the ground has been cleared for roadways, trails, and developments. Protector plants root quickly into the land to fix nitrogen in the soil, replenish its nutrients, and prevent the soil from washing away. Blackberry rapidly transforms devastated land into an impenetrable vine forest that offers food, shade, moisture, and safe habitat for birds and small animals.

Applying prickly borders is something we can all understand. Think about a time you may have insulated an ill or elderly friend from outside stressors, stood up to a bully, pulled a frisky dog away from a baby, or demanded solitude to catch up on badly needed rest or finish a creative project.

Protector energies are a feminine expression of fierce nurturance.

In the plant world that explosion of yellow on the border of northwestern highways, known as Scotch broom, is also a protector. European immigrants imbibed an extract of Scotch broom as an herbal remedy and beverage, but it can slow your heart and make your feet and hands go numb if you ingest enough of it.

These potent defenders are the land's immune response to threat. In contrast, the indigenous Blackberry Plants that grow in the remaining virgin forests where I live in the Pacific Northwest are small, low bushes with feathery leaves and soft, tiny thorns. Like their giant foreign cousins, they, too, are sunseekers. Yet, as native Blackberry Plants grow in balanced ecosystems, they seem happy with the plants that surround and grow with them.

No natural area is completely safe from human exploitation, and if we fiercely steward our own lands, protector plants may not take over and try to do the job. We can also take a fresh look at invaders

and weeds when, due to our own action or inaction, resistant plants take over.

An interesting story is of a Washington state couple that cleared a section of rural land. When massive Blackberry thickets resulted, they decided to bulldoze them.

An Earth-revering friend asked them, "Do you ever wonder why we seem to be the only animal that's bothered by the hard thorns and poisons of protector plants?"

This friend pointed out the obvious—that from nature's vantage point, humans are the invaders. He suggested that since they had invited her in, the couple find a way to coexist with Blackberry Plant, rather than bulldozing her.

The people followed their friend's advice and mowed a wide

figure-eight margin through the brambles, making a path through the vine maze that left most of the plant mass intact. The owners routinely snipped any vines that ventured back to the path. In a few seasons the vines stopped growing onto the path. Everyone who walked through the infinity symbol bramble enjoyed it, especially when the berries were ripe. Plants and people appeared content.

The overrun Blackberry Plants reflected to this couple their own impact on nature. In finding a respectful solution, they took responsibility and gained appreciation for the plant's exuberant response to their clear-cutting of the land.

Fresh exchanges like these open new possibilities between people and nature and deepen our sense of belonging with the natural world. Getting close to plants, as this couple and their friends eventually did, opens us to ecstasy.

From my own experience, one evening I entered a dense, prickly Blackberry thicket intending to fill my bowl with late summer berries for breakfast. The plants grew like wildfire alongside a path cut into a hillside near the home where I was staying. Tantalized by one particular fat, dark berry, I leaned far into the bushes, weaving my hand and arm through the prickly maze.

Was it just my imagination, or did Blackberry tease: "Love me or be ready to fight!"

"I love you," I whispered.

The single berry was alluring, as if aching to be plucked. I leaned deeper into the bramble, driven by desire for this black-purple jewel. I moved slowly and softly without fear for the barbs. The vines seemed to relax, some even gently swayed toward me, enveloping me in a loose embrace.

That no thorns caught my clothing or bloodied my skin was a feat. The nature being captured my heart. The Blackberry Plant was beautiful and, as all of nature's creatures are, responsive to the love I radiated.

I had similar interactions with honeybees and rattlesnakes on a vision quest some years earlier. A honeybee visited my altar daily and walked gingerly over each of my bare hands and bare feet on the final day of my quest. Snakes are calmed by singing, and I sang eye to eye for some moments with a rattler that eased its striking pose.

Science supports such experiences: water, plants, and animals display measurable molecular and often observable responses to human intent and sentiment.

What level of relating is possible between humans and nature?

Beyond what science validates, we can all open our hearts to ecstasy and sensibly explore.

Whether native or from other lands, Blackberry is a seductive lot. Her plump, mature berries release at a gentle tug, and the flesh and meat are so tender at this time they practically melt in your mouth. Having to pull at the berry any harder may pluck it off the vine, yet it will not be at peak sweetness. However, in waiting too long the taste turns bitter and the meat, pulpy.

A fierce nurturer and a generous teacher, Blackberry also guides us back to the natural rhythms of the way things grow.

Everything shares the cycles of birth, growth, and fruition—or transformation via death. The Blackberry was revered by the Celts because it taught these three goddess phases: its fruit in its early stage is green, ripening to red, then seasoning to a rich purple-black. So honored were these feminine rhythms that succulent Blackberries were often left as food for the faeries.

I can't help but contrast Blackberry's patience for the way things grow to modern practices that interrupt natural cycles. As a few examples: commercial harvesters collect and stock fruit in our stores before it's ripe; an infant born in the United States has a good chance of arriving on someone else's schedule; ancient trees are still felled despite the centuries that old forests take to grow.

Sensual Blackberries that happily soak in the sun seem to say: "What's the hurry? Slow down! Allow things the proper time they need to grow."

Blackberry Plant gently evolves its fruit from flower to juicy berry, demonstrating how to appreciate nature's pace—whether we are raising a child, writing a book, building an organization, or restoring lands, waters, and forests whose growth cycle extends hundreds and thousands of years beyond our own.

In the temperate rain forest where I live, it's easy to see that cut forests know how to replenish if left on their own. Some forest rhythms appear rapid to me, such as ferns, yellow dock, oxalis, nettles, wild Blackberries, salmonberries, and countless other ground covers that seem to sprout up overnight. Alder trees, which also restore clear-cut land, grow much faster than the spruces that develop through decades and even over centuries.

Each nature being has its cadence. Life thrives in the fertile mystery of rhythm.

Blackberry Plant tells us as much about fruition as it does about growing. Ripe Blackberries practically drop off the vine. On the other hand, berries that cling too long turn sour. Similarly, neither is it healthy for us to try to hold back when we need to change. Just as color and plumpness lure us to sweet berries, life signals to us when we're ready for a new phase.

This message of release is poignant, as the signs are everywhere that "life as we know it" is changing. Humans have birthed wonderful creations, but at a cost of separation from the Earth and Spirit. The challenges we face now, personally and collectively, invite us to bridge these gaps and live in more whole ways.

So many of us feel and confront this push to change. Opening to the wisdom of Blackberry Plant helps us to see that: "The time is ripe. We can trust and let go to a new way of being."

All things natural experience the feminine cycle of birth, fruition, transformation, and death/renewal. In the forest where I live, the dead trees, as well as the single moss-laden limbs of old-growth maple trees that fall to the earth, become food and habitat for other life.

As Blackberries transform in color, they also shapeshift into the birds and small animals that eat them. Then they drop to the soil to seed, finally growing into new Blackberry Plants.

Death is real. Yet, nature makes it challenging to draw a clear line between life and death. Rooted in this blur between what is alive and what is dead are tree beings that witness the passage of hundreds (some, thousands) of years. As I live amidst such ancient trees, I watch the impact these beings have on the humans who come to the forest to meet them. Urban mindsets loose their grip in the face of these giants. Without interruptions from the computer, cell phones, television, and other distractions, people hear the forest sounds. They see amazing sights and smell the sweet scent of decay. Stepping onto the spongy mosses gets them out of their heads and into their bodies. Their desire to be tied to schedules and machines gives way to a craving for deeper living.

Old trees appear almost timeless by human measurement. Trees and plants don't know time in increments. As Blackberry Plant so gracefully suggests, honoring the natural cycles of growth takes us into innate rhythms and thus into life.

🌿 Practice

Blackberry Plant is a profound teacher of the deep feminine: her growth often mirrors human imbalance with nature; she shows up to aggressively protect tender life; and she invites ecstasy with the plant world and encourages us to honor life in all its phases.

To touch the heart of organic rhythms, make friends with the natural world and immerse in nature as often as you can. Drop agendas and schedules; forget linear time, if only for a while.

Listen to all of nature's sounds and smell the earth's scents. Feel the waft of breezes and the caress of plants against your skin. Look with the eyes of your heart at the birth, growth, and death/transformation all around you.

Go deeply into the rhythms of the natural world. Nature's rhythms are your rhythms. As you transition back and move through the normal tasks and activities of modern life, try to remember the innate pulse that runs through life and transcends artificial rhythms.

We live in a relative and contradictory world. We go to work, care for our family and friends, and manage ordinary details every day. And yet we are timeless. We are the rhythm of life.

When you find it impossible to go outside, here's a practice that will help you open to expansive rhythms and find your way through times of rapid change.

Find a comfortable space where you won't be disturbed for some time. Lie or sit comfortably and take a few deep, refreshing breaths. Let each exhale release naturally. Relax more deeply with each out breath.

Honor the full rhythm of each breath. Feel its beginning, middle, and end as it rolls into the next. How does this feel?

Keep breathing this way for a few moments.

When you are ready, continue to relax as you simply notice the subtle body movements as each breath moves in and out of your lungs.

Allow the gentle and natural movement; enjoy that gentle undulation.

The breath is a physiological rhythm to which we can always return. As we relax into it, we can return to center, no matter what may swirl around us.

As you breathe and your restfulness deepens, reflect on daily life. As if you can look at each day in your mind's eye, see how you breathe, move, sleep, and eat. Also note how you relate day to day with friends, family, and your work or craft.

Blackberry Plants invite us to ask: "Do I experience my life fully? Are my rhythms complete, or do I rush the moments—hurry on to what's next?"

You may also ask:

"Do I express genuinely? Do I honor my fierce nurturing qualities— the protector within me—in daily life? Am I comfortable using prickly, even sharp boundaries when I need to do so?"

Take time to reflect. How do you feel about these questions?

What might you want to enact differently in your life?

Take all the time you like to consider these things.

When you feel complete, take a deep and cleansing breath. Allow the out breath its natural release; with it, invite thoughts, ideas, or lingering feelings to ease, as well.

Take another long and refreshing breath. With the exhale, let go of whatever is ready to let go. Ahhhh.

Continue to breathe and release what's ready to go with each exhale.

There is nothing to do or be in these moments. The ordinary constraints of linear time dissolve into the rhythm of each breath.

When fully relaxed, invite deep stillness. Allow noises, thoughts, and feelings to simply flow in and out with each breath.

Take your time.

Travel with your breath to "no time."

Merge with, or slip beneath, bodily rhythms to the unconditional pulse of who you really are.

Allow what arises during this time to simply be.

Thoughts may come and go.

Allow everything to dissolve into one rhythm—the All.

Take all the time you desire. Sink in as deeply as you can.

When you are complete with this experience, or when it's no longer fresh, release a long and relaxing exhalation.

Then let out another big breath.

Now begin to gently wiggle toes and fingers. Move and stretch your whole body to bring your awareness fully back into the room. Open your eyes whenever you feel ready.

Look around.

What do you see?

If inspired, you can write in a journal or contemplate your experiences.

How would you like to bring these insights to daily life?

Then drink a glass of fresh water and take a leisurely walk in or out of doors, preferably with bare feet. Ground and integrate the deep intrinsic rhythms you invited.

Wild Rose

Sandra

Wild Rose says, "Tread lightly as you walk on this earth."

Wild Rose thickets grow after a fast-moving fire and bloom in spring. Many of us perceive the Rose as a symbol of love and connection to the power and beauty of the feminine. We are touched each spring as Rose blossoms brighten the earth with delicate color and the air with a sweet fragrance. Roses are one of the first flowers we think of sending to someone when we want to show our love.

Take a few minutes to reflect on Rose. Close your eyes and imagine inhaling the scent of a rose. The fragrance immediately connects you to the goddess. The sweet scent and folds of the colorful petals might remind you of the magic of life and the amazing beauty that surrounds us on this Earth. With your eyes still closed, bring to your mind's eye your favorite color Rose. As you imagine breathing in the sweet fragrance, feel your heart expand. Notice how your body begins to relax, creating a sensation of inner expansiveness. You feel more energy coursing through you and your eyes soften as you gaze on this exquisite flower.

When you feel ready, open your eyes while continuing to experience the expansiveness of your heart.

Every morning while I drink my tea, I gaze out my window, where there is an abundant thicket of pink Wild Roses. This is my time for reflection and meditation before arising and being consumed by all the responsibilities of my life. I take my time sipping my tea, and as I gaze into nature, I attune to myself, to my helping spirits, and to the Earth. I give gratitude for all that sustains my life and for my loved ones and friends. I give thanks for my life and for all that life brings to me. This is the most precious time of my day. I gaze further, to the piñon and juniper trees that stand tall on the land, but I spend most of my time staring aimlessly into the expanse of thickets of Wild Rose.

The Wild Rose informs me of the change in seasons. It blossoms in spring, the leaves drop to the ground when summer shifts to fall, and the bright red-brown branches dull as autumn turns to winter. I delight in watching the migration of birds who eat the flowers and fruits during spring and summer. I am always happy and excited when I see the return of the bees to collect pollen for their hive.

The Wild Roses growing just outside my window are hearty and healthy, for there is sufficient groundwater in the land where they are rooted that no extra is needed. My favorite time is when the Roses are in bloom and I can smell the gentle fragrance from the abundant small pink blossoms. And I love to watch the red fruits—the rose hips—bloom after the blossoms die. This fruit of the roses turn bright red in summer. They become ripe in late summer through autumn. Rose hips contain high levels of vitamin C, and I love the tangy taste of rose hip tea that I drink when I feel a cold encroaching. Wild Rose hips provide sustenance to many animals and are an important winter food.

Although I spend a great deal of time walking on the land, the dense, thorny Rose thickets are impenetrable. To me this is sacred ground that cannot be disturbed. The beautiful Wild Rose prevents humans from disturbing the earth.

As Llyn so eloquently wrote, a variety of plants and trees grow after land has been disturbed to protect the soil during the process of regeneration. In New Mexico oak and aspen trees are the first to grow after a fire. Wild Rose can also quickly regenerate after a fire. The growth of trees and plants after a fire is part of the cycle of death and rebirth on the land.

People in native cultures understand that we must honor and respect this great Earth, our home. To native peoples every day is a day of thanksgiving and gratitude. Their ancestors walked on this Earth throughout time speaking words of gratitude with each step and each breath. Prayers and thanks were given for the life received from the Earth so that all life might thrive. Honoring the principle of reciprocity, the Earth gives to us and we give back to the Earth with gratitude. As we care for her, she sustains us.

People in native cultures understand that nature is intelligent. Nature is seen as a helping spirit. The Earth is a living being and has all the information encoded in her to create necessary changes to ensure the continuation of life.

Earth, air, water, and fire are living beings that together make up the body of the Earth. We ourselves are earth, air, water, and fire. Our body is earth. We are also made of mostly water. Oxygen flows through our bloodstream. And the flame of our spirit is a reflection of the power of the sun and the fire that burns within the earth.

The earth is the ground on which we live and walk. She provides an abundance of food while surrounding us with beauty, color, fragrance, tastes, and textures for us to enjoy. The earth shares with us her bounty.

Water held us while we were growing in the womb, protecting us and helping transport nutrients to us. As the water breaks in the mother's womb, the child is ushered into the world carried by the beauty of water. There is no life on Earth without water. Water reflects the beauty of our souls and also nurtures and cleanses us. Earth is called the water planet, as water covers the majority of the surface of our planet.

There is no life without air. Air is the first living being that greets us and welcomes us to life when we are born, for life begins with our first breath and ends with our last. We are in relationship with air with each breath that we take throughout life. We are often caressed by the air through a gentle breeze and cleansed by the air in a strong wind.

Fire is also an intelligent living being. Fire in the form of the sun gives us the energy to live. It is not electricity that gives us energy, but the sun. The sun is a teacher of unconditional giving as it continues to give us the energy we need in order to thrive and asks for nothing in return. Fire mirrors back to us our inner passion for life, the unlimited sustaining force.

When landscapes are in need of regeneration, fire comes to heal the earth. Humans are traumatized by forest fire, and we feel deep compassion for all the living beings that lose their lives and homes, but in truth the Earth needs fire for her continued health and well-being. It consumes what has died to provide nutrients for new life. Just as fire alters our outer landscape, so, too, our inner landscape changes over time.

Once fire has cleansed and healed the land, new life is born. Seeds that require intense heat to burst them open start to grow and blossom. Seeds carried by the wind are the first to recolonize. There are a variety of plants and trees that bring new nutrients to the land and protect it during this time of healing and evolution.

In the nursery industry there is a powder that contains the chemicals found in smoke. This family of chemicals mimics the chemicals found in soil after a burn and "convinces" seeds they have been through a fire. The smoke powder is added to water in which certain kinds of seeds are soaked before being germinated in potting soil, acting as a catalyst for seed germination. Seeds of more than 1,200 plants species respond to smoke.

Nature teaches us that death is not an end but a transition. In life we go through many little deaths before we experience the "big death," leave our bodies, and transcend again to Source, Spirit, and a state of oneness.

The little deaths are all the changes and rites of passages we go through in life. And when we experience a life change, we might feel raw and vulnerable as we are sculpted into deeper beings with a new evolution of consciousness.

Just as the Earth protects itself, we must protect ourselves during times of transition as we would protect a newborn baby, because it's not unusual to feel thin skinned during and after a major life change. We want to make sure that a newborn baby is held in love but also protected from too much energy that might overwhelm a new, unformed consciousness. In caring for a precious new life, we want to make sure it is not being overstimulated by the outer world.

That which we love, we protect. Just as we care for new life, the Earth protects the newness of life after a great change has occurred. The Earth is a master gardener.

The other side of protection is the innate desire and passion for life, which nature constantly mirrors back to us.

In our culture we are socialized and trained to fit into society. At a young age we're told there are only a few creative geniuses and most of us are not one of them. We're conditioned to compare ourselves to others and to follow the rules. "Do not shine your light too brightly" is a message given to many of us in a variety of ways; don't stand out. Conformity has been, and continues to be, encouraged.

In our world today the light has gone out of many people's eyes, replaced with blank stares and a lack of presence and joy. When the light goes out of our eyes, the light goes out of the Earth. People living in the Western world are not, in general, living a creative life filled with passion and meaning. And our lack of passion for life is reflected in the number of emotional and physical illnesses afflicting us.

Nature teaches us about the power that comes from allowing ourselves to grow wild and be passionate. Nature teaches us about the beauty that is revealed as we grow in vibrance and vitality, mirroring the plants and trees around us. We must shine our lights as brightly as the sun on a clear day and the stars in the night sky. In this way we caretake our inner gardens and create fertile soil, which leads to a life filled with laughter, joy, peace, health, and well-being.

Our destiny as humans is to caretake this great Earth. We are the caretakers and gardeners of our inner and outer sacred Earth.

🌿 Practices

Go outside and dig your fingers into the earth. Allow your hands to fully connect with the earth. Feel the energy of that connection traveling through your fingers into your hands. Feel the texture of the earth against your fingertips. Notice any changing sensations in your body as you connect deeply with the earth. With eyes closed, start to repeat to yourself, "Earth is my home. My body is the home of my spirit." As you continue to do this over time, you will feel a deeper connection with the preciousness of life.

Take some time to engage in a simple meditation. Imagine that a beautiful garden grows within you. Life is filled with change and your garden changes during different cycles of your life. Old plants, representing old beliefs and attitudes that no longer serve you, need to be removed. Life might have brought so much change that it is time to simply let the soil in your garden rest. You can feel this in your cells. There is an intuitive knowing that a cycle has ended, a new one is germinating, and you must protect the soil.

Imagine yourself as earth. What might you grow in your garden to make sure it is protected during this time of regeneration before the newness of life begins to take shape again? What boundaries do you need to create? This is a time of turning your focus and attention within as new thoughts, beliefs, attitudes, and visions are born.

We were born with a DNA program encoded with the knowledge of what we need in order to thrive, including the information we need to heal ourselves. This same knowledge is contained in every seed planted in our inner and outer garden.

When change occurs, if we sink into the depth of our own inner knowing and allow ourselves to simply be and rest, we allow nature's intelligence to operate. As humans we tend to immediately look at what we need to do, to "fix" it, but there are times we must rest and allow the energy to build inside us before new birth can occur.

The elements clear the land through climatic events, such as storms, fire, and drought so that rebirth and evolution can occur. The earth we live on and the earth within each of us is intelligent. Let us not interfere with the process of evolution. Death, change, rebirth, and evolution are all part of life. We must learn to go with the flow rather than against it, not fight what life is bringing to us. And as the earth protects new life, we must learn how to protect ourselves while the inner process of life grows into a cycle of new beauty. Nature always informs us of how to flow with change versus resisting it.

Take some time to reflect on what you love in your life that you wish to protect and caretake.

Listen to a drumming track or other music that invokes a meditative state of consciousness, or you can drum or rattle for yourself. As you listen to the music, ask yourself: "What activities and creative endeavors would make me feel inspired and bring joy into my life?"

This writing practice will reveal your inner desires to you. As you listen to some meditative music, keep your eyes partially open. Write this question on a piece of paper: "What activities would bring passion and meaning back into my life?" Allow your pen or pencil to automatically write. Allow what is germinating in your unconscious to burst up through you and reignite your inner creative fire, so that your eyes shine with joy, vitality, and passion. Allow yourself to blossom into the great beauty that you are.

Commit to a hobby, whatever interests you, or to spending some time sitting on a park bench or walking through a garden. You will notice that you can add activities or hobbies into your life that spark the flame of inspiration and excitement. Would you like to learn a foreign language, garden, or perhaps tend beehives? Have you always wanted to play with watercolor paints? When was the last time you danced? Maybe you would like to take up a craft such as knitting, crocheting, carving, or sculpting. It is important for your health and feelings of well-being to wake up the strength of your creative fire. Starting with simple steps will lead you on a path to diving deeper into your own creative nature.

4
ARTESIAN SPRING AND MIST

Artesian Spring

Sandra

I walk out the door of my adobe house on a beautiful day in the high desert. The sky is bright blue and no clouds block the sun. I absorb the warmth and light as I walk down a narrow path surrounded by piñon pine and juniper trees.

After a short walk I come to a marsh. It is not common to find abundant natural water sources in the desert, and I have the privilege of living on land where there is an Artesian Spring bubbling up from deep within the earth. Marsh grass, cattails, and willows grow here in abundance, nurtured by the water. Even during times in the year when water is not visible on the surface, it is still plentiful deep in the earth.

When the water flows above ground, it attracts a variety of life. Colorful dragonflies appear only when there is standing water. Birds

and animals not typically seen in other areas of Santa Fe come to drink from this sacred place.

I live on the Old Santa Fe Trail. With my imagination I can see the horse-drawn wagons of the past coming through and weary folks grateful that they have finally arrived at a source of water.

Where water flows is sacred ground. Our planet is mostly water and all of life depends on it to thrive. Water is precious and we must always honor it as a living being. When we sit with water, we are in awe of its beauty. We find deep inner peace when we watch ocean waves, experience a deep state that allows our inner wisdom to come forth as we sit by a river, and experience stillness as we reflect while gazing into clear lake water.

As we experience times of extreme drought in the Southwest, I find myself turning to prayer to give thanks for the rain that will come so that all life might thrive. Giving thanks and knowing that the spirit of the land and the elements will provide what is needed for life to continue is crucial.

When I journey to my spiritual teacher, who is the Egyptian goddess Isis, and ask her about the drought, her response to me is always the same. First she tells me that if I believe we will not have water and rain, we will experience a scarcity of this precious resource, for our belief and perception creates our reality. Living this teaching is a work in progress for me. It is not an easy process to disconnect from the collective trance that supports the belief in scarcity versus abundance.

She also tells me that it is time to embrace the feminine principle of recognizing that all that we desire in the outer world lies within us. Isis says to me, "You are always looking to the sky for the rains from above to come. You need to call the deep waters in the earth to bubble up and feed the trees, plants, and all of life."

This is a powerful teaching on a metaphorical level, for in the Western world we look to the outer world to give us what we need. We try to amass material goods and money to feel wealthy, yet true wealth lies within. And when we stop looking outside and embrace the feminine, the gems—the inner knowing, inner health, inner peace—bubble up and create true joy. This is the reflection of the sacred well that lies deep within the earth waiting to be experienced, acknowledged, and called up to feed and support all of life.

In the late 1980s I had a powerful experience of Isis while on a vision quest in the high desert of northern New Mexico. Isis came to me in a vision and told me that she would be my teacher in my spirit world journeys and would guide me in teaching how to bring healing and balance back to the Earth.

Then in the late 1990s one of my students asked me if I would bring a group to Egypt to visit the temples and sacred sites. I have always felt a connection to Egypt and its history, so this idea intrigued me. And of course, as Isis was my spiritual teacher, I was even more drawn to accepting the invitation.

I journeyed to Isis and asked her for her guidance, and she answered me in a metaphorical manner. Speaking and teaching through metaphor is the way the spirits communicate.

I had asked her, "Should I bring a group of students to Egypt?" Her answer was, "The power of the land is the water that runs through it."

I interpreted her response to mean that the land in Egypt holds great power due to the Nile River running through it and that her answer was yes. Thus I did bring a group to Egypt, and we had special and profound experiences during our time visiting sacred sites and temples.

Over the next year I thought about Isis's response to me that the power of the land is the water that runs through it, and I reflected on this in terms of the places I've lived. I grew up in Brooklyn, New York, near the ocean, and then I moved to San Francisco, where I lived for many years until moving to Santa Fe. In the coastal cities where I lived, I found the energy of growth and also the personality of people to reflect back the effervescence of the ocean waves.

In contrast, Santa Fe is high desert. Beautiful trees and a wealth of plants grow here, and there is a deep silence in the land that supports the spirit of creativity. Growth in the desert is slow, but the land supports deep growth, because roots must grow very deep to find the water needed to thrive.

In my workshops I started having participants meditate or journey to connect with the land where they live and experience the water running through the landscape. I asked them to notice if the people who live there reflect back the qualities of the waters, and this has been a valuable way for all of us to learn about the land where we live.

Water reflects the nature of our soul. It symbolizes the principle of "as above, so below, as within, so without." When we examine how our inner toxicity is reflected in our environment, water is a great example of this.

A solution to our current ecological crisis is working with the feminine principle of *being* versus *doing*. I teach that it is who we become that changes the world, for we can be a healing force through our presence.

My love for water led me to the study of marine biology. I thought I would be spending my life working through a scientific model to look at reversing pollution in the waters of the world.

Destiny led me in a different direction, and in 1980 I was introduced to the practice of shamanism. As I learned about the power of spiritual healing work, I focused my attention on how we could use spiritual methods to not just heal the waters of the world, but to reverse all environmental pollution. Spiritual traditions teach that everything in the outer world is a reflection of our inner world, which means that from a spiritual perspective the toxicity we see in our environment is a reflection of our own inner toxicity. That we are experiencing severe drought in some parts of the world while other locations are experiencing extreme flooding is a reflection of how out of balance our inner world is. To support our environmental health, we must embrace this feminine principle: "It is who we *become* that changes the world, and not just what we *do.*"

In the practice of shamanism, it is understood that thoughts have substance. It is also understood that words are seeds and have the power to create. In its original Aramaic, the "abracadabra" famously used by magicians derives from *abraq ad habra,* which literally translates as, "I will create as I speak."

In indigenous cultures the difference between expressing problematic thoughts or emotions and sending the energy associated with them is well understood. In our Western culture, where we do not validate what is happening in the energetic and invisible realms, we often find ourselves filled with toxic thoughts and emotions that we then send to ourselves and into the world. Without realizing it we can end up sending poisonous, dense, or heavy energies to others, the planet, and even back upon ourselves. We often end up polluting our water within and without, as we are not conscious of the impact of our thoughts and words.

The key is to learn how to acknowledge the depth of our feelings. Experiencing fully a range of feelings from joy to anger is part of being human. We do not want to repress or deny our feelings. The key is learning about how the energy we send out affects our personal health and the health of the planet.

Start changing that energy by taking some time to get centered and reflect on the nature of your thoughts and feelings. Once you acknowledge a feeling through the use of intention and creative inspiration, you can transform the energy behind your thoughts and words into love. Then you can send loving energies through your thoughts and words to yourself, loved ones, and into the world. In this way you can express what you are feeling while feeding yourself, others, and the planet with love and radiant light, which will bring you back to a state of inner peace and harmony that will be reflected back to you in the outer world.

In 1997 I had a powerful dream in which the Egyptian god Anubis appeared to me and told me that the key to the spiritual work of reversing environmental pollution is transfiguration.

On awakening from the dream, I had to look up the meaning of transfiguration and learned it means what is referred to in shamanism as "shapeshifting." I had heard stories about shamans shapeshifting into animals such as wolves and ravens, but I could not at first connect that practice to reversing environmental pollution.

An important insight about this came from my neighbor, also a client, who was dying of liver cancer. One day Kathy and I were sitting and chatting as friends. When I told her about my dream, she became very animated and started to share stories about Jesus. A fundamentalist Christian, she knew quite well the biblical accounts of how Jesus had transfigured and shone with bright rays of light. While in this transfigured state of divine light, he worked miraculous healings.

Now I understood Anubis's message to me: light heals and transmutes. This is true in various spiritual traditions that offer countless references to shamans, healers, and spiritual masters transfiguring into divine light while performing miraculous healings. Since we are essentially spiritual light connected to all of life, spirit is who we are beyond our skin. When we drop all that separates us from our divine light, everything outside of us mirrors back to us a state of divinity, light, and perfection.

For years I worked with groups of people on a community experiment trying to transmute pollution in the environment from a toxic to a neutral substance. We took deionized (pure) water and polluted it with ammonium hydroxide, which is a common pollutant in the environment and is a strong base. It is easy to check its presence with the use of pH strips that measure alkalinity.

Our ceremony involved letting go of egoic states that separate us from our divinity and achieving a state of union with the power of the universe, the divine source of light and universal love. We worked with the understanding that water will reflect back to us our state of inner harmony. As we radiate our light, everything around us reflects back a state of health and luminosity. I have presented this ceremony to many groups, and every time the pH of the water has dropped one to three points toward neutral. The actual ceremony lasts about twenty minutes and the pH changes within this time frame. From a scientific perspective this would be seen as impossible.

Since these initial experiments I've started using a gas discharge visualization (GDV) camera that can capture the physical, emotional, mental, and spiritual energies emanating from a person, plant, liquid, powder, or inanimate object and translate those energies into a computerized model. In other words, this diagnostic camera measures and evaluates the energy of the auric field and integrates that information into a computer-generated report with pictures.

The camera enabled us to document the change in energy of the substances present in our circle. And time and time again, as we experienced and radiated our divine light, we saw the field of light of the water in the middle of our circle increasing.

The teaching Isis and Anubis encouraged me to share is how we can heal by our presence. In the work I share on this topic, we do not pray for the water or send light or healing energy to the water. We simply radiate our spiritual light in the way that the sun or a star shines. When we allow our light to shine, our outer world reflects back to us our divine nature.

Our bodies are mostly water. As we experience our divine light, the water within us is transformed into a state of harmony and health. As we transform our negative and defeatist way of thinking and consciously work on our thoughts and the words we use throughout the day, we heal our inner water as well as the waters in the world around us.

❧ Practices

Find a body of water—either a beautiful place in nature or a nearby park that has a lake, pond, or stream—and sit near it. Moving water, such as a river, stream, or waterfall, can help to transport you away from ordinary concerns so that your inner wisdom can emerge. Watching the waves in the ocean creates a state of opening so you can listen to the messages of your soul. If you sit by the ocean, feel the waves welling up inside of you. If by a river or stream, drop into your sensory awareness of the flow of your inner water. A lake or pond might put you in touch with the stillness within you.

Listen to some music you find relaxing and expansive or to a drumming track. Lie or sit down, close your eyes, and hold the intention that you wish to experience the waters that run beneath and through the city where you live. Experience the waters and learn about the qualities of the water that runs through the land where you sit. Open to your sensory awareness and notice what you feel in your body as you do this.

Reflect on the people, trees, plants, animals, and other nature beings that live in your area. Meditate on how they reflect back the qualities of the water.

When you feel you are finished, return from your meditation. You may want to take some notes. Take a walk outside and tune in to the feel of the water running beneath the land. Even in a city there is groundwater in the land.

In some places the mighty rivers and oceans run strong. In other locations there might be gentle streams and still lakes feeding the land. Sometimes there are deep pools of water beneath the land that sustain the life that grows roots deep enough to find the water below.

Merging with water is a wonderful way to experience becoming one with the flow of life. Water flows in a natural and graceful way. It is a reflection of the divine feminine and reflects the nature of our soul. We can learn about the power and nature of water by merging with it. When we merge with an element, the teachings we receive go beyond mental understanding to have a physical impact on us as we become one with the energy of another living being.

In the natural world, when water is allowed to flow without restriction, it flows in the same form as a snake. Snake medicine teaches us about flowing and becoming one with the heartbeat of the Earth, with which we are all connected.

Listen to some drumming or relaxing and expansive music. Imagine becoming one with a source of water, such as a still lake, river, waterfall, the ocean, rain, or mist. Go deep within and experience yourself losing your own boundaries and becoming one with this water source. Learn about water by becoming water. Once again open your sensory awareness and notice all the feelings in your body as you do this.

Relax into being water. This is such a powerful and regenerating practice.

When you feel ready, disconnect from the water source you are merged with and gently come back to yourself and into the space where you physically are. Feel revitalized from your experience. Feel yourself grounded and present.

If you need some help with feeling more grounded after such an expansive practice, imagine deep roots growing out the soles of your feet into the earth. Or imagine sitting by a tree and leaning your body against it.

Make it a daily practice to honor water. As you wash yourself, the dishes, and so on, connect with water and give thanks for the way it sustains life.

It also heals and cleanses us. As you drink water, give thanks to the life and nourishment that water brings to you. As we give thanks and bless water for all it shares, water will bless us in return.

We need to be conscious about what we put into water and not pollute that which gives us life. We can all start helping to clear it by radiating love while in the presence of water.

Listen to a piece of music that creates an expanded state of awareness. Set your intention to travel within to experience your inner light, your inner sun. Some people find it helpful to imagine merging with a star. A star does not try to shine; there is no effort involved. Nor does a star choose where its light shines. A star simply radiates light and brightens all of life. You can also meditate and simply imagine yourself stepping out of the coat of your body and sinking into your inner light.

Allow your divine light to nurture all the cells in your body. Absorb this light deeply into your cells and luxuriate in this light.

After about fifteen minutes of experiencing your divine light, return from this experience without disconnecting fully from your true spiritual nature as a luminous being.

Now drink a glass of water, and notice as you radiate and experience your light how smooth, fresh, and sweet the water tastes. It is the same water you drink each day, but as you allow yourself to experience and live from a state of light, water will always reflect back your luminosity.

Stay connected with your light as you function in the world. Notice if your perception shifts about others and the world as you experience your light shining through you. Go outside and observe how everything in life has a glow to it.

Incorporate a practice of lighting a candle in honor of your inner light. The flame of the candle will reflect your luminosity back to you.

Mist

Llyn

Imagine traveling far from Sandra's desert environment with its hidden Artesian Springs to a land that is saturated by water most of the year. You sit on cool, damp earth surrounded by luminous green plants. Tiny dewdrops cling to each leaf and blade of grass, and you breathe in the same pristine vapors that craft these watery jewels.

This is a world unto itself. You could gaze and smell and drink in its nuances for hours. Maybe even for weeks or years. Yet this verdant pocket is a threshold looking out to a large expanse not of water, but of gravel.

The river that carved this rocky bed is low. The spring rains have lightened, although the snows of higher altitudes have yet to melt. Look intently across the stretch of stone and sand, an ever-shifting stream of earth. Virgin plants—willow saplings, tender wild mountain lupine, and river grasses—root in the rocky bed the river possessed just weeks earlier. Nothing remains static in the Hoh River Valle
constantly change.

Allow your gaze now to drift across the gravel b
hills where old growth is mysteriously draped in a lo
wispy shapes look surreal, as if you are truly in a dr

light varies with temperature, time of day, and the wafting of air. It is hard to fix upon these forms that constantly morph and evaporate. In trying to focus on the shapes, you merge with the white phantoms, as if you also float and dissolve. The sensation is euphoric.

It is during such moments that I invoke Mist's sacred feminine wisdom: "Teach me. Teach me."

Mist is condensed vapor—fine water particles that are suspended in the atmosphere. Mist reminds us that we, too, are mostly water and space, not solid at all, but one with nature's harmony.

Mist also teaches about nourishment. Deceivingly translucent, it carries loads of nutrients to the nature beings of this cloud forest—mammals, insects, fish, and plant species unbeknownst to lands beyond these. The misty white cloaks infuse abundant life into all.

In the similarly shrouded cloud forests of the high Andes, I hiked with Quechua shamans descended from ancient Incan peoples. There the highland trees display lavish orchids that feed on air steeped in moisture and organic matter.

Airborne plants also grow in the Amazon basin and here on the Olympic Peninsula in the world's largest temperate rain forest. There are almost one hundred types of epiphytes—nonparasitic plants that grow on other (host) plants and feed off nutrients and moisture in the air—in the Hoh Rain Forest. Instead of orchids a primary northwest tree-hugger is moss. Moss hangs heavy with moisture on the tree limbs. Contrary to what most people think when they first see them, mosses aren't parasitic. They don't draw from the trees but from nutrient-dense vapors that drift inland from the nearby Pacific Ocean. The trees, in fact, root into the moss mats to absorb organic debris and water, enabling them to grow and thrive at heights not otherwise possible.

In the same way that rain and cloud forest plants draw moisture and bio-residues from Mist—and humans draw oxygen from air and essential substances from food—people can absorb good influences from subtle particles in the atmosphere. These are more energy than matter, less dense than oxygen. We receive nourishment not only from food but also from the sunlight, natural spring water, fresh air, and invisible subtle energies that are also essential to our health.

In his book, *Spiritual Wisdom from the Altai Mountains* (translated by Joanna Dobson), spiritual elder Nikolai Shodoev writes of such sublime phenomena that occur in the Asian Altai. "Often in the Altai Mountains you can see a light bluish haze (*ynaar tyudyuzek*) which seems to have formed as the result of the unification of different elements, including radiation from the sun, 'the breath of the earth and vegetation,' moisture, and the movement of air currents. Such natural phenomena are very wholesome for the human body and soul and can impart a huge charge of energy."*

---

*Shodoev, Nikolai, *Spiritual Wisdom from the Altai Mountains* (Moon Books, 2012), 33.

Shamanic traditions around the world espouse nature's life-giving powers. The spiritual myths of diverse cultures even include beings who have lived only on essential forces transmitted via the air and sunlight for hundreds of years.

This diaphanous enrichment is the sacred feminine wisdom of Mist reminding us that, as with ancient shamanic and Altai traditions, we can enliven with sublime forces. Likewise, as Sandra reflects in her work with water, we can positively affect everything around us with our own near-invisible, radiant force.

Nature's luminous energies are visible to some, such as those who see the bluish Altai light of ynaar tyudyuzek. Yet Mist teaches that there are many ways to perceive, and also converse, through nature's subtle pathways.

In the foothills of the Olympic Mountains, I hear singing—captivating chants that roll up and down this glacial valley. Sometimes the melodies sound like many female voices, and at other times the harmonies sound like male voices. Sometimes the choruses are combined male and female voices. I don't hear musical instruments or words, only entrancing tones and chants. Just as Mist nourishes all life in the Hoh Valley, this valley's own rhythms feed my soul. Some who visit these lands also hear the singing.

We each have our own way of relating to nature's mystery. It's possible that some people will perceive the subtle influences (such as the Altai light) I hear. Alternately, one may taste or smell energy while another may sense it.

One morning when my forest guide, Mick Dodge, stepped into the barn attached to my cabin, he felt a tug of expectation. Mick instinctively turned to look at a fallen branch he'd hauled into the barn a few days before, intending to do some carving. Barren when he had first brought it in, the log had literally mushroomed overnight. The tug this man felt was the life glow of tender new mushrooms.

Indigenous wisdom ways help us revive such passionate interchanges with nature that are innate to all humans. Nikolai Shodoev implies that the survival of the human species depends on our ability to connect in these ways with the natural world.

"Biological energy is also the informational channel by which man can communicate with the animal and plant kingdoms," Shodoev tells us. "Through this energy man can find common language with plants and animals learning to feel and understand them. This channel is more reliable for preserving a unity between man and nature than contemporary technological attempts to solve ecological problems."*

I have given up wondering whether the singing of these lands comes from the mountains or the trees, or the water, stones, wind, or other aspects of nature, or people, or spirits. I can't see the answer. Nature is sentient but some things are known only by the heart and through experience. When I stop trying to figure it out, I simply hear the spirit, joy, and love of the Earth—the vibrant harmony of life. These voices move my soul and have a profound impact on my work. They are part of the natural mystery of life, of which we have much yet to discover.

Interestingly, indigenous teachings as well as Christian doctrines reference the singing of the land and trees. These lines from Isaiah in the Old Testament express it well:

"The whole earth rests, is quiet: they break forth into singing. Even the cypresses rejoice at thee, the cedars of Lebanon: 'Since thou hast gone to sleep, no one will come up to lay the axe upon us.'"

When drifting, floating high, Mist and I touch age-old treetops on the ridge above the river. A sentiment wafts from tree, through misty vapors, to me:

"This enchanted world of trees, land, nature beings—all unite in spirited harmony. When humans forget their place in this harmony, we nature beings are vulnerable to you, ever so sensitive, even to your thoughts and feelings."

I live on a small strip of private land bordering state and national

---

*Shodoev, *Spiritual Wisdom from the Altai Mountains*, 33.

parklands. There are about fifteen cabins here, most times empty. Some owners are here only during hunting season and others show up for occasional weekends. The elk that visit my cabin, and the singing, stop when these folks arrive. The winter elk return after they leave. One time forty elk showed up on my land after everyone drove away. Elk-sense is uncanny. The singing also resumes.

To open the subtle pathways, empty out. Drop agendas. Let go of time. Walk barefoot, softly on the earth, and listen from the heart. Work, move, and play on the land and listen from the heart. Sleep and dream on the earth and listen from the heart. As with a human friend, offer your time and loving attention to our invisible kindred. Mist teaches such things and more.

My eighty-two-year-old father tells of sitting at the border of hidden marshlands in New England. In the spring he intently listens to the thriving, ecstatic life of the marsh. My dad fights the urge to walk into the marshlands to see all this amazing life, yet he cannot bear to impose a human footprint here; he instinctively knows his place in the spirited harmony of this ecosystem.

The deep feminine wisdom of Mist opens us to subtle enrichment and to delicate exchanges with nature. Mist rouses the mystic that lives within each of us.

❧ Practice

Let us listen deeply to, and protect, our wild natural places and open to invisible kinships with nature. The insights above will help. We can also encourage nature's vibrancy and open to her subtle communication anytime and anywhere. Below is a simple way to cultivate this.

If possible, take a barefoot walk in a natural environment where you live. If this isn't possible, or if you live in a city, walk to a park. If you can't go walking, sit in your backyard, gaze at an indoor plant, or take an imaginary stroll.

As you begin your walk (or experience), take a few deep breaths. Relax your mind with each exhale and with each step and movement.

Walk aimlessly; wander like a child. There is no goal but to explore and open your heart and senses to nature.

Move slowly, feeling each footstep upon the earth and the movement of your body. As a child might, sense what is around you as you move. What do you see? What do you smell?

Enjoy the experience.

When something catches your attention (tugs at you)—whether flower, tree, field, stone, sky, stream, or other—linger for a while. Take time to appreciate this nature being and to invite the subtle channels of communication to open between you.

Study this nature being's physical details. Ask permission to touch and smell it, if this is appropriate. Speak aloud to this form; share from the heart. Or share in another way, such as by singing, gently moving, praying, or simply being in silence. Notice what feelings arise in you as you offer good energy to this nature being. What are the sensations in your body? What do you sense beyond words?

When you feel ready for the next step, prepare to listen deeply to this being. Close your eyes, if that feels right. Or move in ways that call you. Drop your expectations. Desire nothing from this being but to extend interest, appreciation, and a gentle presence. Listen with more than physical ears; open your whole heart and being. Relax and notice the subtleties of what you feel in your body. Do you feel warmth, or tingling, or another sensation?

Where in your body do you feel this, and how would you describe it?

What do you feel in your heart? What do you *feel?*

When you note these experiences, relax into their texture. Settle the mind, open the heart, and drop into body awareness.

Spend as much time as you like in deep listening. This simple practice will restore you and it extends good vibrations to nature. Feel what exchange occurs between you and the nature being. Notice any tangible signal back to you from nature, such as a waft of air, a bird's trill, a shaft of sunlight, an insect's hum, a leaf that gently falls from a tree, and so forth.

You may enjoy consciously breathing in the light, beauty, love, or whatever good forces you feel radiate from this nature being. Allow these qualities to infuse you. In turn, you can breathe out to the plant, tree, or other form your gratitude, radiance, harmony, or whatever good energy you feel. The more you open, the stronger the invisible pathways will be.

Take time. Stay in your heart and be aware of what you feel in your body. Breathe, be, and listen. In addition to how you feel, also notice any subtle messages that come.

Take your time.

When you feel complete with this exchange, express gratitude. Then say goodbye for now to the nature being.

On your return stroll, walk, move, and breathe with these vibrant qualities of nature. You can also set an intention for some of the good energy that radiates from you to extend to plants, stones, winds, waters, other aspects of nature, or people who may benefit from it.

The more you practice, the deeper will be your experience. Over time your exchange with the subtle aspects of nature will become a natural and powerful part of your life.

5

WILD PLUM SEED AND EARTH GODDESS NUNKUI

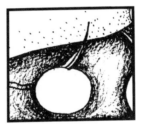

Wild Plum Seed

Sandra

Spring is a time when awe-inspiring creativity in nature abounds. The spring winds carry seeds that the earth readily receives to nurture. Actually all life carries seeds from place to place. Some animals pass seeds through their digestive systems, or seeds cling to a paw and get carried from location to location. Birds carry seeds in their beaks or in their bodies and drop them into the earth, and insects scatter seeds as they travel. Many species of ants actually carry seeds into their nests. Water that flows through the lands also helps to carry seeds around the earth. And, of course, humans intentionally plant seeds in our great earth garden.

Earth waits patiently for these seeds to be planted in her body, her

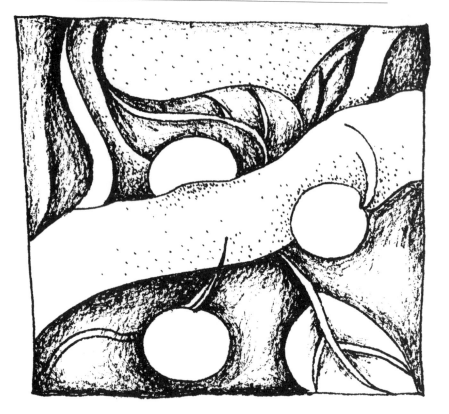

soil. And then she nurtures each seed without judgment of what is carried in this seed and what will grow and blossom from it. She just nurtures the seeds with unconditional and universal love.

Due to drought conditions my husband and I have to depend on rain and snow to water our garden. We have to be very conscious of how much of our well water we use. Because there are minerals in our soil and we need to conserve water, only very hearty seeds tend to grow deep roots and mature into healthy plants.

One year I noticed a new bush growing in our garden. It seemed to have appeared overnight. I had no idea what this little bush was but was happy to have a beautiful green bush now growing in a place that had been bare.

During the summer fruit appeared on this bush. The fruit was about one inch in diameter and a beautiful deep red. I decided to pick one of the pieces of fruit and taste it. To my absolute amazement it was a plum. This was a great omen to me, as plums are my favorite fruit.

Over the summer I noticed these Wild Plum bushes growing everywhere in our garden. The bushes started growing in such abundance that I had to start cutting them back to protect the root systems of our other fruit trees.

Wild Plum is a drought-tolerant bush that fills the land and wild places of its natural habitat with the scent of sweet white flowers. It is a deciduous shrub with reddish-brown bark covering its low, slender branches. Deep green, small, tapering oval leaves emerge in the spring. With the arrival of fall, Wild Plum's foliage brightens to golden yellow before dropping. Its enthusiastic root-sucker production requires time to manage and control its vigorous spread. I find myself walking around the plum bushes carefully, as their branches can be quite prickly and scratch my skin when I walk carelessly and get too close.

It is so interesting to watch the wealth of plants that grow in abundance in a desert environment, even with the lack of water. Nature is always teaching us about the strength and passion for life.

All over my land I watch during the heat of summer the abundance of growth of mallow, mullein, beautiful purple asters, lilacs, grape hyacinth, and even a type of bluebell. I walk in amazement as I observe the beauty of these plants growing and looking so vital even without receiving water. I realized I could benefit from their strength and knowledge of how to thrive in a harsh, challenging climate, so over the years I made flower essences from these healthy plants. When I feel I need a reminder of my own strength to support me in challenging times, I drink a few drops of the essence of one of these desert plants that calls to me as an ally.

All plant life starts with a seed. A seed is filled with potential. Nature's intelligence has created a blueprint that programs each seed to thrive and be healthy. When we learn about the power, potential, and inner wisdom that each seed has, we learn a lot about ourselves. For we are part of nature with a passion for life and a blueprint that informs us of how to be healthy and thrive.

To explore our state of health and well-being, we can use the metaphor of a garden. We can cultivate rich inner gardens filled with seed words and seed thoughts we would like to see grow strong.

We also have to pay attention to some of the wild seeds we scatter and plant in our gardens, for we often plant and nourish seed thoughts and words without knowing it. Sometimes we end up scattering seeds of defeatist thoughts or words that grow strong and take over our inner gardens. We nourish these plants and encourage their growth due to our lack of awareness of the growth we are feeding. We often use words and have thoughts that don't align with the positive vision we have for ourselves and for the planet.

Conversely, the more we feed our positive visions, the deeper those roots will grow in our inner gardens, producing a life of inner joy, inner wealth, and inner health.

If you plant a pinecone in the earth, you get a pine tree, not an oak tree, yet we often plant seeds of defeatist thoughts and attitudes and expect to see a positive vision grow from them. This is not the way nature works.

We also want to see change happen miraculously in our external world. We forget the feminine process of birth. A baby just doesn't appear in the world; a fetus grows within the womb and the baby is born when the time is right. A plant or tree starts from a seed. Deep roots grow into the earth, and then the stalk or trunk grows and develops branches that lead to flowers and fruit. Flowers and fruit don't just spontaneously appear.

Everything we see in the external world begins from a deep inner process. This is the feminine process of creation, gestation, and birth.

We can look to our inner gardens to give us clues about what inner process is manifesting and growing in our external world. We can use the metaphor of a seed and garden to explore what is growing and flourishing in our lives.

In indigenous cultures we witness a power, strength, and light that is seen in the eyes of people living in harmony with nature. The internal state of strength and joy is not dependent on what is happening in their outer world. The deep-seated power and laughter comes from the depth of an inner well and fertile inner landscape that leads to joy for life itself with no conditions. This joy comes from having cultivated a very rich inner garden.

Many of us attach the experience of joy to what is happening in the outer world rather than allowing joy to flow through us. When we attach our joy or love or any feeling to outer events, we become dependent on what is happening outside of us in determining how we feel on a particular day. When we do this the good feelings of joy, love, wonder, and harmony will be fleeting, as conditions of life change moment to moment. Safety and security fall into this principle also, for as our outer world changes, one day you feel safe and then the next day you do not. For example, one day you feel secure in your job and then the economy changes and your job security might now be at risk. You might start to feel as if you are riding a rollercoaster of emotions.

As the world continues to change, transition, and evolve, you must engage in a deep inner exploration and find joy, love, safety, security, and peace that permanently live inside of you and are not dependent on changing outer conditions.

It is important to notice, work with, and deepen the minute-to-minute experiences that tap you in to your inner well and garden of joy, love, safety, security, and peace. Take a walk and just experience the beauty of nature, independent of what is happening environmentally. No matter what is happening, the planet is still filled with great beauty.

Think about and reflect on the simple joys of life that are not dependent on what is happening in your life.

Sit with this principle, meditate on it, reflect on it, take walks holding your questions, and notice if you can begin to find some doorway into the inner core of your being that experiences safety, security, joy, love, and peace independent of what life brings to you.

As our lives and the planet keep transitioning through intense changes, many of us start to reflect on the meaning of life. At some point we realize that focusing on the outer world does not create happiness. We realize that accumulating more in the material world does not create meaning and purpose. As we grow and evolve, we start to see that true meaning and wealth lie within each one of us.

For me personally, as I continue to go within and experience the wealth of my inner garden, I find meaning in being a channel of love and light. For what else is there as you evolve in your life's journey?

We have a tendency to attempt to over-domesticate our inner and outer gardens. We need to find a state of balance in allowing the wild seeds to take root and grow, as well as in caring for what grows into strong and healthy plants.

Just as wild seeds often grow into the most magnificent plants, sometimes wild, spontaneous ideas grow the deepest roots and most beautiful manifestations. There is a wonderful place for the wild and spontaneous woman in each of us.

Reflect on your life, and you might be delighted to remember times when your spontaneous ideas created very joyful and meaningful experiences.

Start to cultivate your wild and spontaneous side. Delight in the wild aspect of the feminine.

Plants that grow wild are vital, strong, and healthy. They represent the undomesticated power of the feminine. It might be time to break free from the domesticated part of yourself and explore your inner wild feminine.

Finally, it is important to remember that seeds germinate in the right time. They can wait for years until conditions are right for growth. We must surrender to right timing and not lose patience when we make a judgment that growth in our lives is not happening fast enough. It is important to keep fertilizing, nurturing, and watering our gardens to create the right conditions for growth.

🌿 Practices

Listen to a drumming track or meditative music that has no lyrics. The music will assist you in traveling within to your inner garden.

Lie down or sit in a chair in a place where you will not be disturbed for about twenty minutes. You might want to close the curtains or blinds to darken the room. As you listen to the music, imagine yourself traveling within to your inner garden. This is a continuation of the work you began with your inner garden in Wild Rose.

You can ask to meet a master gardener who can help you inspect your garden.

First, examine the earth in your inner garden. With your fingers feel the richness, texture, and levels of moisture that determine how healthy it is. Bring the soil up to your nose and notice if the fragrance is moist and rich. Examine the health and strength of the flowers and plants that are growing. Notice if the flowers and plants are bright in color and look vital, or if they seem to be tired and struggling. This information will give you some clues to the care that your inner garden requires.

Next, observe the wild seeds you have already planted throughout your life—the thoughts, words, attitudes, and beliefs that are growing into strong plants in your garden. Notice what wild plants need to be removed. Start to plant seeds of love, inspiration, and hope for yourself and the planet. Imagine the words you use and your daily thoughts as seeds. Plant the seeds you want to see manifest in the world.

Scatter some seeds filled with your wishes, compassion, and forgiveness.

Now imagine yourself planting small areas of your garden with seeds of good memories and gratitude for what you have. Water the soil with your love so the seeds can take root.

After you have experienced your inner garden, just be still as you continue listening to the music. Reflect on the experience you just had. Set an intention to continue to visit your inner garden so that you can continue to nurture the soil. Observe over time how rich and fertile the soil becomes. Set an intention to continue to plant the positive seeds you would like to watch grow into strong and healthy plants that will produce a state of inner strength, peace, harmony, and joy.

Use your imagination, and scatter some wild seeds in your inner garden, trusting that with the right conditions they will take root and grow into plants of joy.

When you feel ready, bring your consciousness back into your physical space. Take some deep breaths. Experience an inner feeling of peace, an inner smile, and let your own internal light flow through you.

Life will continue to bring change. Cultivating a rich inner garden will help you to stay centered and harmonious in the midst of change.

This practice will give you the experience of the power of a seed. As we are part of nature, we have the same potential and power that a seed has.

Take a walk in a park or a garden, and find a place where you can sit by a tree or plant that attracts you. Close your eyes and engage your imagination. With your imagination travel down into the earth and meet with the original seed of this tree or plant.

Feel in your body the unpotentiated energy and passion for life that this seed holds. Experience the blueprint that holds all the instructions for a healthy life. Notice the flow of strength, power, and energy that you feel in your own body as you attune to the power of how this tree or plant was born. Now take some time to experience yourself as a seed of life and feel all your innate inner information. Appreciate how much knowledge you have to help you flourish.

When you feel ready, take some deep breaths and state how grateful you are for your life. Seeds of gratitude that are nurtured in your inner garden create a beauty and power that ultimately will nourish you on all levels.

Open your eyes and gaze upon your chosen tree or plant. Feel the strength of the connection you have established with it by experiencing its growth, intelligence, and vitality.

Commit to paying greater attention to the seeds you plant and nurture in your inner garden.

Earth Goddess Nunkui

Llyn

I loved Sandra's story about Wild Plum Seed. How magical that those seeds found their way to Sandra's garden to grow into trees that bear her favorite fruit.

Earth Goddess Nunkui is a wonderful complement to wise teacher Wild Plum. I was first introduced to forest spirit Nunkui many years ago when I co-led groups with John Perkins to visit a remote Amazonian tribe in Ecuador, accessed by small aircraft landing on a machete-shaven airstrip. The Shuar, unconquered by both the Inca and the Spanish, were headhunters who lived harmoniously with the forest.

Twentieth-century missionaries shifted Shuar lifestyles so that even remote tribes began to seek outside resources for their daily needs, such as for clothing to cover their bodies and school supplies for their children. Their population also increased beyond what the forest alone could sustain.

Today, historically undefeated Shuar warriors fight oil interests that threaten their ancestral lands. Juxtaposing both the loss of traditional Shuar ways and the threat of devastation to their rain forests is the earthy Shuar deity Nunkui, who nurtures all that grows.

Living under the earth by day, Nunkui tends the seedlings and

roots of the plants beneath the soil. When night falls Nunkui spirals up and out of the earth like an unfurling seedling, or a water fountain, to nourish the burgeoning plants.

Untiring Nunkui goes unseen as she nurtures life underground, and it is too dark to watch her careful tending after dusk. No need for pomp or praise; Nunkui's ecstasy is life itself.

When I muse with Nunkui here in the Pacific Northwest, I see her waist-length auburn hair dampened by dew and, clinging to it, bits of twigs and soil. She smells green to me, like the spongy forest mosses and luminous streambed plants.

Midnight-haired spirit of the forest Nunkui is of the Shuar. I am Celt and in kinship with a different forest.

The feminine spirit of the Earth has names and appearances that are as diverse as the lands and waters that span the globe. Not bound by geography, description, or even time, this revered goddess is ever here, and she is everywhere. We can entice her presence through our care for the Earth.

Feminine archetype Nunkui opens us to the Earth's abundance and the mystery of what flourishes in the dark—children may grow an inch overnight, we restore through rest, and a dark night of the soul can transform us. Tragedy, and even death, can initiate a fresh cycle of life. I have found that Nunkui can enrich our own dark passages and also support us as we face the suffering of people, animals, and nature in the world today.

Here is a story of how the spirit of the forest, by whatever name we know her, helped me.

In the Hoh Rain Forest, I am blessed to have many old-growth maple and spruce trees near my cabin on the strip of private land where I live. When I first moved here, I used to walk and run through a second-growth forest near my cabin that borders the expansive, untouched old-growth areas that remain. This made me cry. Mature stumps sat as gigantic phantoms amid dwarfed, new-growth trees. The original forest must have been magnificent. It no longer existed.

I spoke to the stumps, the grandmothers and grandfathers, and shared my gratitude as well as my grief. I felt hopeless and angry as so many trees are still being cut, here and elsewhere. In many areas even the stumps that hold the genetic memory of old forest in the soil, to generate new life, are now being removed.

Amazon tribes engage in a noble fight to keep their trees standing. North Americans who help them may be shocked to discover how much of our own temperate cloud forest is being cut right here in Washington State, our trees felled primarily for foreign buyers.

Feelings are signposts. I honored mine. Yet I couldn't get beyond my despair.

One day the woman of the forest showed up on my walk. From my bottomless pit of grief, through my tears, I saw her light as if for the first time—in the joyous, unstoppable growth all around me. Countless plants and trees—ferns, oxalis, hemlock, spruce, mosses, and more—brothers and sisters spiraled up from the rich dark soil, feeding on death, the genetic material of the old growth. Ecstatic life was everywhere, visible and palpable. So absorbed was I by loss that I had missed the beauty right in front of me.

I recalled a time long ago when a dear friend died and my tears wouldn't stop. I learned then that those tears pouring from my eyes, and the grief that broke my heart, reflected the pure force of love I felt for my friend. So I dipped into that bottomless well of grief, knowing that it was love, and committed to generate more love to benefit the life in this forest and the life here that was yet to be.

I sang with this love and joy as I ran and celebrated with tree brothers and sisters, offering them good energy and strengthening my intention "to join people with nature." Like composting food wastes to enrich the soil, the Earth Goddess recycled my difficult feelings into fortitude for what was growing and hope that we can revive the old forests.

Nunkui gives us hope and reminds us of the opportunities in personal pain and challenge. Her light shines when there seems to be no light; she is a guide through difficulties that can evolve us. The spirit of the Earth is an alchemical midwife who nourishes essence.

Nunkui is associated with the night, and each night unfolds the classic cycle of dark to light. She says, "Relax what you desire as well as what you fear. Rest in my spiraling movement and perceive the dark as light."

We can tap in to the light of Nunkui in the dark every night by paying attention to our dreams and awakenings, and sensing what blossoms, or stirs, in the wee hours. As the light dims the veils of reality woven of personal and collective hopes, fears, and conditioning grow thin. The sacred that is always there is easier to see.

All aboriginal shamanic people I've met respect the potency of night. Those traveling on the vast expanses of the Asian steppe, which is known for bandits, or sleeping amidst wild animals in the Amazon wake to the sounds and bumps in the night as a natural protection. In the Amazon Basin, Mongolia, Tibet, and elsewhere, indigenous people wake to dreams and spirits and use the power of the night to pierce through to other worlds.

Nunkui says, "Open to the fertile night. Attune to me, spiraling and abundant muse."

Nunkui, who coaxes seedlings to unfurl into the plants the Shuar rely on for food, is inseparable from nourishment. Legend tells that Nunkui sent a child to help the Shuar grow food on the land by their long houses when the plants they had wildcrafted from the forest and along the river grew scarce.

Like women of all original cultures, Shuar women still sing the ancient secret songs (*anents* for the Shuar) to the plants and Earth Goddess so the crops will thrive. Sandra shares beautiful insights about singing to the nature beings and land in her writings on Corn.

Interestingly, science notes that extra carbon dioxide is released when we sing, making plants in the vicinity grow more quickly. Sound waves can also positively affect growth; everyone's heard that harmonious music helps our houseplants and crops to grow.

As validating as science can be, its tendency to dissect the mystery into parts and pieces can deny other subtle factors that encourage life to flourish.

A Shuar woman will tell you in simple terms: "When a woman sings the sacred anents as she tends her garden, Nunkui is happy and so, the plants grow."

Shuar women invite and intensify the life force of the food they grow by carefully tending their plants while singing sacred anents to invoke Nunkui. The women's piercing, high-pitched voices are beautiful and induce an expanded state within which they merge with the spirit of the forest. The Shuar know that life needs more than physical elements, and that it flourishes when the spiritual force is strong—when Nunkui is present.

As the women sing to Nunkui, they *are* Nunkui.

When we extend love and goodness to the Earth by singing, tending plants, being respectful, making offerings and ceremony, preserving nature, bestowing good sentiment, celebrating, and in other ways living peacefully with nature, we also can merge with this deep feminine spirit.

When Shuar women do not honor Nunkui, the spiraling movement of life, the Earth Goddess moves on to other tribes. The plants suffer and the family's food source is in jeopardy.

Old tales say that Nunkui's child taught the Shuar to make the mildly alcoholic beverage *chicha,* from manioc (yuca, cassava) root that the women chew and then spit into a gourd bowl. Chicha is the staple drink, served only by Shuar women. Shuar of all ages drink chicha, a thick, pleasant beerlike brew, throughout the day in lieu of fresh water, which locally contains too much organic matter to drink.

Nunkui's child also taught the tribes to hunt and cook. The old ones say the Shuar were at first excited about all they learned, but later became greedy. Nunkui's response was to take her child back. The Shuar learned from this tragedy. Mothers taught daughters to care for the gardens and maintain good rapport with the Earth spirit. Men were expected to hunt and cut trees in balance with nature and not take more than was needed.

The story of Nunkui who took her child back from the Shuar mirrors where we are now—cut off from the seed of life and the earth by greed and immaturity.

To restore stasis we care for the earth and strive to live in balance and engage her mystery. Deep trust returns to us as we do. Yet it is strikingly easy for us, even those who strive to stay close to the earth, to feel disconnected.

When I first began practicing shamanism and energy healing, many considered them cults. Over the years holistic interests grew. As Reiki and shamanism became widespread, I traveled more to teach, but the practice of accepting every teaching opportunity caught up with me. I flew in airplanes, ate in restaurants, and stayed in hotels far more than was good for me or felt good. What irony, as the shamans I knew were rooted in the earth and drew their power from the land, especially the land on which they were born.

During this time the Earth Goddess kept showing up in my dreams. She appeared in different forms and dream scenarios, yet her message to me was always the same: "Come back to the earth; sink your feet more deeply into her than ever."

I listened and got my feet as deeply into the earth as I could.

Not everyone needs to live at the edge of the wilderness, yet we all need to touch the wild places that remain. They teach us how to revive the land, which also revives us.

Nunkui says, "Mature land and waters—and reverence for your own elders—have faded from your reality mirror. Only in maturing yourselves will the reflection of the old and wise return."

When we open our hearts we hear the forest spirit's voice. She appears in myriad forms and speaks in countless ways. Loudly, clearly this Earth Mother calls her children to come back to her now.

Many interpret the Shuar as saying that all women are Nunkui. Others say Nunkui is Mother Earth, or the spirit of the Earth, or the spirit of the forest. Still others say she is the plant seedling itself.

Nunkui is each, as well as all, of these. And she is more.

Indigenous people do not compartmentalize as we do. The seed and life force, as well as the spirit of life, the forest, and the earth—and the womb of the Earth and the womb of women where life is nourished—are not separate. All comprise the sacred feminine.

🌿 Practices

Nunkui nourishes under the ground by day and above the earth by night. We can invoke her spirit in our own gardens. If you don't have a garden, find one to explore or go to a wild place in Nunkui's honor to learn how plants and trees grow to maturity.

Also watch what grows every day where you live. Check each morning for changes and new life. See what the Earth Goddess has inspired in the night.

Give good energy to the plants you engage with and grow. Feel what it's like to be part of a growing garden. Shuar women invoke Nunkui and also take loving care of their plants. Good energy is action as well as sentiment.

As Sandra speaks of tending your inner garden of thoughts and actions, also give your good energy to people, projects, and passions, as well as problems. Then put these aside at night as you rest in the fertile gap—the goddess's realm of potential. The nourishment will continue under Nunkui's care. Release to her tending. You may wake with an insight or dream the answer to your struggles.

How does the archetypal Earth spirit appear? How do you know her?

If you stir in the night, be curious. Consider rising before dawn to the muse's spiral dance. Breathe and stay clear to feel her. The feminine spirit of the Earth is there, alive and radiant. In the space between dark and light, at the edge of awareness, she abides. Empty out your preoccupations and make space to know her.

We touch the movement of the sacred with our hearts and subtle senses. Nunkui is one with the rhythm of night, darkness, and life, all part of Earth's mystery.

Another good way to connect with the mystery and attune to natural rhythms of night and day is to go without unessential electricity one day a week.

Light candles or ease into the dark instead of turning on lights. Cook on a woodstove or eat leftovers. In lieu of watching television or using the computer, tell stories. Or go out and walk barefoot, watch the sunset and speak with the plants, water, sky, animals, wind, and stone people; then listen in turn to the animals, insects, wind, and trees as they speak to you.

Day releases to dusk. Twilight becomes night. Night is deep and full, then morphs to dawn. Morning breaks a new day.

What blossoms in the fertile time of night? What feelings or experiences stir?

These simple practices wake up the life in us. The magic is always there.

In a dark time of the soul, ask the feminine spirit of the Earth to support you in using this experience to alchemize suffering into power and love. Nunkui can help. Just as fevers in children often precede visible behavioral spurts, our darkest periods of loss, illness, or chaos can make us strong, wise, and compassionate.

Call upon the forest spirit, or Earth Goddess. Offer her the rich humus of your pain and confusion. You can even dig a hole in the ground and offer food that symbolizes your angst. Offer from the heart, feel your pain—cry it, yell it, move it, offer it to the Mother. The Earth can compost this good energy.

Afterward, rest. Trust the unseen force. Feel the life force course through you.

Nunkui says, "The center point of dark is light." When the light floods back in, share that feeling with the Earth. Plant some seeds. As she has put the life back into you, offer life back to her.

Chaos and pain unfold in every moment, as do life and love. As we honor our difficult feelings, they can lead us to the rich center of the dark, which is love. We can find nourishment in this deep well and also offer it to others in need.

6

BANANA SLUG AND EARTHWORM

Banana Slug

Llyn

Imagine strolling along a mossy trail in a dense, wet forest. Thousands of tiny migratory birds alight in the treetops overhead, chirping above the sounds of rain and raging glacial streams.

You breathe in the freshly scented air, rich in oxygen and negative ions. It is springtime in the rain forest. Everything is green and flowing and blooming. The rains will cease in a month, yet right now the earth is a sponge and water drips from every moss-bearded tree limb.

Seeming to walk with you on the lush and sopping trail, yet moving so slowly that you barely see it move at all, is a small, plump, snail-like creature with no shell. Of the countless nature beings I live with in the Hoh River Valley, the Banana Slug is a prolific and intriguing presence.

Why are Banana Slugs called Banana Slugs? The skin of a Banana

Slug is colored yellow with brown spots, like the skin of a ripe banana. Although you may love to eat the mature, sweet, brown-speckled banana fruit, you would likely gag if offered Banana Slug snacks. But for many indigenous groups, slugs are a good source of protein, raw as well as cooked.

Tourists who visit the Hoh Rain Forest of the Olympic Mountains are mesmerized by Banana Slugs; their images adorn coffee mugs, posters, and tee shirts. For many who live in the Northwest, slugs are not so alluring, as they wreak havoc in people's gardens, often consuming carefully planted seeds before the plants can sprout. If Slugs could speak, I imagine them to say: "Oh, how thoughtful of you to provide us with food!"

Even for those who do not maintain gardens, these small slimy life forms can elicit intense reactions from humans. Some find them ugly. I recently heard of a man who squashed every Banana Slug he encountered.

Many of us in commercialized cultures have a narrow range of what we consider to be beautiful. We also tend to project onto nature what we reject in ourselves.

Soft, fleshy, and fragile, the Banana Slug has no protective shell like its snail cousin. Does Slug mirror our underbelly? The divine feminine knows there is power in being vulnerable.

Sensitive as a lover's heart, Banana Slug is likewise moist and spongy like female genitals and the fleshy insides of our mouths. Does this tiny being cause us to bristle because it hints at those parts of us that we deny or conceal?

The sensual, sensitive aspects of the sacred feminine are still something many of us hide as well as hide *from,* and they have been abused and misinterpreted across time and cultures.

All nature beings in the rain forest thrive on the rich, the dark, and the wet; these are not sun worshippers. In fact the Slug, which can remain under water for long periods, needs moisture to survive. Temperatures can drop into the twenties during Hoh winters, and

snow and hail fall. In contrast to this, the hot, dry months of August and September would desiccate any wormy, wet life-form not under cover. During these times the Banana Slug crawls under a protective log, cocoons itself in slime, and trances out in ooze till warmth and/or wetness resume.

Slugs love to nuzzle into the moist, mushy, lightless places of the forest, adjectives that also describe the environment in which babies are conceived, grow, and emerge into the world at birth. Sensuality is prime to nature and to life.

The endlessly patient Slug helps us reframe distortions that arise when sex is marketed and virtual, the earthy sacred feminine forgotten. The exquisite nature being Banana Slug does this by calling us back to what is rich and real—our bodies and the earth.

How do we honor Banana Slug medicine and touch back into tactile earthiness?

One way is to learn from wholesome young children who love to lie on the grass gazing up at clouds and stars, run through summer downpours, squish mud between their toes, roll down grassy hills, and smear face paints, cake frosting, or dirt onto their skin. My toddlers also loved to run their fingers through my hair, as well as through gooey cookie dough, and rub wet, salty-gritty sand all over their legs at the beach.

The simple, sensual explorations that occupy healthy youngsters signal robust curiosity and a hearty connection with their bodies and the earth. These kids are in touch.

In North America we say to one another, "I'll be in touch," "Please touch in," "That's a nice touch," "I feel out of touch," "I want to touch on this," and so forth.

In developing countries I observe that people don't talk as much as we do about touch. They touch.

College friends in India hold hands—boys with boys and girls with girls. Children and women in the Andes not only hug visitors, but they also hold each other's hands and stroke their arms and hair. One woman on an Ecuador trip in the Andes many years ago proclaimed that although the shamanic rituals were powerful, the most healing aspect of her journey was the unconditional love she felt in being petted by the Quechua women and children. Innocent touch changed this woman's life.

There are times in my healing practice when I have known that gently holding a person for a longer-than-normal hug in a noninvasive way would heal and allow grace to flow. I didn't pray, chant, caretake, pity, strategize, or send energy, but simply felt goodness grow with every breath. The effects can be profound.

Spirit and body are inseparable. We are also one with our planet's body. Touch is innate to who we are and how we know self and world.

Banana Slug suggests we get back in touch, with each other and with the earth.

The Slug body is primarily water, as are we and as is our planet. Banana Slug breathes through wet, porous skin and moves oh-so slowly on its foot muscle, gliding most easily in the rain on a thick protective trail of slime. Old timers in this region say slug slime is antiseptic; some even borrow slime from Slugs to apply to scrapes on their own skin.

Banana Slugs may stubbornly not budge while you watch them. Turn away and they seem to glide huge distances in no time. Once when I lay down for a nap by the river about an hour's walk from my cabin, I made sure no Slugs were near; I did not want to squash one or get slimed in my sleep. Twenty minutes later I opened my eyes to see a Banana Slug dozing next to me on my wool blanket.

Life would take a different spin if we also hugged the land as do trusting and tender Slugs.

The unguarded Banana Slug freely shares her deep feminine teachings: "Remember the sensual and the power of little."

Nourishing our children and friends, preparing a delicious meal, and much of the goodness of life involves simple details and interactions that make all the difference. It's the little things that matter most.

My children, Sayre and Eben, are now twenty-six and twenty-three. When they were young it took me insane amounts of time to get things done, yet young childhood is precious and short. I strove to put distractions aside and invest in little joys, such as reading stories and making up games, picking berries and visiting Lady Slippers in Sayre and Eben's secret forest places, or serving picnics under the dining room table on snow days. With children little things rank big. And they keep parents grounded.

With my children grown and living on their own, since living in the Hoh Rain Forest, I again focus my restlessness in order to honor the little. One has to be like a Slug—slug-(g)ish—in order to see, let alone appreciate, these tiny camouflaged beings that play an incredible role in forest ecosystems.

Banana Slugs are vital to the decomposition of plants and spread seeds and spores across the forest floor. They are also amazingly sentient. Come to Slug with malice and it retracts and plays dead or asleep. Speak in a soothing tone and this fellow being may lift its head and turn to look at you. Chatting with Banana Slugs can make me weep.

I traveled out for a workshop while writing this chapter and happily wrote on Banana Slug on my flight back to Seattle. Upon return I stayed for a night in my friend Ryanne's minimalist house on Whidbey Island, a 120-square-foot space with a sleeping loft. I climbed the loft ladder and went to bed musing about Banana Slugs. I woke up at 2:00 a.m. musing about Banana Slugs. I got out of bed the next morning musing about Banana Slugs. This is the way of things when I write.

In the morning I climbed down from the loft and stepped barefoot through dewy grasses to my young friend's little kitchen building, eighty paces from the sleeping house. The cooking room, reminiscent of a New England summer kitchen, had windows on three sides looking out to tall trees and an inlet. A tiny bathroom was built onto the backside of the kitchen.

Musing with Banana Slug and staying in this elfin dwelling brought a happy simplicity to my return. I made some hot tea and sat on the little kitchen veranda enjoying the morning smells and sounds.

Later I washed my face and brushed my teeth in the tiniest sink I have ever seen, in a teensy-weensy bathroom, which fulfilled every toiletry need including a shower.

Banana Slug's teaching of the power of small is big in current times when hoarding is at the same time diagnosable and prime-time entertainment. Our households and storage units are packed, yet our lands are stripped and our hearts are vacant.

The power of the small was very apparent in a water ritual I shared with shamans on the Mongolian border, which included a silent sunrise ceremony. It felt powerful not to impose—to be silent and move softly, allowing space for dawn's delicate expression. No words were spoken as a creation fashioned from nature was passed from person to person. Then as the sun rose, it was presented to the lake. We watched the gentle ripples as one person placed our gift in the water, knowing our love would touch every shore.

Despite our conditioning to be big, loud, in your face, more, complicated, bigger, and louder again, the sacred feminine is alive and well in the simple, the silent, and the small. Even in the invisible.

Banana Slug posits: "The feminine spirit awakens; honor your heart to feel her caress."

When I stepped out from Ryanne's bathroom on that cool island morning, I felt a tug and glanced to my right. There in a wee love nest of glistening grass blades was the first Slug couple I've seen in my four years of living in the Northwest—a visual feast of two Slug arcs almost creating a heart shape together, with translucent white forms conjoining in the heart's center.

It was auspicious to find these little lovers at this humble home. The lightly treading dweller of this place is thirty-two years old. The world was different twenty-five years ago when I was Ryanne's age. Instead of ignoring the state of things or indulging apocalyptic gloom, she contributes by example, understanding the largeness of small. There are many like her who do not wait or plan for or boast about a new societal dream; they live it. The benefit ripples out like water blessings in a lake.

A barred owl flew over our heads the night I arrived at Ryanne's home, and now pure Slug ecstasy played out in front of me. All was well here between people and nature.

For those of us who still worry and wait, or endlessly scheme a new dream, what locks us in old paradigms and keeps us from being living examples of ecstasy and harmony?

"Oh, this one little thing will free you," Banana Slug says, sliding up to join the conversation: "Know that you are enough, just as you are."

Though humble and little Banana Slug's slow fertilization will help to bring back an old-growth forest. This requires the patience of a Banana Slug, as it is a thousand-year investment. It also depends on whether we humans can revere the small and let nature restore.

Patience comes naturally to Banana Slug, which is what it is, and does what it does, unfettered by even the baggage of protection.

We, also, can stay uncomplicated—root in who we are as we do amazing things for our planet.

The little creature Banana Slug does not even need a partner to procreate, though it may choose one. Efficiently, the sex organ is eaten after coitus. Banana Slug is definitely a world unto itself.

It may not always seem so, yet we also carry within us everything we seek. We do not have to strategize our way back to wholeness, as grace is here for us to touch right now.

Banana Slug holds up a hopeful mirror: "You and I are not so different, and who we are is enough."

🌿 Practices

Through the stories and suggestions above, we engage Banana Slug wisdom, get back in touch, and empower the small.

Think about tiny aspects that largely have a positive impact on your life right now. Envision and appreciate these. Give energy to the little.

Banana Slug helps us recover childlike curiosity and sensuality. This can be as simple as dipping our fingers into a cold stream or under faucet water, sifting our hands through beach sand or in a child's sandbox, stroking a baby's silken cheek or the soft fur of a pet, or sniffing our favorite cooking spices or an indoor flowering plant. Open your heart and senses and see how alive the small makes you feel.

As important as it is to be in touch, all of us know how it feels to be panicked, stressed, or overwhelmed—to lose touch, feel out of touch, and forget the power of the little.

Consider a gentle approach at such times; for example, lying on a carpeted floor or a natural covering outside; taking some luxurious deep breaths and moving with the breath in slow, minuscule ways as if cozying up to the earth; and hugging the land like a tender Slug magnet.

Take all the time you like gently touching and stretching. Allow your body to show you how it wants to move; engage the sensual.

Breathe with whatever feelings arise, allowing them to bubble up and wash through as you move.

Our bodies instinctively know how to unwind, free unexpressed feelings, and absorb good energy from the earth. This is how we find our way back to ourselves, our breath, and what we really feel.

The small will return you to yourself. The power of the little is key to healing naturally. In ayurveda, for instance, practitioners suggest small life shifts to support greater well-being. As another example, in homeopathy tiny amounts of remedy can trigger big healing responses.

In moving like a sensual Slug, little by little you will start to again feel happy to be in a body here on Earth.

Ah, what a good feeling!

This may be just the right time to review the life patterns that put you out of touch.

After reading about Banana Slug, muse and journal about other ways you're inspired to empower the small and reclaim the sensual.

What is right for you and what presents itself auspiciously?

Little by little—and a little at a time—is the way.

People will notice and wonder. They may say, "Wow, you glow! What are you doing?"

Applying the little is often invisible, yet the effects can show in a big way.

Slugs are vulnerable. They sometimes get squashed. Sometimes humans do, too, when life truly falls apart. For example, they may lose their homes or families to floods and fires or their loved ones to the military or to post-traumatic-stress suicide.

Remember little Banana Slug, which is what it is, and does what it does, nourishing and seeding the earth despite the surrounding devastation of cut forests.

During times of crisis we also can be who we are and ground ourselves in the small. Search out the little things. Focus on the small and tangible. Act and gesture in ways that touch the heart and also get done what needs to be done. Banana Slug medicine helps us stay humble and focused in order to recover our touch and purpose during unstable times.

The world is at a tipping point instigating great reality shifts. Neither we, nor Banana Slugs, can escape being vulnerable. Yet as uninviting as being unguarded feels, it teaches us to be open and fluid as change washes through.

Throughout all, meek and wise Banana Slug encourages: "Stay simple and in touch. You and I, we are just enough."

Earthworm

Sandra

"We need to get some earthworms!"

This is a statement my husband hears from me continually as we examine the soil in our garden.

When we moved into our house, there was a beautiful garden right outside our door, abundant with brightly colored flowering plants and fruit trees—apple, peach, pear, cherry, and apricot. All received lots of water and the garden was healthy, vital, and flourishing.

Due to drought conditions we could not continue to give the garden sufficient water to support the growth of so many plants. The hardy desert-growing plants continued to flourish, but plants that needed to be watered daily did not survive. Our fruit trees survived, although they are not as vital as they were in earlier years.

One quadrant of our garden does not support much plant life, but the tall apple tree in that quadrant is healthy and produces very tart apples each year. Some years the bounty is enormous, and I have brought an abundance of apples to my workshops to share with others. Although the apples are a beautiful bright red and look perfect, animals do not eat them. Some years they are even too tart for me to enjoy, but to honor the apple tree for producing such an abundance of fruit, I eat them to honor the gift that is shared. Some years, due to late freezes and drought, only a few apples appear.

The dark brown cherry tree did not survive the drought. It was a very old tree with fissured bark, and each year the tree produced less and less fruit, until one year it died. Initially I could not bear to cut it down, hoping it would come back, but eventually I succumbed and down it came.

We have consulted with many landscapers regarding the soil in this quadrant of our garden, for we have mulched and fertilized to no avail. It seems something in the chemical makeup must have changed for it to go from supporting plants to sustaining only the very hardy. The issues seem to be beyond water.

I even called in the Hidden Folk, whom I wrote about in my final essay, but they have not helped with this situation. Therefore I know there is something important for me to learn as I explore the issue on my own.

I believe the issue is that the soil has become so hardened by minerals and drought in this area that the only solution is to bring in an army of Earthworms.

I certainly cannot say I have ever been "attracted" to the appearance of Banana Slugs or Earthworms. Truthfully, I've always jumped back when I have come into contact with these nature beings, which some people describe as squishy, wriggly, and slimy.

As Llyn wrote, we tend to have a narrow range of what we consider beautiful. Earthworms are tube-shaped and segmented. They are hermaphrodites—each individual carries both male and female organs. They are both blind and deaf, but their skin is covered in cells that allow them to taste the soil and sense light and dark. Earthworms live in soil, burrowing into various levels, naturally allowing oxygen to get in, which is beneficial for plant growth. They turn leaves, leftover food, and anything able to be decomposed into fertilizer. They breathe through their skin and have five sets of double hearts in segments that are close to their heads.

In 1881 Charles Darwin wrote:

"It may be doubted whether there are many other animals which have played so important a part in the history of the world, as have these lowly organized creatures."

In our modern world we tend to compartmentalize the way we view nature and our bodies. We create gardens, but bring in trees and other flora from around the world that do not interact well with local life forms. In caring for our own bodies, we go to specialists when we have a physical issue. Sometimes we go to so many specialists that the true diagnosis of an issue is missed, as the body is not examined as an entire organism. We buy food, furniture, clothing, and other material items in stores and do not reflect on all that went into creating the final product.

Many years ago I had a vision in which I met a descendant from thousands of years in the future. She was short with a slight build and had beautiful shiny black hair that just touched her shoulders. Her large eyes were also black and filled with peace, light, and joy. She shared a very powerful message with me. She said that in today's world we act as the fingers of a hand that have dropped to the floor thinking that each finger can have a separate life on its own. That, she said, is preposterous. The work is to reconnect the hand to the body and to understand that every aspect of the body is interdependent on all its parts to sustain the life of the whole.

We can take this literally—our body is a whole with our blood, cells, organs, body parts, microorganisms, and good bacteria all working together. And we can also use this as a metaphor when we look at our Earth garden—every single living being is connected to the Earth and vital to the health and well-being of the entire garden.

There is such a weaving of mystery in creation, and we often miss the magic of how each and every creature in the web of life serves a role in creating, maintaining, and sustaining life. All in the web of life have something vital to share in creating a healthy Earth garden. All life is interdependent on other life forms.

More microorganisms germinate in half a cup of fertile earth than there are humans on the planet. Every acre of well-cultivated land contains up to half a ton of thriving microorganisms, not to mention up to a ton of earthworms. The earthworms can create a ton of humic castings that are essential for the health of the soil. The castings nurture the soil with much-needed nutrients that promote healthy plant growth. The mucus that the earthworms produce, along with the castings, promotes the growth of helpful bacteria and fungi.

❧ *Use your imagination to leave your ordinary life behind, and take a journey with me into the world of the Earthworm and the gift of its life.*

Close your eyes and imagine yourself in a rich and fertile garden. As you examine the soil, you are led to the small life forms that are the tenders of the soil.

Using your invisible senses notice how microorganisms built the soil, but nature's true tiller of the soil is Earthworm. Observe how these small blind beings are powerful diggers and earthmovers, capable of burrowing as deep as fifteen feet. Watch them force air through tunnels as they move. Be amazed at the way they burrow and aerate, mix up the soil, break down clumps, and bury stones. Watch as they carry down leaves and other organic matter, while others bring nutrients and humus to the topsoil. Earthworms cannot live without enormous amounts of decaying organic matter.

Return to your ordinary awareness with a sense of gratitude for how Earthworms create healthy soil that supports the growth of food that sustains us.

Ten thousand years ago the Earthworms we are familiar with today were found only in certain areas on the planet, such as in the valleys of three great civilizations—the Indus, the Euphrates, and the Nile. These are places where crops easily grew in soil enriched by the presence of Earthworms.

In *Sacred Medicine of Bee, Butterfly, Earthworm, and Spider,* Linda Star Wolf and Anna Cariad-Barrett wrote that Cleopatra and the ancient Egyptians viewed Earthworm as sacred. They shared that this view probably originated from Earthworm's contribution to the viability of agriculture along the Nile.

In my further research I read the amazing book, *Secrets of the Soil,* by Peter Tompkins and Christopher Bird. I learned that ancient Egyptians were forbidden to remove Earthworms from the land, and farmers were told not to trouble the worms for fear of interfering with their role in creating fertile soil.

Many lush meadows found in other locations in the world are attributed to the introduction of the Earthworm. Earthworms can produce more compost in a shorter time and with less effort than is required by any other method.

In the 1940s German researcher C. Merker wrote that Earthworms have voices and can actually sing. He found that by opening and closing their mouths, they produced sounds made of changing rhythms.

This was considered an astonishing finding, as Earthworms do not have lungs and breathe through their skin, but I was not at all surprised to read what C. Merker wrote about Earthworms singing. My own time spent in nature has revealed to my visible and invisible senses that *all* life sings.

Using modern technology we can hear Earthworms making gurgling sounds when they are disturbed in any way as they burrow. All of life tends to complain when being disturbed.

It is sad to note that this amazing life form, Earthworm, is being killed by the pesticides and chemical fertilizers we use today. But as long as there is soil and organic matter, Earthworm will continue to proliferate and gift us with the miracle of its life.

When we look at how all in the web of life contributes to the health of all of life, there are many lessons we can learn. As you read some of the messages I received from examining Earthworm, take some time in reflection and notice what emerges from your deeper inner well.

We often judge the importance of the role of a person or a nature being. We tend to compare the power of life forms based on their size and how colorful and loud they are. Llyn reminds us to honor and acknowledge the power of small.

When you honor the small beings that are vital to life, you start to let go of your judgments and comparisons of appearances. You can, without judgment, tune in to yourself and acknowledge the gifts you personally contribute to the web of life. And in doing so you feel on a cellular level that you are enough.

Many seek to be noticed, and we give accolades to public speakers, authors, and teachers, forgetting about the millions of people around the globe who are quietly or anonymously doing spiritual work and contributing to the health of their communities and the planet.

There are so many who pray for peace and for the health of life. I have met extraordinary people who work in grocery stores, banks, restaurants, and other businesses who stop and engage in conversation with each person they meet. Their smiles, care, and laughter cause every person they engage with to brighten up and smile in response. Each person feels seen and leaves feeling light and filled with joy from being in such a person's presence. But these people are not famous and have no need or desire to be known or recognized.

Every person has a role to share in life's play, and it does not depend on external recognition. Millions of people go about their work looking not for fame, but to be in service to, and help to sustain, all of life. They are guided from their hearts and souls, not by how they are seen or the acknowledgment they receive.

When we travel back to the power of Earthworm medicine, we can easily understand that the earth cannot rely on only a few powerful Earthworms doing their vital work to create nutritious soil that sustains life. It is a community of Earthworms all working together that creates rich soil, and together as a community they are sacred.

We live in a time when the process of individuation is supported and valued. And of course it is essential to appreciate and grow into who we are as individuals and connect with our unique talents and gifts. In this way we become healthy members of our community. Healthy communities in native cultures depend on each member knowing what she or he contributes to the health of the entire community. Each person's gift is acknowledged from the time of birth.

We often look to "leaders" to change the world for us. We want someone "out there" to make life better for us and cure the problems we face in the environment and in the challenges we face politically and economically.

But in truth it is the power of community that is vital to creating needed changes. We see the power of people coming together in communities already—helping to rebuild after a natural disaster, growing communal gardens that feed many, speaking out against abuses and, with their joined voices, changing policies that have an impact on the environment and all of life. Many join together in prayer and other spiritual practices, and we see the effects ripple throughout the entire web of life.

In the 1990s I received a powerful message while performing a shamanic journey. I was shown how children in the future will no longer read fairy tales about how one hero or heroine saved the world. Rather, they will read stories about communities of people coming together to create positive change. The power of community working together on behalf of all of life will be recognized in future generations.

Earthworms have an amazing ability to dig in the earth and process waste in a way that fertilizes the soil and creates a healthy garden.

When I go into a pharmacy, I am struck by how many shelves of pills and tonics are sold to help with digestive problems. As a culture we deal with an abundance of issues resulting from our lack of ability to digest what we eat. Of course some of this can be attributed to the kinds of food we eat and the way we eat our food. In addition, we take too many antibiotics and eat foods that have antibiotics in them, thus killing the microorganisms and beneficial bacteria that we need to keep our inner soil healthy.

On a larger level is it that we no longer know how to digest life? If you cannot digest life, you cannot digest your food. This is worth pondering.

🌿 Practices

Honor and appreciate all the different aspects that make up your entire body and the beautiful, radiant living being that you are.

Take some time to give gratitude to your cells, blood, organs, and all of your body parts. Your body is one organism and needs to be fed, nurtured, and cared for as such. Avoid focusing on different symptoms. See how whatever physical symptoms you might be dealing with are a statement about the health of your whole organism—body, mind, and spirit.

Honor the microorganisms and good bacteria that fertilize the soil in your own inner garden and contribute to your health and well-being.

As you go about your day, notice the people you meet who are in service to the community and to the planet who do not need any acknowledgment.

Honor the power of anonymity while doing your spiritual work and practices on behalf of all of life.

Put on some music and meditate on the gifts, talents, and strengths you were born with that add to the health of your family and your community. Or take a walk in nature appreciating the importance of all of life while you reflect on the beauty of your contributions.

Everything that occurs in your life is a gift. Life brings things for you; it does not happen to you. As you learn to flow with life and accept the changes that are occurring personally and at a global level, you will be more adept at digesting life. In so doing you will start to feel positive changes occurring to your physical health and sense of well-being.

7

BLACK BEAR

Black Bear

Llyn

The densely forested lands where I live on the wild side of the Hoh River are known to be bear country. The nearest town is a forty-minute drive, assuming a fallen tree or swollen stream hasn't blocked the road. Intending a quiet weekend in the wilderness, sometimes people become stranded here for a week. The Black Bears, however, fare just fine.

When I was driving into town recently, a Black Bear sprang out from the forest and bounded down the road ahead of my car. Imagine a two-hundred-pound animal running in front of you; how fast Black Bears move and how strong they are.

"Black Bear, why does your power enthrall us so?"

Anyone who's encountered Bear in the wild will know.

Black Bear is reclusive and silent, with the exception of a mother with her cubs. If she senses a threat to her young, the nurturing female becomes a violent defender.

Earlier in my life, while living in New England, I occasionally chanced upon Bears. One time I was walking on a dirt road when a mother with two cubs ventured from the woods. Luckily for me, though I was standing within feet of the Black Bear family, they passed by and reentered the forest on the other side of the road.

Another time, upon hearing garbage-raiding raccoons, I ran out my front door to scare them away from the trash. No coons in sight I was suddenly eye to eye with a Black Bear. I ran one way and was grateful that the Black Bear ran the other.

Many of us know that awesome feeling in the presence of a large, wild creature of nature. If you have not experienced this, perhaps you've felt similarly as ocean waves crashed at your feet, during a powerful hailstorm, in close range to a lightning bolt, or at other times when nature's potency was close.

In musing with Black Bear, the sacred feminine reveals, "This primal force is who you are."

Old Norse warriors directed this natural, often dormant power by wearing *bear-sarks* (bearskin shirts rubbed in herbs and oils) to elicit fearlessness in battle; this may be the derivation of the word *berserk*. These men also likely ate—or painted their skin with—plants that evoked bearlike strength.

The solitary and gentle Black Bear mother, a supreme nurturer, is ferocious if she needs to be. And males may attack if food is scarce, for intensity is about protecting and surviving.

We may not wear bear-sarks, but people fight to stay alive and keep out influences they fear, just as a mother Bear does with her cubs.

Black Bear models an easy, uncensored flow of expression: from wild, intense, or forceful to tame and gentle, and back and forth. Healthy toddlers who play, cry, laugh, throw a temper tantrum, and then fall fast asleep are just as versatile.

Intense energy can invigorate and stimulate creativity. For instance, although I need calmness to write, I take frequent breaks outside. Taking a few barefoot steps in the snow or freezing river, getting drenched by rain, or running in a sharp wind inspires my writing.

Like a guileless child, the divine feminine sees everything as the one. Just so, every aspect of us, whether we judge good or bad, or agitated or peaceful, makes the whole of who we are. Just as agile Black Bear rolls around on the earth for the pure pleasure of it, that same type of playfulness and movement helps us stay authentic.

"Embrace all of who you are to touch your natural power," says Black Bear. "Trust and relax. Play."

It was hunting season when the Bear lunged in front of my car in the Olympic Mountains. In sobering contrast to that amazing surge of life that bounded down the road, my weekend neighbor shot a Black Bear a few days later.

Black Bears have few predators, and humans are among them. Black Bear hunting in these mountains traces back to honorable pursuits of the original Hoh tribe, whose descendants live nearby. Hunting practices have changed, however. Bear pelts yield a high price, and using guns instead of arrows distorts the balance between land, people, and animals. The old ones revered the land the Bears roamed and used the animal's meat for food; fat for waterproofing; pelts for rugs and warm garments; teeth, claws, and bones for totem energy and jewelry; and so forth.

As hunting Black Bears in these forests is a fact of life, and one was shot while I was writing this chapter, I went over to see the freshly killed Bear stretched out in my neighbor's truck bed.

Imagine burrowing your fingers into the thick pelt of a freshly killed Bear, its luxurious fall coat the blackest of blacks. I did this and stroked the Black Bear's head and fingered its long, curled claws. I held a heavy Bear paw in my hand and touched its leathery footpad.

The hunter, my friend Monty, eyed me inquisitively.

"You're sad for the Bear, aren't you?"

I admitted my heart was heavy. Struggling for words, I stopped trying. The Black Bear had given its life and was soon to be skinned. I just wanted to admire it.

Imagine gliding your hand over the length of an almost six-foot-tall Black Bear's furry leg. My fingers and palms still recall the Bear's coarse hair and the firm muscle under its hide. I was grateful to appreciate the Black Bear soon after it died and to wish its spirit well.

Monty pressed on, "You feel bad for the Bear, don't you?"

I smiled, touched by my friend's sensitivity. Perhaps he, too, felt for the Bear he had killed.

As Monty and his son skinned the Black Bear, I discovered its inner physical landscape. Most striking were the intense smell and pure white fat packed between skin and muscle, although there was nothing about this nature being that didn't amaze me.

I used to cringe at death and find such scenes appalling before I traveled to the Asian steppe with my friend and colleague Bill Pfeiffer and saw how indigenous Siberian people relate to the animals they kill.

In the Shor Mountains years ago, Bill and I watched a community slay and dismember a cow. Every member helped, and every part of the animal was used. It was mid-November and fifteen degrees below zero when this occurred. Having ample stores of meat is essential in this part of the world where winter temperatures drop to sixty below zero, just as animals need ample food and fat to manage long winters.

Many Siberian shamans still practice animal sacrifice. Bill Pfeiffer and I saw some that were horrible and belabored. However, in the Republic of Tuva, the rams died swiftly. A small cut was made in the chest and the shaman reached in to choke the heart. There was ceremony and communication with the animal. The ram was honored and every part of it used, including the intestines. I watched the women adeptly flush these with water, fill them with blood, and tie the ends to make sausages. Though it's difficult to watch the killing of a ram (rightfully so), nowhere else have I witnessed such beauty and honor in the taking of an animal's life.

There was no bringing back the Bear on the skinning table in front of me. Although I eat little meat, I very consciously and gratefully ate the delicious rich stew that Monty made two days later. I should always be so aware. Having known the Bear that became this stew, and the hunter who related with the animal from beginning to end, the connection of food to its source was strong. This made the eating of it an entirely different experience.

That life lives on life, the "universal game," as renowned mythologist Joseph Campbell described it, is visibly true in the wilderness. Dying and killing are part of the life cycle, although ironically, the powerful body of Black Bear grows mostly on plants and berries with just a little meat. This gives us much food for thought. In modern times of trophy hunting, commercially raised and slaughtered animals, and rapidly disappearing animal habitat, it would be wise for us to adopt the Hoh way of honoring life, to take on Bear's fierce protectorship qualities to guard the health of our lands and natural ecosystems.

Our fascination with Bear spans centuries and has been diversely expressed. For instance, fairy tales are filled with Bears. Bear has inspired clans and cults all over the world for centuries, and we can still draw upon Bear power today.

Bear spends most of the winter in sleep, making it a natural ally for the dreamtime. The teddy bears our children dream with are a twentieth-century expression of this that continues to this day. Teddy bears got their name when President Theodore Roosevelt was scoffed at for refusing to shoot a trapped older bear.

Like hibernating bears, shamans dream and mystics incubate in caves, forests, and the desert—to heal, see the future, and seek counsel from spirits. The dream chamber is revered in indigenous cultures, and the dreamer's solitude is fiercely protected.

Few of us will ever live in a cave or become a hermit in the forest, yet we all need to isolate sometimes as if in a dark cave to rest and restore. We also need to dream and touch deeply into the Earth.

Unlike ancient seers who mused as Bear does, belly to the earth, Black Bear is neither visionary nor healer. Nor does she distinguish goddess, guide, god, or deity or—as humans do—dissect life's rhythms into time. For Bear there is only the sense, movement, and texture of now.

Resting in winter's womb, Bear's physiology slows as she attunes to Mother Earth's heart. In also slowing, we can relax habits and ideas of who we are to muse humbly upon our Earth Mother's heart.

In these powerfully shifting times, Black Bear guides us to a deeper way of knowing and being.

"The dreamer is the Earth. She is the wisdom whisperer," says Bear.

As Black Bear releases into this dreaming Mother, so can we.

🌿 Practices

This practice is intended to revive the ancient art of incubating to restore, dream, and connect with the Earth. Enact this alone or have a friend protect the dream space for you; then do the same for your friend.

Whether inside or out, ensure you are safe, comfortable, and uninterrupted.

If inside, create a dark, cozy space perfect for a human bear to hibernate. You can dedicate such a spot in your home. Fiercely protect your time for solitude.

If outside, create a special place on the land and incubate when you travel. In closing our eyes, or upon simply taking a full, deep breath, we can touch the earth wherever we are, even in a busy setting.

Incubate directly on the earth when possible or on a natural fabric blanket so the earth's energy flows unimpeded. Sense where you are called and ask permission to be here. Note the nature beings that surround you, who form a sacred circle to support your experience. Make an offering to them and to the spirit of the Earth: a prayer or song, some breadcrumbs or tobacco, or simply place your loving hands upon the earth.

If you are indoors, create a simple opening ritual such as drawing with your fingers an imaginary circle of light around you so the area where you rest will be held as sacred and offering to the spirit of the Earth a poem or a spontaneous prayer that comes from the heart.

Next, stretch, breathe, and invite Black Bear's presence. Call upon her ageless body wisdom. As the silent Black Bear, stretch and unwind to find a quiet inner balance.

When you feel relaxed and fully present, sit down or lie curled on one side as if in a fetal position, with palms flush to your forehead, which opens the portal of your third eye vision. Or lie with your belly to the earth, or lie on your back. See what feels right.

Take some full, cleansing breaths, relaxing further with each exhale. The Earth can handle whatever emotion or energy releases with the outgoing breath. Unleash fully into the earth. Relax into the Mother's loving embrace.

Now, whether you are indoors or outside, sense nature all around you. Sense the land extending to the far horizon. Imagine animals, trees, sand, and soil; also insects, birds, stones, minerals, and roots. Note mountains or flatlands, rivers, winds, and lakes. Most important, feel deeply into the earth through her many layers. Sense her heart.

As you travel in imagination, feel the Earth's spirit—the radiant intelligence that flows through every nature being and you.

Words may not describe what you experience; words can get in the way. Relax. Feel. Breathe with the Earth. Breathe out love and breathe in love. Harmonize with this expanded field of energy; be it.

Take all the time you like.

Civilizations have come and gone, yet the Earth remains. Buildings, people, plans, and schemes all recycle back into the Mother. We are all one with this powerful intelligent force. Feel beyond the givens of our time—including time itself—deeply into this Mother.

When this feeling is strong, stay with the sensations. The Earth is you. Feel who you are. You may relax so much that you fall asleep, as you deeply integrate Earth rhythms.

Take all the time you desire.

To transition, freely stretch, as Black Bear does when rousing from slumber. Stay with the feeling, the Earth force that is you, throughout your day.

You can journal on visions or insights. Most importantly, feel the Earth—in your waking moments and even as you drift to sleep.

As Black Bear is in intimate relationship with the large, contiguous tracts of land (now quickly disappearing) it roams, get to know your own lands and those to which you travel. Wander. Be curious. If you can't walk the land, open your heart to feel it. Notice what occurs as you do. Through intimacy with the land, you may be called to activate Black Bear's fierce protector qualities to safeguard it.

When fragmented, fearful, and at any time, feel the Earth and sense her spirit. Harmonize with her until you feel a deep sense of belonging. In turn, give back to this Mother all that you can. Life will change. The Mother will manifest her dreams through you.

Black Bear teaches oneness with our sentient planet. She reminds us to honor death as much as life and that polarity is part of a larger whole. Here's a practice to rouse your Bear power and explore opposing qualities.

Ponder some of your contrasting personality traits, or parts of you that you find pleasing (smart, happy, beautiful) and the aspects you may not like (shy, temper-prone, undisciplined). Call upon Black Bear for help and remember that all aspects of you are welcomed.

Similarly, you can bring to mind a seemingly either-or situation, such as: "Do I quit my job or stick with it?" or "Do I dig deeper into this relationship or move on?"

Look at divergent traits or choices, then settle on a set and focus your attention.

In a space where you won't be disturbed, stand, relax, and take some full, deep breaths. Call in Black Bear; invite her body to meld with yours. Take all the time you like.

Now, hold your bear paws in front of you at shoulder height, palms facing forward yet with hands close to your chest.

Choose a paw for each opposing quality, for example: "Left paw for my quiet side and right paw for my wildness," or "Left paw for staying at my job and right paw for leaving."

Gently and slowly move your left paw forward from your chest, and then take your time to move it back again. Next, keep this paw close to your chest as you gently and very slowly push your right paw forward. Then gently and slowly bring it back. Let your breath flow with your movement.

Move unhurriedly, alternating each paw back and forth several times. Let the feelings connected to each choice or quality come up as you move in this leisurely manner.

Listen to your body. Note what you feel as you slowly move.

When the time feels right, as if you were a Bear rolling in the sun, play with these tensions. Engage your body. Step, move, or even dance as you press left paw forward, then back. Then repeat with the right paw. Let the movement rise from within you. Begin slowly, then find your pace.

After some time consider moving one paw forward, and the other back, simultaneously.

Be fluid, keeping a good footing on the earth (Bear footprints resemble human footprints). Allow the mystery to move you.

Bear prods: "Try replacing the word 'or' with 'and.'" Rouse energy and see what joins in the play.

Black Bear says, "Dance with me. Things are not separate; every moment is fresh. Charge your primal force; ask your body to show you how to integrate all the parts that make up you."

Dance with Bear all you like, until you lose interest. Then take a gentle stroll. Step with gratitude, thanking Black Bear and releasing her with every movement.

As you walk, note how you feel in body, heart, and mind.

Also note how you feel now about the issues you explored. Is this different from when you began? If so, how?

You may later want to take some notes or reflect more on how to invite Black Bear's wisdom into your everyday life.

Black Bear

Sandra

When I was four years old, I went with my mother and brother for summer vacation at a bungalow colony in upstate New York. I loved escaping the heat and confines of the city. It was so freeing to be able to roam through lush mountain forests and be enveloped by nature. When I developed a severe case of the chicken pox, I had to lie in bed in this very rustic bungalow staring at the beauty of the tall trees through a window next to my bed. During my time of healing, it was as if some inner knowing guided me within to find the rest and peace needed for full and speedy recovery.

My father used to drive up from Brooklyn on the weekends to visit. One such visit was during the weekend holiday of July 4. I was lying in bed gazing out the window when I saw the bright smiling face of my father appear. He had something very large in his arms.

My father then came into my room revealing a large reddish-brown stuffed bear that was almost as big as I was. I immediately fell in love with the bear and named him Brownie. He still sits in my office today, propped up by some other beloved stuffed animals. Brownie does look his age, and he's not "aging well," but I celebrate his birthday every Fourth of July by bringing him a cupcake with candles, and I sing

"Happy Birthday" to him. Throughout my life Brownie has accompanied me on some of my travels to different cities. We've been through many adventures together, and he remains precious to me.

Teddy bears provided great comfort for many of us when we were children. We slept with them, felt protected by them, and knew when we whispered secrets into their ears that they would not tell a soul. Many of us feel a deep connection with Bear as we remember our connection to our beloved stuffed animals.

In the 1970s I worked at San Francisco State University. My position was for nine months of the year, and I had to find work elsewhere for the three summer months when classes were not in session. At the time I had a dear friend living in a small rural town in Tiller, Oregon. She always helped me find work with the forest service or with a private crew, and I was able to spend three months of the year working out in nature.

Many of the people who lived in Tiller had gone there to escape the pressures of society, and some lived on the land many miles from civilization. I had some friends who lived in such an isolated area that we had to swim across a river and then hike a few miles on a trail through a lush forest to get to their home. The sparkling South Umpqua River is quite wide, so a true effort had to be put into such a journey.

One day after work I had set out on the long journey to visit my friends. I was tired and my mind was wandering. I had swum across the wide, clear, blue-green river and was a couple of miles into my walk on the trail. As is often typical for someone who grew up in a big city, my gaze was at the ground rather than around me. I was paying no attention to any other life that might also be on the trail.

Out of the corner of my eye, some movement caught my attention, causing me to lift my eyes. At that moment I saw a small Black Bear about twenty feet in front me. What happened next is a sequence you might see in a cartoon. The Black Bear had also not seen me. We both looked up at exactly the same minute, saw each other, raised our startled arms/paws in the air, and turned and ran, while looking back to make sure the other was moving in the opposite direction. It must have been quite a sight, and the memory still makes me smile.

I had another very humorous meeting with Bear in the 1990s while I was leading a five-day Soul Retrieval Training to forty or fifty people at a retreat center in Phoenicia, New York. Soul Retrieval is a healing ceremony that is performed to help people, animals, and the land after a trauma has occurred.

In the first experiential exercise, I asked participants to journey into the invisible realms to meet a power animal or guardian helping spirit who would assist with their work of performing a Soul Retrieval. We were indoors and I was standing in the middle of the room drumming with my assistant while the group journeyed. When we drummed a change in beat, signaling it was time to return from the journey, people opened their eyes and started laughing, all gazing at a window in the room. There was a Black Bear looking into the window watching our group. This was a wonderful omen for our circle.

In the practice of shamanism, Bear is considered to be a very sacred living being. Native cultures considered Bear's hibernation phase to be a process of dying and being reborn. Bear's death and rebirth is seen as a miraculous event. In some shamanic cultures it is also understood that Bear has the incredible ability to heal itself.

In Native American traditions in the Southwest, Bear is honored as a healer. I have a Hopi friend who used to tell me that shamans worked with the spirit of Bear in their healing work, and the Zuni create bear fetishes that provide both healing and protection. Painted images of bear claws are often seen on various sacred objects, such as rattles and ceremonial objects. In many native traditions Bear is seen as the shaman.

The Bear cycle of "dying" and "being reborn" each year relates to the shamanic initiation practice of dismemberment. In dismemberment a person might have a dream or vision of being eaten by an animal, ripped apart, torn to bone, or even burned to ash. In this process the person is returned to spirit as a reminder that we are more than just body and mind. Who we are beyond our skin is spirit. The dismembered person experiences a state of unity with Source and often has a profound experience of being one with universal light.

In shamanic cultures dismemberment marks an initiation that might be called the "shaman's death." There are no practices or exercises that can prepare you for a shaman's death. Life brings this initiation to you, and if it occurs in a shamanic journey or dream, it typically happens spontaneously. An initiation such as this cannot be planned and has no safety net. In such an initiation you lose the identity you are attached to on an egoic and personality level. And then "remembership" takes place over time as your old identity is replaced with your authentic self.

Life circumstances that provide such a death experience can often be harsh. But in the end, once we surrender to our new identity, we emerge reborn and refreshed. As I wrote in my essay on Sand, our ego is truly sculpted, allowing our spirit to shine through. After these initiations we stop being led only by our ego and follow a path of spirit. Going through an initiation is akin to a snake shedding its skin; we let go of the old and birth new aspects of ourselves.

I have been through many harsh initiations in my life. The messages I have received during these times are to not dwell in the darkness; that the strength of my spirit will carry me through; and that the only way out is through the process.

At the same time a shaman's death can bring beautiful experiences that teach us how precious life is. Through surviving an initiation we learn how to live. We wake up to the strength of our inner spirit.

Part of the initiation into becoming a shaman is experiencing some type of life-threatening illness or a near-death experience in which the initiate loses any sense of ego or separation from Source. In this numinous state we remember that we are one with all.

Among Eskimo shamans these types of initiation experiences bring the initiate a feeling and vision of the body being renewed; often the initiate returns with magical and healing powers. In the Eastern tradition it is taught that it is only when we allow our attachment to our material nature to be destroyed is resurrection possible. We sacrifice identity, ego, and beliefs to the Divine. Death is not an end but the doorway to the eternal.

In a shamanic culture, when one reports a dismemberment dream or vision, the community perceives that this person has been chosen by the spirits to be a shaman. This understanding is reflected in modern psychology; Carl Jung wrote that children often have dismemberment dreams marking an initiation into a spiritual path or a new cycle of life.

Many of my students in workshops have a spontaneous dismemberment experience as they perform their very first shamanic journey. They report that they were ripped apart by an animal, such as a bear or a bird, and deconstructed to spirit. Their bones and organs were cleansed, and all illness was left out as they were reconstructed. They always report that although the experience was unexpected, it was filled with peace and they returned feeling regenerated by the process. Some of my students journey with the intention of experiencing a dismemberment to receive healing or to help them move forward on a spiritual path.

Dismemberment is akin to a Bear dying each year and being reborn. As we are dismembered or go through any initiation that life brings us, we are reborn and come back refreshed from our experience. We are cleansed of impurities on the physical, mental, and emotional level. We begin again with a new awareness and consciousness as we emerge into a new cycle of life. This is like Bear waking up refreshed in the spring after a long winter's sleep.

Nature is a true teacher about flow and movement. Seasons flow into one another, as do the cycles of the moon. The sun rises and sets each day. Bear flows into a deep winter sleep and awakens slowly to greet a new season of life. Times of light flow into times of darkness. This is all part of nature.

We tend to think of shifts, changes, and transitions in linear ways instead of in the circular fashion that the Earth teaches. We have judgment about the darkness of the season of winter, both internal and in nature, and hang on to the "sunny days." But everything in nature changes. Death and rebirth are part of the natural flow.

We have many Black Bears in New Mexico, and when they wake from their long sleep, they roam populated areas looking for food. We have to bring our bird feeders into the house at night, because even though we hang them on a strong metal rod, Bear twists the strong metal as if it were a thin plastic stick, and all the seed spills onto the ground.

When the peach tree in my garden produces fruit, I pick it off the branches and leave it on the ground for the animals, so that Bear doesn't climb the tree and break branches while foraging for food.

Due to continued drought in New Mexico, less food is being provided by nature for the bears living in the mountains. As they continue to roam into populated areas looking for nourishment, they are being captured or relocated and sometimes killed to protect residents. In other words, they are being displaced, as are thousands of species of nature beings around the world due to land development or changes in the environment that no longer support their life. This list includes humans who lose their homes due to environmental changes that no longer support life in certain areas.

We need to be more responsible as we cut down forests and develop land for factories, businesses, and homes to make sure that we do not kill or displace entire species of animals. We live on Earth in partnership with other species who also have a right to life. We have a responsibility to make decisions that decrease our negative impact on the environment, for our choices often lead to destruction of many parts of the world that once were a beautiful and bountiful home for many living beings.

This is a sad topic but must be addressed. We are the caretakers of our planet and there is a web of life that connects all life. When we displace or kill species of animals, there is an impact on all of life. There are consequences to our lack of care for the environment.

I believe that as a collective, humanity is entering a new phase of an initiation process. There will be a death of an old way of living replaced by actions that honor the Earth and all of life.

At the same time the feminine teaches us about the natural process of evolution. The face of the Earth is changing and will continue to change with age. Species will die and new ones will be born. Life that continues learns how to adapt to the changes. The feminine continues to teach us about the cycle of death and rebirth.

🌿 Practice

Llyn provided us with some beautiful and powerful practices, and there is one I would like to add.

Bears do not have a good sense of sight, but they have a very strong sense of smell, which helps them in foraging.

A well-known herb used for preventing and healing colds is osha root, which Native Americans call "bear root." This root has a very strong, earthy, bitter fragrance.

Once a year my friend Ann Drucker, who teaches brilliant herbal workshops in Colorado, leads her students into the woods to forage for osha root. But she has her students do this as a bear would; she asks everyone to get down on all fours. They all put their noses to the ground to follow the scent of the osha root. This is a powerful way to connect to the Earth. Try to find a place in nature where you can be alone and not disturbed by others. Get down on all fours and close your eyes, and let your sense of smell be your guide. Explore your surroundings. Have fun with this practice while also noticing how deeply you connect with the feminine, the Earth herself, as you smell the wonderful fragrances of nature.

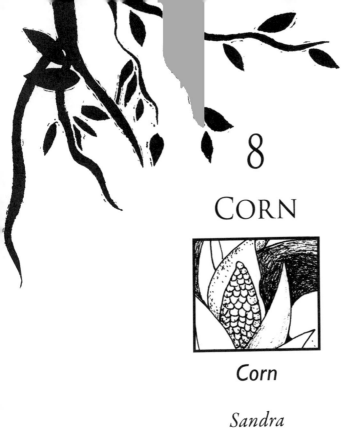

8

CORN

Corn

Sandra

The nature being Corn has had a long life on this great Earth. Scientists have found fossilized corn pollen in sediment in Central Mexico that dates back 80,000 years. It is descended from indigenous wild grasses that were called *teosinte*.

About 7,000 years ago the Indians in Mesoamerica began domesticating corn—then known as maize—and there are several varieties, but the one we enjoy eating at cookouts is called "sweet corn."

Eating corn on the cob is a tangible and rich experience. My mother, at 98, refused to have corn taken off the cob for her, though that would have made it easier to eat. She still wanted that experience of chewing each kernel off the cob.

When I look at all the corn kernels in ceremonial bowls that I keep around my house, I experience brilliant light coming through each kernel. There is a beauty in each kernel and a knowing that each

kernel holds the blueprint of perfect health. I have ears of corn in a variety of places, and they serve as reminders to me that the universe is abundant and we are always given what we need to thrive.

🍃 *Remember back to a time in summer when you were at a cookout. Bring yourself fully into this experience. Imagine how soft the warm air feels, perhaps even a bit humid, depending on where you are. Smell the wealth of fragrances of the foods being cooked. Listen to the laughter of friends and family during this time of fun and celebration. Many of you probably remember eating corn on the cob during a cookout. Visualize the bright yellow or white kernels waiting to pop between your teeth. Feel yourself holding the hot corn and taking that first bite. Taste the sweetness of each kernel as you chew it.*

Now shift your attention and imagine being in the desert of the Southwest. As you gaze at the landscape, notice how the land looks dry. You wonder what might grow in a place like this where water is sparse.

As you look into the distance, you see a garden filled with stalks of corn growing. You walk closer, and once at the garden you notice and hear people with rattles singing to the corn. You are observing an ancient ritual of how people sing up the Corn—a spiritual practice that is used to honor the Corn, encouraging it to grow.

Modern agribusiness has changed our relationship to Corn. Many people no longer honor the spirit of the nature beings we eat; they are perceived simply as "food products" that we buy in stores. It is time to reflect on the sacredness of Corn and all the plants that sustain us.

When I first moved to Santa Fe, I received a message while performing a shamanic journey that I did not understand with my rational mind. I was told that Corn is the most sacred plant. At that time I didn't fully understand why.

The native people of the Southwest call Corn "the mother" (Corn Mother) because of their mythology about its origin and its emergence from the primary mother, Earth. They also depend on it as their primary food source. Ground corn or corn pollen is used in ceremonies and prayers as an affirmation of the connection between Earth and all of life.

Among the Hopi, Navajo, Apache, and Zuni tribes, Corn has been elevated to a high cultural status. The Navajo believe that Corn is a gift from the Holy People. For the Navajo people the Holy People are the deities who live in a world beneath the earth's surface or what some would call the Lower Worlds. The Hopi developed a dry farming technique for growing Corn based on the Earth's cycles, which they incorporate into their religious rituals.

In pueblo mythology Corn Mother represents the feminine aspect of the universe. Beautiful and powerful Corn Dances are performed in many of the pueblos to honor her and offer her pollen.

While living in Santa Fe, I have had the wonderful opportunity to attend many different Corn Dances. There is always great excitement as the dancers come out in colorful costumes, dancing in a way that has been passed down through generations to honor the sacred living being we call Corn. Drumming supports the dance and the power is tangible and timeless.

The Zuni people are known for making fetishes that honor certain animal and plant spirits. Fetishes share power with those who feed them, honor them, and care for them. Fetishes are often offered cornmeal as a form of respect. The Zuni people teach that when you sprinkle a fetish with cornmeal as an offering, you will be blessed in return. Zuni fetishes are made from a variety of materials such as mother of pearl, coral, turquoise, fossilized ivory, bone, or deer or elk antler.

There are Zuni fetishes that contain the power of Corn—Corn Maidens and Corn Mother. The six young Corn Maidens have the task of keeping people supplied with Corn—the Blue Corn Maiden, Red Corn Maiden, Yellow Corn Maiden, White Corn Maiden, and Black Corn Maiden; the sixth is Spotted Corn Maiden. There are varieties of corn that grow in these six colors.

Corn is food and is seen as the seed and symbol of life. The Corn Maidens bring the power of life to the people. Corn is given life by the sun; the Corn Maidens bring us life through the power of the sun, giving us the health that the Creator designed for us.

There are various stories of creation taught in the Native American traditions of the Southwest as to how Corn came into being. The stories are so numerous and contain such a wealth of symbolism that an entire book would need to be written to share them all.

In the Hopi tradition blue corn represents the rising sun and the beginning of life, wisdom, and understanding. The Hopi believe that blue corn symbolizes long life. The Acoma Indians teach that corn seeds hold the potential to generate life.

Corn seeds are literally kernels of ancient wisdom. They can be stored for many years and remain vital until they are planted. Then they sprout with new life as a new plant is born to nourish life.

You can only imagine that growing food in the desert during

times of drought and intense weather is challenging. The people who have inhabited the land here have always honored the spirits of the plant and animal life that bring nurturance.

Corn is not that easy to grow in the desert and needs a lot of attention. I tried to grow blue corn—blue is my favorite color—and planted kernels in my garden, where the land was dry and hard. There was rock beneath the top layer of soil in my garden so it took a lot of effort to dig holes where I could place the seeds. I felt enriched by giving my attention to growing blue corn and doing my own ceremonies that came through direct revelation to honor the plant and give thanks for its growth. I have been so inspired by how the Hopi people sing up the corn that I did this myself and was excited to watch the corn grow. Due to the condition of the soil, the plants did not grow tall, but they did produce corn.

I remember cooking up the first ears of blue corn that I grew in the hot summer. I bit into the small cooked kernels and was overwhelmed by their sweet taste. As I ate the blue corn, I felt the potency of this ancient plant. I fully absorbed the wealth of nutrients that are known to support health and a long life.

Every solstice and equinox I walk around the land where I live giving offerings to the ancestors of the land, the Spirit of Santa Fe, the Hidden Folk, all my helping spirits, and the spirit that lives in all things. I join my heart with them to welcome in the new season and also give gratitude for all the protection and help I am given in my life. For my offerings I sprinkle blue cornmeal as I chant words filled with gratitude and blessings to all of life and welcome in the change of season. I give thanks to earth, air, water, and the sun. I end by giving thanks to my personal ancestors and also for my life. I offer gratitude for having the opportunity to be a caretaker of the land where I live.

In addition to the corn kernels in ceremonial dishes around my house, I have a corn doll on one of my altars and Zuni Corn Maiden and Corn Mother fetishes that remind me of the power of life and the abundance that is shared through the creative forces of the universe.

There are a couple of sayings I love that originate in different traditions in the Southwest. When someone is about to embark on a business venture, it is often asked: "Will it grow corn?" The meaning of this is, "Will your venture bring abundance your way?"

I also share a teaching in my workshops that I learned from some Native Americans in the Southwest, which is that as long as you have two kernels of corn, you will never go hungry—physically, emotionally, or spiritually. I often give two kernels of blue corn to each of the participants to carry with them in a medicine bundle or to plant. In later seasons I have been gifted back with ears of blue corn grown from the two gifted kernels. These ears of corn represent sacred blessings I receive.

🌿 Practices

Buy a small pot, some potting soil, and herb seeds. Parsley is very easy to grow, and the seeds germinate quickly.

Plant the seeds and begin a daily practice of singing to them. Notice how you feel as you share your energy with this growing plant. Feel what it feels like to establish a deep connection with a plant.

As it grows continue your practice of singing to the plant. Nurture your plant with loving words and thoughts. From time to time close your eyes, open your invisible ears and psychic senses, and intuit any messages the plant shares with you. You might see an image, hear a telepathic message, or get a feeling in your body or "in your bones."

At first you might feel as if you are forcing the communication. But once you settle into a relationship with this plant you will notice a flow of conversation emerging. Children easily communicate with nature beings. We have to open back up to the psychic gifts we had as children.

You can also engage in this practice with a houseplant you have been tending. And if you have a garden, sing to the plants you grow.

May this practice inspire you to do the same with the seeds of the words and thoughts you plant in your inner garden.

This practice will create a desire to be conscious of energies you share through your thoughts and words. For we want to feed our inner garden and our Earth garden with love.

In shamanic cultures people sang and drummed up the sun to thank it for coming up another day and bringing the energy for all life to thrive.

Find days when you can sing to the rising and setting sun, the moon, the stars, the land, the trees, and the spirit that lives in all things. Notice how this practice of singing to the nature beings makes you feel more connected to nature and the cycles of life.

There are many creation stories in Native American traditions, and Corn is often featured. It is seen as sacred food and a gift from the gods and goddesses who created the Earth and all of life.

Take some time to meditate on how the creative forces of the universe collaborated with the Earth to bring together energies that created spirit into form. Imagine how you also were created as spirit into form. Feel the power, intention, and love that all came together to create form with power, intention, and love.

Find a way to express the energy of collaboration between sky and earth, the alchemy that brought forth the elements of life.

You may want to use watercolors, acrylic paints, or crayons to go beyond a rational expression and just let color and shapes flow through you onto paper. Or put on some music and dance the flow of creative energy that birthed you into form. You can also use your imagination to write a story about how the sky and earth joined together in love to create you and other nature beings. If these ways do not speak to you, let what I have suggested inspire your own form of creative expression.

Then go outside and either lie on the earth or sit in a chair with the soles of your feet touching the earth. Close your eyes and take some very deep breaths. Open yourself up and feel the vibration of the Earth. You might feel the power of the inner fire of the Earth. Let yourself feel the love of the Earth flow through you. Soak it into your being.

ᘁ

In spiritual teachings it is understood that there is a web of life that connects us all. Part of the practice of shamanism is exploring practices where you can honor and respect "the spirit that lives in all things." It is important to find ways to honor the plants and trees where you live. And it is important to honor the animals, insects, fish, reptiles, birds, rocks, and minerals that live with you in harmony.

As I wrote in Wild Rose, the more we can respect nature, the more nature respects us, which goes back to the shamanic principle of reciprocity. In native cultures it is taught that when we live in harmony with nature, it will bless us and reflect back to us a state of balance.

Engage in simple practices that align your energy and harmonize you with nature. Find simple ways to honor the nature beings where you live. When you feel called to do so, you can leave an offering for the nature spirits. Hold your intention that this offering is a way to express gratitude for earth, air, water, and fire (as the sun), which sustain you. Give gratitude to all the beings that live in your area. You might wish to offer gratitude for the helping ancestral spirits where you live and also to your personal ancestors who gave you life. Give thanks to the spirit of the land, the Hidden Folk, and your own helping spirits. Reflect on other nature beings you would like to honor.

You might wish to research indigenous edible plants in your area. What plants were gifted from the holy ones? Give thanks to the plants for the nurturance they share.

I leave offerings during each equinox and solstice, as I like to perform a ceremony during this potent time of seasonal change. You can find your own times when you desire to give thanks to the nature beings.

It does not matter where you live, in a city or in a rural area. There are plants and trees in all urban areas. You might live by the ocean and can visit a beach; you can leave offerings as you connect with the power of the ocean. There might be a park you can visit or a garden where you can leave offerings. Find other places in nature where you can walk and offer gratitude in ways that call to you.

There are no "correct" offerings to give. I leave blue cornmeal as an offering because blue corn has deep meaning for me, but you can leave a bit of your favorite food, flowers, water, drink, and so on as an offering. Please remember that animals and other nature beings might eat the offerings you leave. So please be conscious and make sure any favorite foods you leave are safe for them to eat. The key is holding a strong intention in your heart to give gratitude and to share your love with the Earth. Nature reads your heart, not your mind.

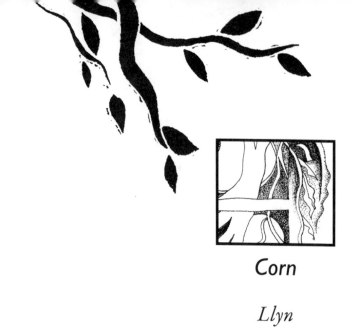

Corn

Llyn

As I read about eating corn on the cob and summer cookouts, my mouth waters. I can taste salty and buttery white and yellow kernels, the succulent butter-and-sugar corn of my childhood. The stalks were so high in the New Hampshire cornfields my brother Steve and I ran through that we children felt lost in a mysterious world.

In reading Sandra's writings about Corn, I also remembered, as if yesterday, the burnt scent and taste of cobs roasted over open fires in India, where I lived for a time in my twenties. People the world over share a sensual love for Corn's rich, lingering smells and tastes.

Sandra describes the Corn ears and kernels laid out in her home that radiate light, and she writes about indigenous reverence for Corn. Imbued with the power of the sun, this staple has sustained people throughout the ages. Given that it is a sacred and primary food, it feels wrong to genetically modify Corn (or any plant food). Mexico, where maize was first cultivated and whose people eat delicious warmed tortillas made of freshly ground Corn at every meal, bans the planting and sale of GMO (genetically modified) Corn.

I first fully embraced Corn's power many years ago after visiting Hopi tribal lands with John Perkins in Arizona, where Corn is synonymous with life. There John and I met Hopi Elder Grandfather Martin Gashweseoma, who gifted us each with two ears of blue corn. After our meeting with Grandfather Martin, I returned home and had a strange dream.

A giant Corn plant appeared in front of me, its husks and stalk stretched to the sky. The plant was so large it frightened me.

The Corn being said: "I want to be at your workshops."

I've had several experiences like this when plants have made it clear they had their own agendas. Plants also appear patient when I am slow to catch on to what they intend. In this case I didn't have time to think on my dream before my next program, but the Corn plant took care of things—a participant gave me a gift of a bag of cornmeal. I put some of the cornmeal into a small silk pouch from Nepal and it came with me to the following workshop. Here a participant gifted me with a tiny Corn ear with golden kernels and soft suede husks. I placed the tiny ear into the silk pouch with the cornmeal.

Corn has accompanied me to every workshop since this time, and a little Corn Maiden doll, another unexpected gift, also lives in the pouch with the cornmeal and tiny ear. As I feed our altars with cornmeal or its flour, I see the ancestral grandmothers of plants and people, of stones and waters and winds, of the lands and of animals, and the grandmothers the stars. Amidst these spiritual matriarchs I am humbled, as I also feel seen by them. The magic is simple—the offerings we make to honor the sacred feminine in turn align us with archetypal forces that are here to support us. There is such potency in offering Corn.

I also offer cornmeal to the earth. As the Corn plant requested, it is always present in my work.

Sandra shares beautiful stories about Corn from the cosmologies of many traditions, all of which relate Corn to life and creation. In my own musing the Corn plant teaches so much about sharing ourselves, just as Sandra speaks of honoring the land, nature beings, and spirits.

Have you ever daydreamed, as a child might, about what it would be like if Corn ears could actually hear? If this were so, what might the

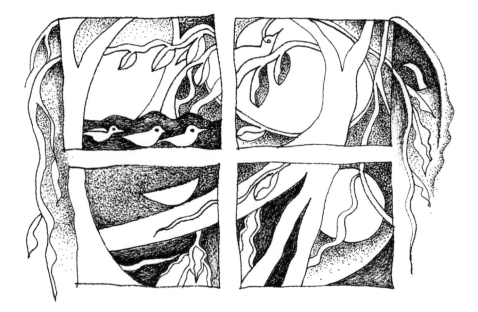

human activity around them sound like? I imagine a fair amount of our chatter could be reduced to a simple mantra: "I need and I want."

It's challenging not to be preoccupied by the trappings of the modern world. When I have brought people from developing countries to gatherings in the United States, they, too, have struggled with material seduction. Consumerism has become a hypnosis that keeps our culture immature, as it keeps us overly focused on ourselves and on material desires, instead of on cultivating deeper soul richness.

Corn teaches that anything in its full maturity gives of itself. The mature tassels of Corn plants generate pollen that is offered out, blown about by the winds to enter that lustrous, silky part of the Corn so those juicy kernels can grow. Mature land gives out to the animals and to us; its rich soil nurtures and feeds all that grows. Mature water bestows moisture and is steeped in minerals that benefit the land, animals, and people. Mature forests offer shade, shelter, beauty, food, and love and wisdom we have yet to explore.

Prosperity means different things to different people. A curious example is of a Mexican folk healer, a *curandera* I worked alongside in a mental health center decades ago in Colorado. This woman was caring with everyone she met. She also looked after her childhood community in Mexico. When money was needed back home, the curandera used to go to a shopping mall and approach a stranger who appeared to be in need. She then bought this person a nourishing meal and shared meaningful time with him or her. In turn, the curandera told me, "Within a week I receive an unsolicited donation for the amount we need at home. I give from my own heart and pocket to someone who really needs it, and that energy unfailingly returns."

It's natural to desire and seek for ourselves and our families. Everyone wants to be happy and prosperous. Yet if we only breathed in and never breathed out, or if we only ate food and never expelled food waste, we would die. In the same way, the soul thrives through giving.

Corn, revered by Mexicans and so many other original peoples, says: "Offer out as abundance loves this movement out, which as a vortex draws goodness back. And always remember that the most sustaining wealth is internal richness."

I had to learn about my own needs and wants in order to more effectively share my gifts. This happened as never before when I lost the sight in my right eye due to an inoperable benign mass pressing against my optic nerve. The traditional and natural medicine, shamanic and spiritual methods I sought absorbed me. I wanted and needed to be healed.

During this time I asked my Tibetan teacher for a divination about my eye condition and it was frightening to hear him say, "The next year, 2012, does not look good."

"However," he continued, "you can change this."

What Rinpoche (Tibetan for "precious one") said next was both shocking and obvious.

"Think on others who have eye problems and of how animals suffer. Give to organizations that help these people and animals. Even small amounts of money are good; it is the intention to help that matters. And free small animals."

The suggestion to give to others instead of wallowing reminded me of the curandera's humble actions. Thinking about people who were blind and donating to help others who also had eye problems immediately lightened my anxiety; I no longer focused just on myself.

What about freeing small animals?

Since connecting with Buddhism in my late teens, I had freed, instead of killing or leaving to die, insects trapped inside my home; the bugs hanging out in my house now really got my attention. I also released trapped mice back to their fields. Now I began having disturbing dreams about dying animals and invested green energy—dollars— to stop baby seals from being killed. The plight of the Earth's creatures consumed me.

One morning during this time, I walked where I lived on the Salish Sea (Puget Sound). No matter how cold the air and water was, I always walked this beach without shoes. My feet stung and vibrated, a feeling I have grown to love. I looked out to a tidal pool. In the water were some small wild ducks with their mother. They were beautiful.

As I watched the duck family, I saw two eagles flying toward the tidal pool. As the eagles grew closer, the mother duck swam to the water's edge, then ran down the beach, I assume to lure the predators away.

The eagles ignored the mother duck, by now far away. An eagle swooped down, plucked a duckling from the water, and flew off with it. The other eagle hovered over the two that remained, then extended its talons, one onto each duckling's head. The eagle dunked the small heads underwater. Moments later, the large bird lifted up from the water and two heads bobbed up from underneath the looming winged body. The eagle snatched one of them and flew off with it.

This was intense, dramatic to watch. Although I knew that baby eagles waited in their nest for fresh food—the baby ducklings, and this is nature's way, my heart knew this was not the surviving duckling's fate. I watched from a distance as the second eagle flew out of sight. The last duckling could have been resting against my chest, the feeling of this baby was so strong in my heart.

As I stood helplessly watching, the last duckling swam from the middle of the tidal pool to the water's edge. It took time for the dark downy body to reach the shore. When its tiny webbed feet hit the sand it ran hard and fast—in my direction.

One of the eagles started flying back. I stood there as the duckling ran closer and closer to me, and the eagle flew closer to us both.

Soon the duckling was about twenty feet away from me. I instinctively squatted and thrust my hands out onto the sand in front of me. The duckling ran right up to me and jumped into my opened palms. I scooped it up and stood, holding a wild panting creature against my own pounding heart.

The eagle soared nearby. I thought it might attack. It didn't.

What had occurred was unbelievable. Yes, it did happen.

What could I do with a wild baby duck with no momma, and eagles in the wings?

I walked home barefoot with a duck in my arms and called wildlife rehabilitation. A small animal was saved. The Earth took me up on my good intentions.

These adventures didn't save my sight, but they saved my sanity and I believe helped me avoid a worsened medical condition. Most importantly, a whole new chapter of living and a deeper way to see—and give—began.

Nature spreads her seeds, spores, and pollen wildly, lustily, like wild Corn tassels that toss in the wind to spread pollen that the silky parts seduce back to the plant to grow kernels. We, too, can be passionate givers and livers, offering ourselves to humans, spirits, and animals. We can feed nature as traditional peoples have done since the beginning of time, and as did folk hero Johnny Appleseed, whose fervor for people and the Earth made him a legend.

Tradition has it that Johnny Appleseed tossed the seeds of apples wildly, with abandon, as nature does by roadsides and into open spaces. Research suggests this is likely fable and that Jonathan Chapman (Johnny Appleseed) industriously planted and managed small apple orchards for more than fifty years. But we don't really know. Maybe Johnny did it all.

Research tries to get the facts straight. Story, however, stirs the soul as it mirrors our untamable nature. It also preserves amazing wisdom that defies convention and leaves no linear trail. Our current cultural story is about learning to bridge these seemingly divergent worlds. Myth and person, feral and methodical, manly and deeply feminine, Johnny Appleseed is said to have had a lot of green energy come his way, which he planted in the ground instead of depositing in a bank. Legend says Chapman dressed poorly and did not live in a house or wear shoes, but walked the Earth in toughened bare feet, even in the snow. In other words, Johnny Appleseed was fed and warmed and enriched by what he gave through his deep love for people and nature.

Those light-filled Corn kernels that remind us, and those who have come before us, of life incepted and nurtured by the sun can guide us to internal wealth and light. Just as Johnny Appleseed was rich in spirit, Corn teaches that life fills us according to how we give ourselves to it; the fire we stoke is the fire that blazes. The Earth offers abundantly to all her children, and when we give back, really put our hearts to it, we entrain with our Mother and harmonize with her creatures. We join with nature in remembering we are the same light and love.

🌱 Practice

Sandra outlines great suggestions for making offerings to nurture beauty, magic, and balance between people and nature.

To add to these consider taking the Corn plant for a walk. Holding a small bag of cornmeal reminds us to look outside of self, to see what we can give.

Offer to land, trees, and water. If you live in a city, there are still trees and land and water. It's powerful for urban dwellers to notice the nature around them and important for nature everywhere to be remembered and loved.

Giving out is a practice that gains more impact over time. As you sprinkle

Corn where you're drawn, talk to those nature beings. Relationships with people deepen because of what we give to them, and connecting with nature is the same. Speak with nature beings as you would to your friends. There's no need to be overly spiritual or serious. Just be you.

In conversing with nature, feel free to ask for help and guidance if you're having a hard time. Don't hold back. Cry if you need to. Voice what you don't feel comfortable sharing with people; plant or dog or river won't judge. Voice it and you'll feel better, with nature as your witness.

Then take a few deep breaths and allow balance and wisdom to flow back to you.

You can also offer your support to the Earth. Nature listens and responds. It may not be today or even tomorrow, but the tree, stone, bird, or other being will make it clear that it did receive your offerings and wishes. Prepare to be taken up on these good intentions.

Here are some examples of what we might say to the Earth:

"How can I help decimated forests grow back? You young fir trees are so beautiful, and you'll likely be gone in thirty years. Instead, I see you flourishing—a diversely abundant forest. I offer myself to this vision. Let me help you."

Perhaps you would like to make a broader offering, such as, "Mother, I am here for you. I offer myself in service as a hollow reed. Please guide me."

Whatever you say put your heart into it. Feelings are a powerful force.

If you live in a city, talk to the water that comes out of the faucet, trees that may have been planted along the sidewalk, skies that hover between tall buildings, and plants that live in window boxes.

Offering to nature opens powerful channels for us to co-create with her. We offer—then honor—by acting with intent, guided by the Earth.

The following two beautiful offerings are adapted from rituals taught to me by my Quechua friends, the Tamayos, a powerful family of shamans who live in the high Andes.

Offering One

Create a circle of yellow flowers or Corn ears, husks, or kernels.

Place a candle made of beeswax in each of the four directions. Beeswax, like Corn, represents internal richness, and the color yellow signifies the fire of the Earth, sun, and stars—Mother Earth, Mother Time, and Mother Universe—*Pachamama.*

Sit in the center of this circle and meditate on the sacred plants and animals and all that is sacred in nature.

Offering Two

Create a circle of yellow flowers or Corn ears, husks, or kernels.

Place a beeswax candle and a glass of fresh water in the center, and then enter the circle and sit next to these.

Say a prayer for troubled parts of the world. Radiate love to Pachamama.

This is a nice meditation to do under a bright yellow full moon or as the sun rises or sets.

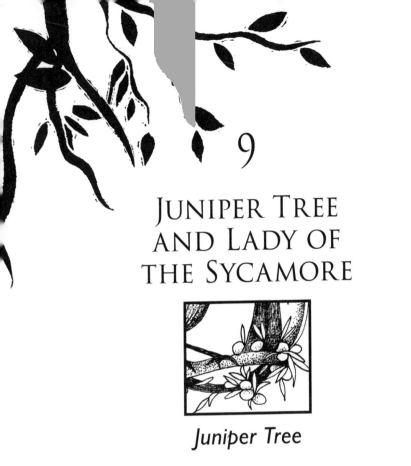

9

Juniper Tree and Lady of the Sycamore

Juniper Tree

Sandra

As I drank my breakfast tea one morning a year or two ago, I was entertained by robins outside my window feasting on an abundance of deep blue-purple Juniper berries. Typical to Santa Fe the sky was clear blue, which created a beautiful contrast to the light, fluffy snow covering the branches of the piñon and Juniper trees. The Juniper branches were filled with red-breasted robins eating the blue berries and ingesting the snow for water.

That year the fruit trees bore more fruit than had been seen here in many years. Branches were heavy with apricots, peaches, apples, and plums. I have an apricot tree that had never produced fruit in seventeen years, but that year it was filled with apricots.

The piñon trees were heavy with pinecones, and there were more Juniper berries than I'd seen in thirty years of living in Santa Fe. Some of the branches of the Juniper were so heavy with the small hard berries that they drooped almost to the ground.

Many years ago a Native American friend taught me that when nature produces a wealth of fruit, nuts, and berries in the summer, it is an indication of a harsh winter to come. Nature in all of its intelligence always provides what is needed so that life might thrive.

Having seen this abundance of food that nature provided during that summer, I did not need a weather report to be prepared for an intense winter. I did not know if we would receive much snow, but I surmised the temperatures would be cold and the animals would need more food.

During that winter we did experience very cold temperatures. As the weather is getting extreme due to climate change, the weather here has gone back and forth between warmer and colder than normal temperatures, but that year we mostly had days of extreme cold.

Robins love to eat Juniper berries. It was great fun to see the migrant population of robins grow to numbers rarely seen in the past, attracted by the wealth of food. And they had enough snow to provide them with drinking water.

Juniper trees and pine trees are both evergreens. Junipers are native to the Southwest, and Native Americans use Juniper's ripe blue berries and dark green needles in herbal medicines. There are a variety of ailments that Juniper berries and their needles are known to cure. Incense is made from Juniper that is used to cleanse one's energy before performing or stepping into a ceremony.

The one-seed Juniper is native to this area. It grows at altitudes of 5,000–7,000 feet, is extremely drought hardy, and is a wonderful example of a tree that has adapted to long dry periods in its native environment.

This Juniper grows very slowly above ground, maybe just three to six inches a year, depending on how much rainfall there is. Although Juniper is slow growing above ground it rapidly grows long, deep roots. Juniper trees that range from five to thirty feet in height produce tap roots almost two-hundred-feet long.

The curve of the Juniper and the texture of its gnarly branches conjure the feeling of ancientness. It survives extreme temperatures, blazing sun, and big snowfalls. There is a deep wisdom in these trees, and they seem to have a knowing of how to survive in a wide range of conditions.

The shorter Juniper trees where I live are interspersed among piñon pines. I love to walk through the piñon and Juniper, inhaling the distinctive scent of their needles. The fragrance is sweet and fresh and is cleansing to my energy. If green were a smell, I would say they smell green. In summer the pine needles blanketing the earth tickle my bare feet. Feeling the needles on the soles of my feet gives me a sense of strength, comfort, and peace flowing through my body. And I continue to be in awe of how old the Juniper trees are.

One of the amazing things about Junipers is how fast they move into pollination. We can have very cold temperatures accompanied by snowstorms for weeks or months. And then the one day the sun comes out and the temperatures warm, suddenly the fine red-orange pollen that all residents of Santa Fe come to dread is seen on the trees. As the spring equinox gets closer, the red-orange pollen floats in the air covering cars and homes.

People's eyes start to water, and the sneezing begins as "Juniper fever" affects all the residents. It is a time that all of us resist. We love the beauty of spring, but most people in Santa Fe fall prey to extreme allergies to Juniper pollen. Common wisdom is that once you move to Santa Fe, you will have a five-year grace period before the allergy takes hold. Once it is activated, for many people the seasonal allergy affects them almost like clockwork.

Although some years I suffer from severe allergies to Juniper pollen, I cannot help but feel excitement at their great power of procreation. As I watch the deep-red pollen emerging, I find myself feeling a deep joy that bubbles up within as my nose runs, my eyes tear, and nonstop sneezing begins.

Juniper tree pollination reminds me of the abundance that nature always provides for us. As I wrote in my essay on Artesian Spring, in today's world we often focus on scarcity. It is quite healing for us to observe how nature is a great teacher of abundance.

In some native traditions trees are called "the standing ones." All native people have great respect for the "tree people." In Siberia trees are seen as the most sacred beings, as they bridge heaven and earth through their branches and their roots.

In Siberia there is a wonderful shamanic tradition of creating "prayer trees." Typically a Juniper is used for the prayer tree, although sometimes another type of evergreen might be used in this way.

Traditional food and drink offerings are left by the tree. The shaman in the community chants and gives thanks to the helping spirits for carrying the prayers of the people out to the universe so that their dreams manifest back on Earth. The ceremony of chanting, praying, and leaving offerings may continue for many days.

Brightly colored cloth ties are hung from the branches of the prayer tree to blow in the wind and carry prayers of individuals for the community and for the world. The cloth ties are hung loosely so as not to choke the branch as it continues to grow. Some prayer trees in Siberia have branches so laden with brightly colored strips of cloth that they just about touch the ground.

Along the same lines Melissa Reading, a colleague of mine, was trained by a Buryat shaman to create a "peace tree" on which ribbons are hung bearing prayers of peace. The peace tree acts as a representative of the World Tree. The World Tree is the "axis mundi," which is the central axis of the cosmos. It represents the center of our world and the connection between heaven and earth.

Melissa had volunteered to create a peace tree where I was leading a workshop at the Sunrise Springs retreat center in Santa Fe. She came early to walk the land and find the right Juniper tree. A Juniper on the edge of the property was found, and there was an agreement that the tree would not be disturbed, because once ribbons containing prayers for peace are tied onto the branches, they cannot be removed.

Melissa led chanting and ceremony for many hours as the tree was honored in a traditional way and prepared to receive prayers of peace. Traditional foods were left as an offering, vodka was offered, and shiny luminescent beads were scattered around the tree. Juniper is the sacred incense herb of the Buryat, and is potent in purification and protection, so it was also burned as incense as part of the ceremony. It was quite lovely to be part of such a powerful calling in of spiritual powers to help send our prayers for world peace. About thirty people were present to support the drumming and ceremony.

The tree was honored in 2006, and it still stands today. I've taught many workshops at this retreat center, and during every workshop we bring ribbons or yarn to the tree and add to the prayers for peace that have been left over the years.

My friend Kappy Strahan and I also taught workshops at this retreat center on the art of spinning fiber into yarn, using spinning wheels and drop spindles. Shamans weave the fabric of reality into being through their spiritual work, and so do people who spin. There is a mystical process that happens during spinning where you know that energies created while spinning affect the entire web of life. And as you spin you move into a place of oneness with the spirit that lives in all things and a door opens into the invisible realms that allow visions, great wisdom, and healing to infuse the work. In spinning the yarn weaves together the physical and spiritual aspects of life.

The focus of our spinning workshop was on learning how to bring spirit into what we make so that we empower our homes and the world with clothing, scarves, and other fiber arts made with intention, power, and beauty. It is important to bring spirit and the sacred into the clothes that are manufactured, the plants we grow, the food we prepare, the objects we make for decoration, and the homes and structures we build.

It was very powerful to spin yarn that was imbued with prayers for peace and then walk together as a group to the Juniper tree and tie on our yarn with intention.

Sunrise Springs closed in 2012, but the prayer tree still stands, sending out prayers of peace to the creative power of the universe. The colors of the ribbon and yarn are faded from the strong sun and intense winds, but the tree still looks majestic and exudes the presence of great spiritual power.

One year when I was teaching in Scotland, I visited a forest in the Trossachs known as the Fairy Forest. People from all over the world had come to the forest to leave letters, drawings, pictures, gifts, and prayers for personal and planetary healing. These were left on the ground by a tree or tied to the branches. It was extraordinary to see this forest of trees filled with colored ribbons, photos, gifts, and a variety of beautiful objects carrying love and hope.

Simin Uysal, a brilliant Turkish teacher of shamanism and dream work, shared with me that in southeastern Anatolia there is a wishing tree on a hill called Gobekli Tepe. This site dates back 12,000 years, and local women still go there to pray and tie their ribbons.

I imagine there are prayer trees, wishing trees, and blessing trees all over the world.

🌿 Practices

I love encouraging people to create prayer trees in their communities. I am such a tree person, and I can feel the powerful energetic connection between a prayer tree and the creative forces of the universe.

Close your eyes and imagine the power and beauty of a tree that has colorful ribbons tied loosely on branches and a variety of offerings left on the ground at its base.

Feel your heart opening to the power of nature, the earth below, and the heavens above. Feel yourself being a bridge between heaven and earth through your heart. Feel your compassion grow as you imagine people stepping up to the tree and tying on a prayer tie with the intention of manifesting a wish or dream for themselves, a loved one, the community, or for the planet and all of life.

You can create a prayer tree in your yard, where you can place on the branches ribbons or yarn that are imbued with prayers, wishes, and blessings for yourself, loved ones, friends, nature beings, and the planet. Also, creating a prayer tree in your local neighborhood or community is a powerful way to bring people together in support of each other. Invite children in your community to participate in this activity. This is a way to teach them about the power of joining together to support each other, all of life, and the planet.

Find a tree in nature that would be appropriate to designate as a prayer tree. Start by giving thanks to the tree in a way that calls to your heart. Intention is the key. Bless this tree with the love in your heart as this living being works in partnership to carry prayers to the creative forces of the universe.

Invite people where you live to tie ribbons loosely on the branches or suggest that people craft their own prayer objects through knitting, crocheting, or carving that contain prayers for themselves, loved ones, others, nature beings, and the planet. Remember that as the branch of the tree continues to grow, you don't want to choke it by tying a ribbon too tightly around it. Ask people to leave an offering of gratitude filled with love such as a good thought for the tree. You might also teach people about leaving an offering such as cornmeal, flowers, or water. Imagine the good feelings and the sense of belonging you will create by bringing people together in this way. When people come together to pray for and bless one another and all of life, their positive energy creates healing for the whole planet.

You can create a prayer tree, wishing tree, or blessing tree at Christmas or another holiday time, and instead of decorating with ornaments, invite your community to place ribbons, letters, drawings, and other objects that include prayers on it.

If you cannot use a tree in nature to create a prayer tree, use your imagination to design and create a tree out of natural materials. There must be a balance between thinning our forests for the health of the forest and cutting down trees simply for use as holiday decorations. This is an issue for all of us to reflect on as we learn how to live in harmony with nature. We must honor the trees that share the Earth with us. They are living beings and vital to the health of the web of life.

If it seems appropriate, you can even create a prayer tree in your work place. This is a great way to bring coworkers together to support each other's prayers, show appreciation, and bless all of life.

Use your imagination. The key is the intention and love that you put into creating this ceremony.

When we experience our gratitude for life, we transform our perception about what is occurring in our own lives and on the planet. For when we feel grateful, we can experience the beauty instead of the pain. We want to acknowledge those who are suffering and feel compassion, but at the same time experience the beauty and gifts that life brings for us. This is an ancient teaching that has been passed down through many cultures and generations.

Let us together hold a positive vision for the planet. Let us embrace ourselves, our loved ones, and all of life with love.

Lady of the Sycamore

Llyn

Sandra's writings on the Juniper tree bring back the pristine smells of the northeastern Juniper of my childhood in New Hampshire. They inspire me to relate freshly with the Juniper of the Pacific Northwest, which carries those same crisp scents.

Sandra shares about prayer tree ceremonies, which are close to my heart. I have facilitated such rituals in the United States for many years since first performing them with shamans on the Asian steppe.

Some shamans' trees in Mongolia and Siberia are so covered by prayer ties, called *chalimars,* that you cannot see the trees underneath the ties. Prayers that are infused into the recycled strips of cloth are energized by the tree, rain, sun, and the spirits of the land. Like Tibetan prayer flags, the prayers and wishes in chalimars are flung far and wide by the winds.

Picture in your mind's eye a Eurasian Juniper prayer tree adorned with multicolored ribbons.

Now conjure the sharp, fresh smell of Juniper berries and needles.

Imagining these trees reminds us of winter solstice or Christmas. As a child I loved having a tree in the house for the winter holidays. I used to lie close to the lighted tree in the evenings, gazing up at it and taking in its fragrance. These days, as special as it is to have a tree in the house, I can't bear to cut one down to enjoy it for a couple of weeks. Instead I find some fallen boughs or ask the evergreens in the forests where I live if I can cut a few branches to grace my cabin with tree energy.

Bringing trees and greens inside in the "dead" of winter during the darkest times, the shortest days of the year, is an ancient custom that cleanses the space and reminds us that life and light will return.

My Ukranian friend, Ludmila, has told me that in the Ukraine fresh greenery is brought inside again in the spring. When light and growth return outside, fresh grasses and branches with new growth are strewn onto the floors inside the home. As people go about their daily activities in their homes, they walk barefoot on the tender greens.

Take a moment to really envision this, as it is such a lovely custom. You may be inspired to ask the nature beings surrounding your home to donate a little greenery next spring so that you can walk barefoot on it, as people have done for centuries in the Ukraine.

Walking barefoot on nature's new growth and inhaling its fragrance is invigorating and healing. Just think of how you feel when you walk with bare feet on the earth, smell a freshly cut lawn, or sniff a wild rose. Perhaps you were lucky enough to get nose-level to the earth as a child, and do now as an adult, and know her sweet scent of renewal.

It's not surprising that so many cultures equate trees with purification, as trees continuously bathe all life on our planet with life-giving oxygen and cleansing waters.

Enriched water travels up a tree's roots and trunk to its branches and leaves. Much of the water releases from the tree, up to hundreds of gallons a day. Tree condensation and shade cool the planet and invite rain to the land; trees make clouds.

Increased carbon dioxide in the air causes trees to release less water, which, combined with the clear-cutting of forests, makes it difficult for clouds to build up steam. The result is that the land becomes dry.

Find a tree you admire on your land, in your backyard, or at a nearby park.

Stand on the earth next to this tree, barefoot if possible. Gaze at the tree and sniff the air. Try to sense the misty, nutrient-dense waters that evaporate from this tree being. Although you may not see moisture, you can imagine its release.

Breathe in the rich vapors that flow from the tree like a fountain.

Then breathe out sustaining energy to the tree.

As you continue to "tree-breathe," attune to this tree's essence. Feel its spirit.

Telepathically, or speaking aloud, thank this nature being for its beauty and for everything it offers. Importantly, feel your gratitude. Just as its invisible waters and oxygen nourish you, the love you release with each exhale is food for the tree; appreciation is a nourishing force.

This is a good time to commit to do what you can to promote healthy trees and air, with the tree as your witness.

Water that flows from the Earth to trees and to us is like milk that flows from mother to child. It's similar to the love that pours from ancient mother goddesses to assist people through every phase of life, including death.

One such mother goddess who ushers us through death's doorway is the Egyptian Lady of the Sycamore Tree. The Lady rejuvenates those who are dying and refreshes the souls of the dead in the afterlife by offering them water from the branches of her sacred tree.

The Nordic deity, Freya, as feared as she is revered, also tends to the souls of the dead and to those who are dying. Nomad and seer, guide to the afterlife, Freya is a *volva,* the ancient Norse word for shaman. She tells us, "Don't think it coincidence that the word *volva* resembles the word *vulva.*"

Goddess lore is steeped in the sensual and in the themes of renewal, creation, and birth. The deep feminine also cleanses and nurtures at death's creative threshold, which is, in so many ways, like the portal of birth.

The earth and goddesses do not fear demise; nature eats dead matter. Tibetans may even chop up the corpse of a person who has recently died and feed it to the birds. Most of us can't imagine this; we perceive it as gory. Ancient peoples believed that consciousness continues when the body returns to the earth. Children raised in such cultures have a folksy relationship with dying. The smells and sights of birth, life, and death aren't hidden but available for all to experience. Not too long ago, in my grandparents' era in New England, people still birthed and died at home. It was not uncommon to lay the dead body out in the parlor for people to visit and pay their respects. These events were no longer happening by the time I was born. When I was a child, animals offered my only direct exposure to death.

I always loved animals and, upon finding a small dead one, often carried it home with me to do a burial ceremony. Other children sometimes joined me in these rituals.

Once on my walk to school, I found a baby bird that had fallen from its nest. I took my sandwich out of my lunch box and removed it from its bag, placing the sandwich back in the box. Then I put the dead bird inside the now-empty waxed paper bag. I slipped the bird bag inside my desk when I arrived at school, so that I could take it home at the end of the day and do a ceremony for the little creature.

Our Catholic school had desks with tops that didn't lift; we had to bend over to look inside of them. If something got shuffled to the back of the darkened desk, it could have been lost for weeks. This is what happened to the baby bird. It's possible that the smell of the decomposing bird was what inspired the nuns to clean out all of our desks after school one day. Guess what they found in mine.

After the Sisters of the Holy Cross discovered a rotting bird "hidden" in a lunch sack in the back of my desk, school life became difficult for me for a while. Despite this the natural curiosity and empathy I held for dead and dying animals lived on.

As an adult I have sat with many animals as they lay dying. Some lost their lives to my own machine—my vehicle. Not long ago, when driving my daughter to my cabin, I hit a rabbit that hopped onto the road. How horrible that felt! I turned the car around to see if the bunny was still alive. It lay there panting, blood dripping from its right eye.

Using a towel, my daughter Sayre and I gently placed the rabbit into a cloth sack. We walked out onto the land, and Sayre placed the bag on the ground and carefully opened it. I cringed as I watched the injured rabbit attempt to hop to what I hoped would be safety.

I dropped to the earth on my knees, emptied myself spiritually, and quietly chanted a Buddhist mantra. In these moments I was Freya. As I softly sang to the rabbit, I was the ancient woman who waters from the Sycamore Tree, and simultaneously I was a tree flowing with renewing waters. In those moments I became inseparable from death's alchemical goddess-midwives, pouring out nourishing energy just as the Lady of the Sycamore offered water to the dead and dying from her sacred tree.

The animal grew calm at the sound of my voice. It actually turned around and struggled to make its way back to me, then sat still and quiet. The rabbit and I gazed at each other for some time until the animal gently fell over onto the earth.

I chanted for a while longer until Sayre and I agreed that we felt complete. We took in the beauty of this being, then left the body where it lay. Other animals would return it to the land.

A few days later I visited the spot where the bunny had died. A mostly eaten carcass remained, rabbit fur strewn helter-skelter.

All of us in modern times encounter hurt or dying animals on the road. Freya would not walk or drive by without stopping. Lady of the Sycamore would sit with the dying one and bestow refreshing waters to prepare the being for the next journey.

During his nomadic days my forest guide, Mick Dodge, walked the highways and byways of Washington State. One time a car sped by and hit an elk that sprang out in front of the vehicle. The car sported Earth-honoring bumper stickers and the driver, a woman, was mortified to have hit a wild, innocent animal. Other people stopped their cars to see if the driver was okay. The elk lay panting in the road.

We do not call ambulances for animals.

Several people helped to carefully move the elk off the pavement onto the earth. Then, Freya, the Lady of the Sycamore, and Mick Dodge sat with this elk for three days until it died.

Trees invisibly channel and diffuse waters. Most of us have numerous fears, ideas, and judgments about death. The trees and goddesses teach us how to sit at death's portal by grounding in the Earth and being present. As we settle our minds and open our hearts, nourishing energy will flow from us like the waters of the goddess's sacred tree; it is a natural force of love.

Freya reminds us, "Honor death as in life and remember who you are. The ancient pathways of the goddess—threads of light and wisdom—will become visible to you."

Is it compassionate to kill a suffering, dying animal? I have struggled with this. Buddhism teaches us to be aware as we die, and the same is true for animals. Pain is often part of the experience. I've witnessed pure grace when sitting with a being as it takes its final breath. Tending a suffering loved one, animal, or person through a long and drawn-out dying process is equally powerful and not without its challenges. The threshold goddesses—Freya and the Lady of the Sycamore—can help.

Freya and the Lady of the Sycamore Tree, alchemical goddesses, encourage us to open space within our hearts (and in our schedules) to resurrect the archetypal death-midwife.

The watering goddess, who provides nourishing waters from the Sycamore Tree to rejuvenate those who are dead and dying, says: "To nourish one who is at death's gateway, hold the space as sacred by having a calm mind and an open heart in the final moments. This is easier when you view dying as birthing—shifting from one experience to another. Support person or animal to die wakefully, and the blessings will shower down upon all."

🌿 Practice

Like the cleansing water of trees, the clarifying scent of Juniper, and the purifying energy of nature's fresh greenery that promise life and light will return, the Lady of the Sycamore is a watering mother goddess who refreshes each person or animal for the next journey.

The Lady of the Sycamore and Freya teach us how we can be present and open with our loved ones as they are dying to revive the power of death's passage in modern times.

Freya, the feared one, and the Lady of the Sycamore Tree, watering goddess, can also help restore vibrant qualities within us that are languishing. For instance, the threshold goddesses can nourish angry, hurt, and fearful parts of us so we can live with less angst. Walk out into the forest on a dark, windy night, and notice what you feel. Nature's intensity stirs dread for many, stimulating whatever lies in shadow or unresolved within us.

I used to be afraid of the dark.

I was afraid of me.

Freya, the shaman nomad, tells us that the forest is an alchemical mirror. Trees and goddesses nurture death equally as they nurture life. Hence, nature reflects what is threatening, wounded, or untamable in us— the vibrancy we've stunted.

Care for the trees and also sit with them. Lie on the earth and gaze up at them. Sleep atop their silent roots and against broad or spindly trunks and under leafy or conifer canopies. Go deeply into their mystery to find the deep mystery of you. The feminine wisdom-waters that flow through and from the trees will transform your water consciousness. You will discover who you are. Greet the power that stalks you. What is shrouded in us and in our world yearns to return to light and life.

Take some undisturbed time sitting indoors or outside near a robust tree. Close your eyes for a few moments, and take some luxurious breaths.

When relaxed, consider Lady of the Sycamore, protector and guide, sacred midwife who births and resurrects life.

Feel the Lady's energy; sense her eyes upon you. See the turquoise waters with which she renews. Sense the sacred Sycamore Tree or your own favorite tree nearby.

Take time to really imagine the Lady of the Sycamore and the tree; see how they appear to you. Or simply sense them.

When ready, look into the goddess's eyes. What color are her eyes?

What do you see and feel as you gaze into the eyes of the goddess?

Take your time.

When you are ready, notice the ancient mirror the Lady holds. The Lady offers a look at your life. If you accept, take some time to gaze into the mirror, considering what reflects back to you. Look deeply.

What do you see?

What do you feel?

What wants to come back to life that you have lost or forgotten? It may be joy. Silliness. A favorite pastime or craft.

It may be dancing or stillness. Or prayer.

It may be time in nature or time with friends.

These are just examples; it may be anything, small or lofty.

Look deeply into the Lady's handheld mirror and feel the goddess compassionately watching. What has been put aside?

Allow whatever feelings are coming to the surface. Let them wash through with each breath. Keep returning to what is being restored—brought back to life. Take all the time you like.

When you feel complete with this experience, allow the image, mirror, and Lady to fade.

When you are ready, notice the sacred tree—the Sycamore, or a tree of your own lands. In your imagining sense the clear turquoise refreshing waters that shower from the tree.

Imagine that you stand next to this tree and immerse yourself in these waters. Feel the tree's spirit and its restorative force. Envision and feel this water, like liquid light flowing over and nourishing you.

Go deeply into this experience. Feel your spirit. Feel the vitality you have forgotten. Allow it to flood through every part of you.

Take all the time you like.

When and if it feels right for you, do the same practice for the collective field. Sense the trees of the Earth, healthy and strong. See their cleansing vapors renewing and restoring the Earth. Also know that they revive for humankind the ecstasy of living in harmony with nature.

Again, take all the time you like. Make this imagining real.

Close the experience when you feel complete. Do some gentle movement and stretch to help your transition back to everyday consciousness. When fully back in the present, close your eyes as you drink a glass of pure, fresh water. Feel the water touch every part of you; nourish what has come back to life. Take time to write about your experience if you'd like. Include concrete ways to honor what you have revived, and to restore and renew your daily life and that of the Earth. A newborn being must be fed and nourished. Start small, but commit to giving energy to your dreams. Commit to vibrancy. Feed it every day.

Take an offering out to feed the land or your favorite tree. Feel the watering forces, the nourishment and light of the trees and the Earth. Speak your gratitude freely, also a nourishing force of love. Thank the threshold goddesses. Say yes to nature and to life.

10

ELK AND SNAKE

Elk

Llyn

Imagine strolling through a magnificent dark forest and sniffing the fresh scent of conifers. The canopy of branches over your head is an intricate lacing of hemlock, spruce, cedar, and fir trees.

I love walking through forests in the Pacific Northwest, and as I do I notice signs of animal life all around me. For instance, whenever I see the telltale nipped tips of bushes, I look to the ground as there are often hoof prints of deer or Elk.

Picture in your mind's eye the tan-colored body of an Elk, with its tufted, dark brown hooded head and white rump.

Can you envisage an Elk bull with antlers that weigh almost thirty pounds?

Sense for a moment what it would be like to wear a thirty-pound, three-foot-high sculpture of shapely bone-hair on your own head.

There is a rough inlet that veers off one of my favorite walking

trails in the Hoh Rain Forest. Taking the narrow path I climb over a large log. The bark is stripped where the hooves of many Elk have scraped against the fallen tree.

Further down the path I come to a clearing with giant trees and prehistoric-looking ferns. When the sun streaks through the spacious canopy, its warmth coaxes a delicious smell from the earth. When sunlight penetrates this place, it also illumines flattened grasses where Elk sleep amidst the giant fern fans. It's exciting to find Elk beds and awe-inspiring to see Elk in the wild.

The Olympic Mountains are home to the largest unmanaged herd of Elk in the Pacific Northwest. This vast wilderness region also boasts the largest Elks in North America. Ten thousand visitors a year pass through the gates of Olympic National Park, tucked into the far northwest corner of the United States. Up to two thousand people a day can drive in when the rain ceases during drought season in August and September.

Some environmentalists guess that only 3–5 percent of original old-growth forest remains outside National Park boundaries in the United States.

At the same time I have heard locals say: "The Elk love the cleared lands; they are great places to graze."

Elk do often browse in manmade meadows where great forests once stood. As they nibble, some *Wapiti* (Shawnee, meaning "white rump") bend to the earth while others stand alert. The herd, whose primary threats are people, bear, and cougar, appears as a choreographed wave of bobbing heads in the open field and is a sight to behold.

Elk are gardeners of the forest. Wapiti hooves that dig into the earth aerate the land, and the health benefits that drive people to search out dropped antlers for medicines and dog chews, are meant for the soil.

Wapiti antlers enrich the earth as they decay. The seeds spread by Elk scat also spawn trees. Animals attracted to treeless meadows attract the trees back to these meadows and reforest the land. Nature knows what she is doing.

We are likewise designed to merge our own with the Earth's desire. To do this we nurture nature and our own wild ways.

Regarding the trees much of the old-growth forest in the United States is either gone or preserved. In the 1930s and '40s, 50 percent of forests in the western coastal states—including Washington—were old growth. Now it is less than 20 percent, and 80 percent of that 20 percent is on federal lands. But since many clear-cut areas are replenished with tree planting, people ask: "What's wrong with clear cutting the land if the old-growth forest that remains is protected and new trees are being planted to replace what is cut?"

What these folks don't realize (and I did not until I moved to the Olympic Peninsula) is that tightly packed rows of the same kind of tree are planted for reharvest a few decades later. Tree crops aren't forests, whose hallmark is diversity. Animals are killed and displaced by tree cutting, and monocultures are not only subject to blight, even a dog would be hard-pressed to get through the thick tree stands, let alone a winter Wapiti herd sporting huge-antlered bulls traveling paths their ancestors forged hundreds of years before. In turn, those traveling paths opened the forest for other animals to roam and also drop scat for a hardy ecosystem.

Seeding the land with new growth is as vital as seeding our communities with new dreams.

In these shifting times the Earth has a lot to purge and renew and she is doing it. We are part of the planet's evolution and also have imbalances to set right. Humanity is prodded to deepen; a new way of living wants to take root. Just as Elk shows up to vitalize barren fields, dropping scat that holds the memory of forests, in our lives circumstances, events, and people appear to restore our true nature.

"Take a breath," says Wapiti. "Relax and lift your gaze. See what steps in to stand with you in this life meadow, your field of experience."

Coinciding with the dismantling of the life we know is auspicious happenstance, an allure to the life we have yet to live—the life that dreams us.

Wapiti encourages, "Be open. Scan your field."

What steps in may be a human, animal, or spirit presence; a provocative thought or memory; a stirring book or piece of music; a message in a dream or from the wind or from a favorite tree; an encounter or event; or something else.

This changing era is plentiful in soul direction; we simply need to open to and participate with it. The grace that floats in may be a miracle. The miraculous is more accessible as we remember who we are. Miracles are our human birthright.

Grace can also be a life lesson or a nudge to grow. As a simple example, a puppy showed up in my life quite by surprise last December. Three days after I took this puppy back to my cabin, my nineteen-year-old cat unexpectedly died. The timing was uncanny, as if beautiful black angora Katie had summoned a soft, furry black animal to take her place.

But Gabu-San was not Katie. A frisky Husky-Aussie, the puppy soon started to nip at me. Hard. Letting Gaby know I wasn't an animal she could herd was an intensive undertaking that felt very demanding after just losing a gentle companion of almost twenty years. Yet grace has its own timing, which is perfect.

Gaby and I have our own sweet bond now and she pushes me to be tougher, a quality I need for the more rugged lifestyle I'm exploring.

Blessings have their own ways and are abundant in these times. When I assume this I see them everywhere, not only when I feel the need. Like little Gabu-San, they often arrive in forms I don't expect and sometimes in those I don't desire.

Ultimately, everything is blessing.

It's good to consider this and also help others to open to and trust grace at play. Ask Wapiti to step in with you when you find yourself auspiciously in another's field of experience.

You may ask, "But what of painful circumstances in nature and among people for which it feels impossible to find the blessings?"

At these times it's up to us to bless, to activate grace. Ask Wapiti who seeds a forest as she walks through clear cuts to help you enrich this barren field and nourish whatever situation you encounter.

Compared to the hundred-head Elk herds I've seen in Rocky Mountain National Park near where I lived for many years, Elk groups in the Olympics are small in number with around twenty Wapiti to a herd, although two groups may come together for a time. One morning last winter I awoke to thirty-eight Elk outside my cabin in the Hoh.

The forest is full of life in winter, when I see many Elk, as on that morning, just as it teems with life in the spring.

It's June now, and two evenings ago a huge Black Bear hung out in the meadow behind my barn. Little Gaby and I stood outside watching as it ate dandelion greens.

This morning as I was driving out of the forest, another, perhaps the same, large Bear lunged from the trees and into the road, right in front of my car. Black Bear enacted an extravagant twirl, then dashed into the woods on the other side of the road.

Less than an eighth of a mile before Black Bear spiraled into the road in front of me, I'd met up with the tail end of a modest grouping of Elk. Twelve elegant, wild creatures, large cousins of the deer family, stepped out from the trees, including a dark fluffy baby trailing a Wapiti cow. Despite the open car window, I barely heard a sound as the half-herd leapt into the forest on the other side of the road.

A cow, a grandmother perhaps, stopped scant feet into the trees. Her long glance in my direction made my heart pound.

Three bulls surrounded the grandmother, baby, and other cows. Their blunt velvety antlers, just growing, will shoot hard bony spirals three feet or more toward the heavens come winter's first flurries.

Wapiti is a teacher of one of the most ancient symbols for the feminine—the spiral.

Antlers, like hair, are spiritual antennae. Elk bulls wield their branchlike antlers in figure-eight spirals when sparring in rutting season. This configuration builds and releases incredible power.

Wapiti channels this ecstasy into the herd. The awesome presence of old stags attests to years of harnessing the potency of the spiral. Cows, like mothers all over the world throughout all time, incubate that spiraling life force during pregnancy, then birth it into form—in this case baby Wapitis. It is no wonder early peoples identified the antlered ones with fertility and power. This regenerative power, not exclusively sexual, infuses us and all life.

The Elk drive this life power into procreation. So strong is this force that a bull can hurl another into a tree, snapping the tree in half. My friend, Monty, has told me that decades ago a neighbor's horse met an ugly death when a rutting Elk spiraled out of control into the horse standing nearby. The animal was buried where it was knocked to the ground.

Humans describe rutting spars as displays to establish mating dominion. Although in essence this is true, it's just a fragment of the whole scenario.

Wapiti invites us to appreciate the amazing energetics animals engage in and to embody these rhythms—reclaim the spiral.

In the Hoh River the water forms eddies at turns and where large boulders or logs lodge. The whirlpools can drive like power drills into rocks and sand. You would quickly get pulled under if you jumped into the water in some of these places.

Cone-shaped pieces of wood wash up on the Hoh River's edge. These branches spiral out from the trees where they grow. The limbs are embedded in the trunks, like screws driven into wood. Thousand-year-old trees fall into and travel the lengths of these rivers, and the massive trunks often fall apart before their dense branches do.

The spiral is impassioned and strong. Ancient rituals from all cultures celebrate and invoke the power of the spiral. Many traditions, such as Tibetan and Sufi, include spinning energy practices. Spiraling snakes form the helixes of our DNA and entwine the axis rod of the caduceus, symbol for allopathic medicine.

Spirals are found everywhere in nature and in us.

Elk follow the same paths their ancestors trod hundreds of years before them. What it means to be a Wapiti is imprinted in the land; the energy of their collective and ancestral memory can be shamanically detected in the paths that the animals create and follow on the earth.

In walking the antlered ones' pathways, I spiral into Wapiti consciousness, feeling the hunt in the land and ancient rhythms of the run in my body.

People and animals have walked, crawled, and run the land for thousands of years, to flee, fight, seek food, find water and shelter, and wander. Wandering was first nature to original nomads of all cultures. Anthropologists and historians say that many early peoples wandered all over the world. As just two examples of walking cultures, to this day there are Bedouin desert walkers, as well as lowland and highland walkers in Wales. Like the Elk, as these folks walk and run, they embody, and also release, the spiraling force.

The word *walk* is Anglo-Celt for "water," and in their travels humans likely used their bodies as natural dowsing rods to guide their search for water. We are 70–90 percent water—walking water. Aimlessly wander and see if you walk (water) the land in a spiral. As water and life move in spirals, it makes sense that one eye, one ear, one foot, and so forth is larger than the other and also that our legs are different lengths.

Semicircular fluid-filled canals in the inner ear, called labyrinths, balance our vertical bodies when we are walking. Labyrinths attach to spiral shaped cochlea, which look like soft nautilus shells.

Everything about us says "spiral." Wapiti reminds us that we *are* the spiraling force.

Shells and galaxies spiral, plants spiral as they grow, smoke swirls and spirals in the air just as our breath spirals into our nostrils and through our body, then out again to the air, the wind, which spirals tornadoes and whirlwinds and dust devils. Water spirals into vortex spouts in the ocean and seawater chisels stones into beach sand, just as rivers make whirlpools that sculpt rich places for habitat, and so on and so forth.

We take in as well as release the spiraling force as we walk (water) the land. This enlivens us and the earth. That good feeling of having our bare feet on the earth is nature calling us home.

🌿 Practice

Wapiti encourages us to engage the field of our experience and welcome the grace and growth opportunities that step into our life meadow as introduced by story and suggestion above.

Wapiti also invites us to reclaim the spiral. Just as a washing machine applies spiraling action to clean our clothes, the whirlpools in natural bodies of water cleanse the water, whirling wind whisks the air clean, and swirling flames purify forests.

Here are some simple suggestions for engaging the sacred feminine spiral:

- 🌿 Gaze at spiraling starlight and muse on the Milky Way and other swirling galaxies. As you do, feel how these reflect your own spiraling nature.

- 🌿 Look at, dream on, play with, and move as the spiraling patterns of water, wind, and fire; circular plant designs and those in pinecones and tree rings; whirling flocks of birds and the swirling forms of clouds; the twirling flight path of a honeybee; and so forth.

- Walk a labyrinth or trace one with your finger.
- Envisage the labyrinths and spirals in your inner ears. Look at photographs of ear spirals and labyrinths.
- Hold a glass of pure water and swirl the water into a vortex with a wooden chopstick. Then, as you drink the water, feel and imagine the fluid spiraling through and brightening every cell—your internal waters.
- Instead of walking a straight line, skip like a child tracing circles and spirals on the earth. Also do this in cities to juxtapose sharp urban angles and lines with fluidity and curves. Those who see you may drink in this watering and catch the spiral's power. You will know it by their smiles.
- Enjoy doodling circles and spiraling shapes.
- As you call in the spiral, watch how it shows up in your life field. For instance, while completing this chapter I stayed at a cabin overlooking another glacial river. A silt-foam ball the size of a human head appeared in the water below my deck. It formed in an eddy among three large stones. A clear mirroring, it was astonishing to watch the white foam-head continuously rotate in the water.
- Invite the spiral by writing, telling, and imagining stories, including your own life story. Instead of knowing what you will write or tell, muse into the tale and see how the story spirals through it.

As an example, instead of planning every detail of my life, I muse with it, see what shows up in the meadow of my experience, and then sense how to dance with what appears.

As you tell a tale and muse with it, the story may circle round and again, though it never comes back to exactly the same place. So it is with spirals, and life. Reflecting this, indigenous people naturally speak and teach in spirals and circles via storytelling. When we open in these ways, it is awakening to see what channels through to us.

The spiral cleanses as it circulates stale waters. As we put a new spin on our stale stories, we will brighten, just as the spiraling kundalini snake and the electrical information in our spiraling DNA strands light up our spiritual bodies. This can happen in an instant, as the spiral is not linear and our stories (and we) are not solid, as we think and have been taught.

Allow ample room for the many stories that may make you cry. Allow your inner waters to spiral up to release feelings so that their expression and tears may cleanse you. We may also cry as we touch into—and in so doing cleanse—the Earth's soulful stories, which are our own. Her deep waters are our deep waters. In musing on the Earth, we recover who we are.

Let yourself explore. Participate with what shows up in your life field and be sure to spiral the gifts out to the world, to brighten it and make it fresh.

Snake

Sandra

Shift your awareness from the lush Hoh Rain Forest where the elk roam to the high desert land of New Mexico. Imagine taking a walk through a forested area where you smell the sweet fragrance of juniper and piñon pine. The sun is blazing, heating the land, and you feel yourself soaking in the warmth of both the sun and the earth. The sky is clear and you can appreciate the unique light of the high desert, which attracts so many people to the area. Walking among the trees you come to a sandy arroyo surrounded by red rocks and short, prickly chamisa (rabbitbrush) bushes.

As you walk on the sand through the dry riverbed, you find yourself lost in your thoughts with your mind drifting to this and that. Out of the corner of your eye, you sense movement. There's something moving through the brush. First you are startled out of your thoughts and daydreams, and your heart starts to beat rapidly as you feel some fear in your body. You are alert. That sense of fear shifts quickly to curiosity and wonder.

You stop and stand very still to see what is moving through the landscape. You might feel startled again as you see a beautiful bull snake winding across your path with grace and ease. Snake in all its

189

beauty—a being with no eyelids or legs—sliding along the earth. Snake has internal ears rather than external, and two sets of eyes. One set is normal eyes that can see color; the other set of "eyes" detects radiant heat and helps them target body parts of their prey. And although they have nostrils, snakes smell with their tongues.

The shy bull snake in New Mexico is a friend to humans. A sub-species of a gopher snake, bull snakes are often yellow with brown or black blotching, average about six-feet in length, and are not venom-ous. There is a false myth that rattlesnakes will not inhabit an area where there are bull snakes; nevertheless bull snakes give locals a sense of comfort, for when we see them we believe there are no rattlesnakes in the area.

As you walk, the snake detects you and turns to move away from you as quickly as you might want to move away from it. But you feel yourself immobilized. There is a part of you that wants to run and part of you mesmerized in place by the Snake's graceful movement across the earth.

Many people have a primal fear that arises when they see a snake. And of course there are those who just love Snakes and seek them out in nature.

There is much symbolism and mythology that goes along with Snake. The Bible teaches that Adam and Eve were banished from the Garden of Eden after Snake tricked them into biting into the apple to gain the seed of knowledge. Other ancient stories of snake medicine and the snake goddess have mostly been lost. There is not much information on what snake medicine offered in ancient times, but still today it is often seen to have curative powers, and rattlesnake venom is being researched as a possible cure for cancer. The rod of Asclepius depicting a snake encircling a staff is a traditional symbol of the medical arts.

There is also much psychological symbolism in that Snake represents sacred sexuality. The ouroboros symbol of a snake devouring its own tail and forming a circle depicts the cycle of life. It reminds us that death and rebirth are part of one cycle; in the eternal cycle of renewal, we are always re-creating ourselves.

The focus of this essay is how Snake can help you reconnect with your body, the feminine, and the Earth. Understanding how you can enliven your senses will assist you in deepening the spiritual practices that Llyn wrote about in Elk.

Our perception creates our reality. We change our reality by changing our perception about what is happening around us. Here are a couple of simple examples: You perceive one person as beautiful and someone else might see only that person's flaws. The energy of people at a gathering seems bright and joyful to you, but a friend you are with experiences the energy as dense and negative. Your reality is based on how you perceive the world.

In the Western world we often pity others when we perceive them suffering. All that exists is alive and has a spirit with a destiny. We shift our reality by changing our perception and focusing on the strength and beauty of others and of the Earth. We can truly support others by seeing them in their strength rather than focusing on their challenges. We can be compassionate while avoiding moving into a state of pity.

To sink into another level of this teaching, we need to acknowledge the power of our senses—sight, hearing, smell, feel, and taste. Using our senses is a way to experience the joy and preciousness of life as we delight in our sensory awareness. Opening to and accessing our senses is essential as we remember how to truly connect with nature. We must use our visible and invisible senses to be able to experience the support we are being given.

Although we live in the physical realm in our bodies, some people don't want to be connected with their physical reality. For a variety of reasons, maybe due to past trauma or illness, being in a body is a source of pain for them, rather than a joyful experience. In the same way we are disconnected from our bodies, many of us are disconnected from nature. For to experience nature immediately connects us back to the power and beauty of being in a body.

We share this Earth with extraordinary nature beings that use the strength of different senses to help them perceive the world. Snake—without legs—is always connected to the movement in and vibration of the earth. I can only imagine what that might be like to be so close to the earth all the time.

Snake is dependent on the warmth emitted by the earth to maintain its temperature so that it can be active and move gracefully through its environment. Water that is allowed to flow naturally snakes through the earth. From an overhead perspective in an airplane, it's easy to see the way a river winds like a snake through the landscape.

As humans we have our internal and external senses, but in the Western world we cut ourselves off from using the depth of our senses to perceive the world around us. Many of us live surrounded by so much external noise that we cannot hear a beautiful bird song, the music of a gentle breeze, strong wind, water running in nature, or rain.

We often overload our senses with so many material objects that we cannot take in nature's beauty. Disconnected from our bodies, we don't let ourselves fully touch all that is in our surroundings. The taste of our food is masked with so many artificial flavorings and sweeteners that we cannot appreciate the fresh taste of food from the earth.

This is all to say we are missing out on a lot that life has to offer. We cannot perceive the beauty in life or connect with nature if we have deadened senses.

The prefrontal cortex is the part of our brain that is believed to orchestrate our thoughts, actions, cognitive behavior, expression of our personality, and decision making. The prefrontal cortex makes up only a small percentage of the brain, but in the modern world we rely on it for information. We lose much of the depth and richness of life when we spend so much time in a cognitive process. We need to wake up our sensory awareness.

To shift our sense of reality and inhabit a richer and more beautiful life, we need to get close to the ground, as Snake does. We must reconnect with the earth and fully enliven our senses to contact the beauty and power of the world around us. And then we can truly appreciate the beauty that lives in all things.

We can also tap into our non-ordinary senses—our shamanic, psychic, and intuitive knowing. But here again so many of us have deadened our psychic senses.

Before an earthquake or other natural disaster occurs, animal behavior changes significantly. During the most recent destructive tidal wave in Thailand, animals had moved to higher ground and safety before the tidal wave was apparent to humans.

Birds, dogs, cats, and most animals, including snakes, become agitated before an earthquake. Most of us have disconnected from the psychic senses that inform us with the information that animals receive. The senses of nature beings are heightened enough to pick up changes occurring in the earth.

One of my frustrations in teaching shamanic journeying is how focused people are on "seeing" their journeys, as if they are watching a TV show or a movie. It has been difficult for me to persuade people to experience the depth of all their non-ordinary senses. For the spirits do not communicate solely by showing us images. Shamans take their bodies into the dreamtime and use all their senses while traveling in the invisible realms.

As we live our daily lives, we can open our non-ordinary senses to perceive a rich and magical world around us. We might hear a message in the wind or see one in the clouds as we walk to work. When our ordinary senses are not so overloaded, we find ourselves in touch with inner knowings where we simply feel the truth of guidance or wisdom in our bones.

The nature beings with all their internal and external senses are great teachers for us in how to reconnect with our inner and outer landscape. As we do this we find our perception shifting about events and transitions occurring in our lives. Life takes on deeper meaning, and we can perceive the beauty that life has to offer and how precious it is to be in a body.

I learned from my mother that having a body is a precious gift. This gift is to be honored, not rejected or judged. When we open our sensory awareness, we see, hear, feel, taste, and smell all that nature offers us, and then we inhabit a universe that right now most of us can only imagine.

Whenever I have a question about choices to make in my life, Snake is one of the nature beings that appears as an omen on my walks in the arroyo. I have come to rely on Snake for showing me a sign about moving forward, that something new is coming into my life.

My father always loved me unconditionally and taught me a lot. We had a beautiful relationship, and he sacrificed much in his life, as did my mother, to provide a safe and loving environment for my childhood. A few years ago, at the age of 97, my father dealt with serious health challenges, and I wanted to take care of him at the end of his life as he had cared for me in the beginning of mine. I was his caregiver and had to make very difficult decisions that felt beyond my capabilities.

One day I felt completely overwhelmed. I felt I just did not have the knowledge or information I needed to make the best choices for him.

I went outside and I cried out to God, the divine goddess, and the helping spirits, "Please help me. Give me a sign that will light my way in making a decision."

It was a cold, rainy October day, and I took a long walk in the arroyo, crying and praying. As I cleared my head, a knowing about the next step in my father's care became clear to me. At that point a baby snake crawled over the toe of one of my hiking shoes. I could hardly believe it; it was way past the time for a baby snake to be born. The season was turning and it was cold. I bent down to watch the snake as it slid away, looking to make sure it was not a worm or a long centipede. Yes, it was clearly a baby snake.

To me this omen symbolized a new birth and change for me and my family. I knew that life was taking a turn. Shortly after Snake appeared my father passed away. I was deeply saddened to lose him, but happy that he was finally free and had found peace. He ended up dying a graceful and peaceful death.

Snake shows itself to me in the wild when I need a reminder that death leads to new life and that a change is coming that will help me re-create my life. Snake appears to me when I need a reminder that spirit is guiding me, and I have a wealth of invisible help. Snake also shows itself during my walks when I need a sign that I am on the right track.

Snake continues to reinvent herself. She sheds her skin and, like Bear, is born anew, fresh, and regenerated. Snake teaches us how we, too, can reinvent ourselves and reawaken not just our ordinary senses, but also the non-ordinary senses so we can engage in deep, rich communication with the spirit that lives in all things.

We can spiral back to the gifts of our ordinary and non-ordinary senses, which teach us how to spiral forward in our growth and evolution.

The spiral is a prominent symbol in ancient petroglyphs. It is a symbol of growth and evolution and of the origin of life, water, and snakes. The spiral teaches us about the rhythms of nature, the seasons, and the cycles of death and rebirth.

In nature it is common to find a snake resting or sleeping in the shape of a spiral. When we spiral out of the deep sleep we are in, we allow our senses to awaken to the beauty, power, and knowledge that is within and around us.

🌿 Practices

Snake is always in touch with the vibration of the earth. One way for you to reconnect to your body is to reconnect with the earth. Leave your digital music player at home, and visit a park or your favorite place in nature. Lie on the earth and let your heart harmonize with her heartbeat. Feel the vibration of the earth, and notice your own vibration moving through your body and into alignment with the earth.

Imagine being a Snake and soaking up the warmth and love of the earth. Feel this warmth, love, and vibration being absorbed into all your cells.

Slowly become more alert, and open your senses to perceive the beauty of nature. When you are ready, get up slowly and start to take some steps. As you walk, stop and smell the fragrance of the earth, air, trees, and plants. Put your fingers into the earth and place some in your hands; feel the temperature, moistness, and texture. Place your hands on the bark of a tree and feel its texture. Gently touch the leaves of a plant that are safe to touch. Run your fingers through the grass and touch the moss. Take off your shoes and socks, and feel the earth on the soles of your feet. If you are on a beach, feel the grains of sand in your hands and around your toes. Smell the salt in the air. Lick your lips and taste the salt.

If you are by a body of water, close your eyes as you place your hands in the water. Feel the changing sensations in your body as you do this.

Listen to the beautiful sounds and music provided by nature. With your eyes closed, feel the wind playing with your hair.

Eat food that has not been "doctored" with artificial flavors. Eat slowly and enjoy the fresh natural taste. As you drink water, focus on the sweet fresh taste and feel it nurturing you as it travels down your throat.

Notice what visible and invisible senses you have stopped using to the fullest. What senses of yours have become atrophied?

If you try to wake up your senses all at once, you might get over-whelmed with too much sensory input. Have patience and slowly engage in awakening your inner and outer senses.

Sit with a plant or rock in nature. Sit very still for thirty minutes with complete focus and awareness, observing this nature being. Notice how your senses become heightened after you complete this practice.

When at home, turn on some meditative music or listen to a drumming track and hold the intention to meet the ancient snake goddess. Using all your psychic senses, notice how the snake goddess might communicate her deep wisdom about snake medicine with you. Ask for a teaching that will help you deepen the connection between your body and the earth.

When you find yourself sitting in nature, play with drawing spirals in the earth or the sand. Don't think about it; just notice what you feel as you do this. Allow your own insights to come to you.

Shamanism is a practice of direct revelation. This means that we all have access to the spiritual wisdom we need in order to thrive and experience the beauty of life. We have access to the insights that enable us to glide through life with the grace and beauty of Snake.

As society has taught us to disconnect from our bodies and the earth, the key to healing the planet and ourselves is learning to connect again to our own psychic wisdom and psychic senses. This will enliven the adventure of being a spiritual being in a physical body.

Llyn wrote about Elk and I wrote about Snake. These are obviously very different nature beings that attracted each of us on a spiritual level. Take some time and reflect on the wildlife where you live. Notice if a specific nature being in your area is asking for your attention right now.

11

WOOD SORREL
AND MUSHROOM

Wood Sorrel

Llyn

Imagine unexpectedly finding yourself among thousands of Wood Sorrel plants rippling across a rich, decaying rain forest floor.

Wood Sorrel patches are magical, summoning visions of nearby faeries. When the rain penetrates the forest canopy, its droplets land higgledy-piggledy on stretches of these three-leafed plants that closely resemble clover. Here, there, and everywhere, tender heart-shaped leaflets bow to gentle droplets of rainwater blessing. They spring right back like tiny bells being struck. It is no wonder that Wood Sorrel is often called "Faerie Bells."

Redwood Oxalis, another name for the species commonly found in the Pacific Northwest, grows best in shaded, moist woodlands. Its bright green leaflets are a soft plum color on the underside with a reddish tint

at the base of the stem. In late spring a fragile white flower appears on Oregon Oxalis.

Oxalis plants, sometimes called Shamrocks, radiate pure joy. The little Faerie Bells make you smile and forget about your concerns. Their presence in Pacific Northwest forests is mesmerizing.

So alluring is the "Love Plant" that I urge people to lie down upon the forest floor to appreciate them at close range. Imagine sleeping upon springy beds of moss near tender stretches of this cloverlike plant. Look what happened to Dorothy and Toto when they slept in poppy fields just outside the Land of Oz!

Kansas-bred Dorothy's poppy-induced slumber has sparked some interesting conversations. People wonder if it was their red color or the opiate in poppies that made Dorothy groggy. When you lie amidst lush green blankets of Love Plants for midday naps, you won't care what makes you dreamy.

The three heart-shaped leaves of Wood Sorrel are said to signify the mystery of the Trinity for Christians—as the "Hallelujah Plant"—

and Celts (*Seamróg*, or Little Clover). Everything about Wood Sorrel is enticing, which is likely why it has so many endearing names.

Faerie Bells keep the door to life's mysteries ajar. They grow from rich, moist humus that mirrors the fertile, receptive feminine void. A reminder of what is possible—the place of co-creation with spirit and nature—Sorrel rejects reductionist views and won't even allow us to fix her by name.

Deer Clover, wise as she is gay, asks that we engage life inventively, understanding that not knowing is often potent beyond what others or we conclude or guess. Faerie Bells know how to frolic in the uncertainty of the ever-unfolding current of life. We can lose touch with this wonder-filled flow when we reduce life to what we believe, want, fear, or expect.

As a personal example, for years I held what seemed to be a logical assumption that my lovely black angora cat, Katie (who lived to be nineteen), would require a lot of care from me in her final days. Given this, I sometimes felt concerned over how I would meet an elderly cat's needs.

Katie was a great teacher, as none of what I anticipated came to pass. Vibrant to the end, she simply walked into the forest one night and released her spirit into a giant spruce tree.

We can all relate to fretting over scenarios that never take place. Like Sorrel's name play, we needn't take ourselves so seriously or cast the future in stone.

The elusive Sour Trefoil is also known as "Cuckoo Sorrell" (not to be confused with cuckoopint). Cuckoo shows that notions can make us into complete fools. To obsessively peg life is really an effort to control life, which has little to do with life itself.

This message is timely. As the world shifts all around and we navigate personal twists and turns, why not tune in to our highest dreams—what our hearts and souls long for—instead of mentally sealing off the possibilities or even investing in the worst?

Cuckoo, the little Love Plant, encourages us to stay as centered and spacious through change as we can, leaving room for life's design. My sweet Katie released into this deep place of potential; she literally and consciously walked off into the creative void. She and the forest planned elegantly for how to bring her precious life to a close. Had I relaxed my anxiety and expectations, I believe I would have tuned in to this earlier. Because we humans have so many ideas about things, we can miss the ongoing whispering of the spirits.

On sacred expeditions to indigenous cultures, I train myself, and instruct people on the trips, to get out from behind the camera lens, refrain from idle chatter, and forget about what we think we know and what we need to say, do, eat, or buy. Leave space for the rich tapestry of the moment. This allows the mind to merge with life's creative force.

A compelling example of a person who adeptly blended intellect and inspiration, the mind with the soul, to do good work in the world was my dear friend John Mack, a Harvard psychiatrist whose book about T. E. Lawrence (known as Lawrence of Arabia), *A Prince of Our Disorder,* won him a Pulitzer Prize.

Dr. Mack's impressive career spanned traditional psychiatry, social activism, the transformational effects of alleged alien abductions, and life-after-life. Here was a brilliant man who threw his heart into everything he did.

I once asked him, "John, you've worked in diverse arenas. How do you decide what's next?"

Dr. Mack grinned widely, his blue eyes sparkling, as he answered, "I never do. The next step always appears; I follow my passion."

This resounds with the philosophy of classic mythologist Joseph Campbell. His invitation to the sacred adventure of life—to follow our bliss—has become part of our vernacular. In a legendary interview with Michael Toms on *New Dimensions Radio,* Professor Campbell clarified:

"I'm not superstitious, but I do believe in spiritual magic . . . if one follows the thing that deeply gets you in your gut, doors will open up."

Despite criticism and difficulty Dr. Mack's spiritual direction was clear. He was at ease in co-creating with the fertile realm of potential.

Faerie Bells seem to offer that same encouragement, "May the force be with you, too!" Upon entering its passionate domain, never do you find one Faerie Bell growing alone; it's easy to imagine that these delicate little plants communicate with and relate to one another.

Ants and animal herds function in a collective mind, why not plants? Could the millions of Deer Clover that dapple the forest floor be one organism, like an aspen tree or mycelium fungus?

Beyond possible biological connection, does Wood Sorrel rap with other forest plants in ways beyond what science measures? In other words, do trees and plants engage a group mind? And if so, does this collective field transcend individual ecosystems and unite plants and animals in other places on Earth?

Absolutely.

Are we part of this unity?

Faerie Bells find us so silly.

"Yes, yes, yes!" they chime to such wonderings.

Imagine bright green leaves by the thousands, quivering like school children whose giggles are out of control. Everything is alive and communicating, a conscious field that invites us to participate.

"Explore the wild world and co-create with us!" prod the gazillions of Love Plants.

Sorrel opens and closes its paper-thin leaflets in response to temperature, light, and weather. When its three heart-shaped leaves close, they form a tiny pyramid that protects it and regulates how it receives and releases moisture.

In the same way, people are sensitive to the environment and, like Faerie Bells, open and close. Some of us are reclusive, and others love the spotlight.

These rhythms of opening and closing, expanding outward and withdrawing inward, are innate to life. Whether extroverted or introverted, we all know outgoing as well as quiet times. Likewise, we all take in air and then expel it. Spring and summer are seasonal exhalations, and in fall and winter, nature beings pull in their energy. The lakes and oceans expand as waves roll into the shore and then back to sea.

The swelling and withdrawing rhythms of water can also unfold over long periods. For example, houses built on the shores of Guatemala's Lake Atitlan are flooding. The sacred lake is reclaiming the land and everything on it. Mayan elders in tune with the Earth's rhythms say the lake, a living being, expands for sixty years and then recedes for sixty years. The old ones regard the dramatic rise and fall of water as a natural breathing cycle—the lake's inhalation and exhalation.

The ancient Mayans were master observers of natural phenomena. They even tracked each day's rhythms to harmonize with sacred cycles of time.

The expansive and retracting migration of elk in the Hoh Rain Forest, the ebb and flow of the rain, and the gentle opening and closing of Wood Sorrel mirror basic rhythms that are also within us.

Try exploring these rhythms by exaggerating them in your body:

To begin, wrap your arms and fold your legs tightly to your body, close your eyes, and tuck your chin to your chest, as if you are a snail shrinking into its shell or a Wood Sorrel shutting up in its little green teepee.

How does it feel to close into yourself?

Next, expand out by spreading arms, legs, hands, and fingers wide. Open your eyes and mouth and make a loud sigh, like a lion stretching in the sun.

How does opening out feel?

Wood Sorrel, happiest in shade and pulling back in sunlight, models shameless withdrawal. Yet when Sorrel opens it is unabashed.

"Open with exuberance or hide away in ecstasy!" says the liberated Love Plant. "No excuses are needed; the best design is to be exactly as you are!"

Feel free to continue to play with opening and closing movements whenever you think of it. Your body will become comfortable with these rhythms, which will help to ground you whether expanding or retracting.

Practice also to ease tension between introverted and extroverted tendencies and other in-and-out rhythms that may feel hard to reconcile, such as being in the spotlight or forcing mental energy to get things done in the world and, conversely, feeling quiet or folding in to regroup and/or intuit.

Little Faerie Bells remind us that expanding and contracting, moving inward and extending outward aren't separate, but are divergent expressions in a continuum of experience.

Bridging exhalation and inhalation, solar and lunar, ebb and flow, intellect and instinct, and so forth helps us reclaim the whole of who we are.

Of the many lovely ways to court Wood Sorrel and open to its essence, one is to chew its tart leaf.

Also called Sour Sob or Sourgrass, Oxalis adds lemony, mouth-puckering zing to spring salads. A little goes a long way, as some forms of oxalic acid (which is also found in spinach, rhubarb leaves, beets, chard, peanuts, chocolate, and more) can be dangerous in large quantities. No one seems to know how much is too much, so you must ask Oxalis and start slowly.

The flavorful Love Plant's fresh and dried leaves are also good medicine. Rich in vitamin C, Sorrel has been used to abate fevers, sore throats, swelling and stomach problems, diminish(es) bleeding, and help(s) other ailments.

Despite its being magical, beautiful, tasty, and healing, many view Sorrell as a nasty weed. Hardier than it appears, it stores energy deep in its roots. Deceptively resilient, Sorrel is prolific as well as difficult to kill. Yet those rugged roots that are the bane of gardeners serve a high purpose. Small but effective Wood Sorrel can extract heavy metals from the soil through its tough tubers; it cleanses the environment. We can work with these natural cleansing mechanisms of nature to restore our ecosystems. Phytoremediation elicits the help of plants such as Oxalis to clean up toxic lands.

It can also be transformational. Just note how you feel upon discovering in the forest a seemingly never-ending patch of clover-leafed

Sorrel. Hang out with the gazillions of Love Plants, and just as they extract contaminants from the land, these little light beings will lift the angst right out of you.

It is impossible for me to hold on to difficult feelings when I come across them in the forest. They make the world feel as fresh as forest air. Easily seduced by Sorrel's love spell, my heart cracks open every time.

People often ask how I can live in such a dark and isolated part of the world that receives up to fourteen feet (yes, fourteen feet) of precipitation a year. I sometimes struggle with the wet, dark environment where I live. One of the many gifts of this challenge is to bask in the energy that pours from all the life here. This green-plant paradise gushes oxygen and light, a force we can feel.

Living in darkness also pushes me to seek the light within my being. This light in our virgin forests is the Wood Sorrel, bright spirits ready to teach us that life is but a fluid dream. They support the bridging of divergent rhythms and help us merge and co-create with the creative feminine force.

The little Faerie Bells lift us to love and entice us to remember that nature and we are one. As we work together with the natural world, we transform our environment and nurture our souls.

🌿 Practice

Muse with Wood Sorrel and engage her wisdom in your own backyard or forest. If it doesn't grow near you, muse with nature beings that have similar qualities: a field of clover, grasses or flowers, a grove of trees, flocks of birds flying by, or whatever calls to you.

Find a comfortable place to lie or sit, either indoors or out in nature. Ensure that you will not be disturbed. If you are inside, feel free to turn on a drumming track or other relaxing music.

Take a few deep breaths. Relax more deeply with each exhale, allowing your body to grow pleasantly heavy.

Imagine lying in a moist, lush forest amidst a huge patch of Wood Sorrel. Take all the time you like, simply relaxing and settling more deeply into the earth amidst an endless patch of Faerie Bells. Feel the love and light like a radiant mist all around you; make this experience as real as you can.

With each breath out, Faerie Bells naturally lift and lighten whatever you are ready to release. Don't work at this; merely witness and allow it. Know it is happening.

What is bubbling up to find ease?

Practice this way for some time, simply being with Sorrel; allow its vibration, light, and love to infuse you and to ease whatever constricts you.

Take as long as you desire.

When you feel ready, freely explore the following:

What am I afraid of? At what times do I feel negative?

How do I keep a lid on my deeper expression?

Take some time.

As you explore, imagine where these qualities that limit you live in your body. Where in your body calls your attention?

Place your hands on these areas of your body, and invite Faerie Bells' light to concentrate here with each inhalation.

You do not have to hold to life so rigidly.

Sense these places soften and become more spacious as Faerie Bells' light saturates them with each breath.

Invite the held places to loosen.

Ask yourself, "What does it feel like to open more and relax? What's possible?"

Feel goodness and space. Sense the life glow being breathed into you and awakening the creative feminine force.

As you breathe, imagine how easily a dream could replace a scheme.

Continue to breathe Faerie Bells' light, inviting new possibility and potential to fill places of habit and worry. Soften the grip of limitation.

Breathe love, light, and space. Feel Faerie Bells' light infuse and surround you.

When angst arises listen to the spirit of the Love Plant, which whispers to you about unity with the life force.

Take all the time you like.

When you feel complete with this experience, do some gentle stretching.

Now would be a good time to walk to a park or natural setting. Feel each movement and footstep open you to wonder and possibility.

Consider collecting nature items on your walk, such as dried twigs and leaves. Then select a place to craft these into a form that reflects how you now feel.

Co-create something beautiful, allowing nature to show you what form it would like to take. Have fun with this.

As you fashion an object, invite possibility to come alive. You can even speak aloud to nature and the realm of potential as you craft your item. Let the fertile feminine void hear your desire to manifest with it, to live ecstatically.

When you feel complete with the item you have crafted and the intentions you have infused it with, express your gratitude to the Earth.

You may, in fact, want to offer your creation to the Earth. Or, you can place your nature item in a special place in your home as a daily reminder to open your heart and relax your mind—to allow space for the fertile feminine force so you may co-create with her.

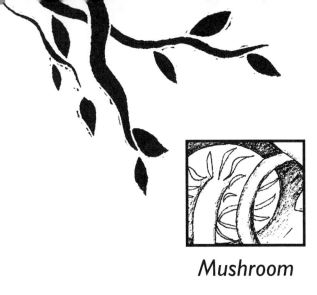

Mushroom

Sandra

I can easily engage my full sensory awareness and imagine wandering through the landscape of a forest floor filled with thousands of clover plants. I can feel an inner smile forming as I come upon patches of Wood Sorrel. I can feel the joy of the plant itself, and I can see the visions of the faerie folk shimmering and dancing. Opening to such a deep experience reminds me of the magic of life, and I sense excitement and passion rising through my body.

After reading what Llyn wrote on Wood Sorrel, I reflect on which nature being excites me, makes me laugh and smile, when I visit with it. What reminds me of the pure magic of life?

At first I tried to come up with a plant that would be similar to Wood Sorrel, but as I sank into my own truth, I kept being brought back to my magical relationship with Mushroom.

Yes, there are plenty of mushrooms in the desert, and I will get to that.

In *Speaking with Nature* both Llyn and I encourage you to open up your imagination to connect with the nature beings that call to you where you live. You might connect with the nature beings in the wilderness or in the waters. Or you might connect with the nature

beings in your garden, or in a park in the city where you live.

There is so much life and wonder in nature! No doubt some of you were surprised by various nature beings Llyn and I chose to write about, such as Glacial Silt and Sand or Banana Slug and Earthworm. We typically limit our connection to certain nature spirits that are spoken about in popular culture and collective associations, so the important teaching to embrace is that all living beings are part of the web of life. Our survival is based on the health of all the living beings in our Earth community, for whatever happens to one life form affects the entire web of life. We are not separate from other living beings; rather, we are all connected. All nature beings are to be honored for their life as well as their contribution to the health of the web of life that connects us all.

There are seemingly unlimited numbers of living beings sharing this Earth with us, and when you spend significant amounts of time in nature, you come across animals, birds, insects, reptiles, fish, sea mammals, invertebrates, algae, plants, trees, fungi, moss, rocks, minerals, and even microorganisms that call out to the depths of your soul. They might not be living beings you normally anticipate when you look forward to time in nature.

As you walk in the outdoors, you may suddenly find yourself drawn to a being that makes itself undeniably present to you. You might find yourself surprised and awed as you are drawn to explore an area caught out of the corner of your eye. Or you might even be drawn off the path by a feeling that tells you to look down or up, turn left or right. A scent or sound might call you to explore its source. As you sit by the ocean, a river, or lake there might be a nature being who lives in the water who attracts your attention.

When you are attracted and called to a nature spirit, it could be that this being is an ally for you. An ally calls to you in the visible and invisible realms to befriend you. It can actually feel like kin.

These allies might not vocalize a message. You may hear a telepathic message, be shown an omen, have a dream, or feel in your bones an invitation from your ally.

When I see saguaro cactus on trips to Arizona, I always remark to people that saguaro and I come from the same home in the stars.

I feel the same about Mushroom. I don't know what it is and I cannot explain this rationally, but when I see a mushroom in nature, I feel joy pulsing through my body. I am simply entranced with mushrooms. I rarely cook or eat mushrooms, so my affinity is not associated with the taste of them as food. It is a spirit connection I feel; Mushroom and I have a deep soul connection. I love them unconditionally and refer to them as the "mushroom people." They are family. Being around Mushroom not only brings me joy, it also gives me a comfort and peace that I do not always feel in my life.

When I come across mushrooms in nature, I take photos of them. I probably have more photos of mushrooms than many people have of their loved ones.

In the Santa Fe high desert, mushrooms grow proud and strong, and most are edible. Many species of mushrooms seem to appear overnight, and some grow and expand very quickly. This is where the expressions "to mushroom" and "pop up like a mushroom" originate.

My husband and I once had a friend visiting from California who happened to be a mycologist. Imagine my excitement! He picked the white button mushrooms growing outside of our house and made an omelet with them.

White button mushroom is a fungi with a stem that grows out of the ground, wide top cap, and gills on the underside of the cap. The spores are produced on the gills and fall in a fine rain of powder from under the cap.

As I tune in to mushrooms growing here in Santa Fe, I immediately feel a quality of earth that is different from what is found in the desert. I have been writing about the dry sand in the arroyo, but Mushroom needs moisture and grows in the shade. As soon as the summer rains come to Santa Fe, mushrooms pop up everywhere on the forest floor.

Then when I close my eyes, I smell the fragrance of moist, rich earth in contrast to the dry-air smell of the desert. I might forget I am in the high desert. I can imagine elves and faeries dancing under the shelter of the mushrooms.

Mushrooms are such special beings, with so many varieties, and many are nature's healers. Mushrooms are used to shrink cancerous tumors and boost the immune system and to consume and transmute radiation and chemical pollution. And there are mushrooms that communicate with and teach initiates on a spiritual path. These mushrooms might provide initiates with healing, prophetic dreams, visions, and the ability to communicate with the spiritual realm. Eating psychotropic mushrooms can lead an initiate into a numinous state.

There are also mushrooms that are deadly to anyone foolish—or ignorant—enough to eat them.

The practice of shamanism teaches that we dream life into being, and Mushroom is one of the nature beings I associate with the power to dream into being what we desire to create for the planet and ourselves. In the essay I wrote on Snake, I encouraged you to practice enlivening your senses. In order to be a conscious dreamer, you must be able to be in touch with all your visible and invisible senses.

Our destiny is to be dreamers. It is how we birth spirit into form as the creative forces of the universe created form from spirit.

I am passionate about teaching people how to dream. We all daydream and use our imaginations with every thought we have and each word we use and send into the collective. Most of us are not aware of the chaos, destruction, and violence we are dreaming into being. We must wake up to our innate creative power. With intention, concentration, and focus, we can create a good life for ourselves and for all in the web of life. If we stand strong together as a global community and use the power of focused intent, we can dream a new fabric of reality into being, because the fabric that no longer serves life continues to unravel. We can dream into being a world that embraces love, light, peace, joy, good health, abundance, and equality for all.

The paradox of stepping into our role as dreamers is also to learn to let go of our attachment and surrender the outcome of our dreams to spirit. Most of us are walking the path of ego versus the path of spirit, and spirit has a different perception of what might lead us to our highest level of healing and evolution.

To move from the path of ego to the path of spirit takes a tremendous amount of personal work, for we really must devote time and energy to exploring how our personality tries to run us. We must examine the unhealthy behaviors we learned as children to help us cope with life and feel safe. I advise people who devote themselves to spiritual practice to add work that focuses on exploring and working through emotional and behavioral issues. It is also important to strengthen the physical body to create a strong, healthy, and vital vessel of radiant light for delving into spiritual work.

Some people shy away from dreaming work due to egoic fear that they will create a dream that does not result in the best ultimate outcome for their highest good. This fear is valid, because from a personality level we often do not know what is for our highest good. As we engage in personal work, we learn to identify what is desired from ego versus Spirit.

At the same time we do dream our lives into being with our every thought throughout the day. Why not focus our daydreams on creating the vision we want to see? We must have a vision for ourselves and the world for life to continue. The key is to establish a dreaming practice with intention while surrendering the outcome. But we must do the work.

Ever since I was a child, I've been fascinated with the process of creation and manifestation—how we can manifest a life filled with joy. As an adult I've read many esoteric texts and performed an abundance of shamanic journeys exploring the process of creation and manifestation and had spontaneous visions over the years that provided great insight into the work. What I learned has become a focus of the practices I write about and teach.

We are experiencing so many challenges in politics, the economy, and the environment that it is important to hold a healthy and positive vision for the planet. To do this we must be able to imagine the world in which we wish to live. We must engage all our senses—seeing, hearing, feeling, smelling, and tasting—to be able to fully imagine ourselves living in a world that embraces love, light, harmony, beauty, peace, abundance, and equality for all.

Take a few moments to imagine what our experience would be if people around the world focused together to use their imaginations in a way that created a return to a harmonious way of life.

What would that world look, smell, feel, and sound like? Imagine the scenes you would see.

See yourself living in a world filled with love, peace, and abundance for all. Open to a wealth of images, colors, people, and other life that inhabit the landscape along with you.

Listen to all the sounds of life and nature coming from such a joyful bright state. Listen to the sounds of children laughing, the birds singing, the wind, and any source of water.

Feel the joy flowing through you as you live in a world filled with love, peace, and harmony. How would it feel to walk on the earth and touch all that is alive? Feel your feet connecting with the earth.

Place some of the earth in your hands and feel it. Touch plants and leaves and branches of trees. Feel the bark of a tree.

Run your hands through the soft fur of an animal you have befriended.

Feel your heart beating and the quality of your energy flowing through your body. Notice any sensations in your fingers, hands, toes, and feet.

Smell the clean fresh air. Take a deep breath in and smell the scent of plant life, the earth, or any water in your surroundings. On your exhale, share the energy of your love and joy for life.

Imagine eating food that was grown with love and without chemicals and pesticides. Taste the clean fresh food cooked with love. Lick your lips. Fully engage your sense of taste as you drink and swallow water.

Connect fully with the beauty of the elements as you daydream. Imagine yourself swimming in an ocean, river, or lake. Feel the water playing with you. Place your fingers in the earth and experience yourself interacting with it in a loving and joyful way. Run and skip in the wind and feel it playing with your hair. Bask in the power and beauty of the sunlight, starlight, and moonlight.

Experience yourself living a life filled with radiance, love, joy, and peace right now.

To project a new vision for the planet, you must be able to engage the depth of your senses, thus fueling your imagination and creative abilities. You also must be passionate about what you desire.

You need to step into the dream fully and live from the dream, occupying and fully inhabiting the space. You want to experience yourself fully alive and living in the dream you are creating. Do not project your creation into the future. Experience it as your creation has manifested now.

The key to doing your dreaming work is to be able to engage your strong inner senses with your own vivid images, sounds, smells, tastes, and feelings. You need to be able to create your own powerful movie by living in the movie, instead of simply watching it. And you need to fuel your senses with intense enthusiasm. Stop allowing the outside world to write your script, and let your new script be created and birthed from your inner world. Use the depth of your senses to make your creations real.

If you cannot get in touch with the true power of your own vivid images, your own internal songs of creation, the beauty of the fragrances you wish to smell, the taste of healthy food grown and cooked with love, and the feeling of touching the beauty of life, there is no power in your creation. If your creation is not fueled by passion and enthusiasm, there is no power in what you project into the world. If your creative work is superficial and lacks depth and power, the world will reflect superficiality back to you.

I feel so strongly that this is a vital missing piece. So much of our creative work simply lacks passion and depth, but we must nevertheless experience compassion for ourselves and be patient with this process. We live disconnected from nature and surround ourselves with continual input from TV, computers, DVDs, CDs, and a myriad of other distractions that mask our ability to get in touch with the depth of our inner senses.

We need to have the patience to awaken the depth of the wealth of our inner senses. We need to revive our passion and remember times when we felt passion that fueled our lives.

Continue the practices I shared in Snake, but now add your imagination to open to your inner sensory awareness. Find times in the day when you can go within to bring up your own vivid images and your own songs. Focus on smelling fragrances that you love and tasting foods you enjoy. Imagine yourself walking around and touching different textures that feel good to you. Practice before you go to sleep or when you awaken. The intensity with which you can experience the senses in your inner world will directly affect your ability to create what you desire in the outer world.

When I engage in practices to get in touch with my inner divine light, I experience the void. The void is the territory prior to creation. In

Buddhist teachings the void is seen as empty, yet full. The void is a powerful territory to experience. It is the place from which form and light are birthed.

While in the void one is surrounded by complete blackness filled with unpotentiated energy. Anything can be created from this place. Once visiting and working with the void, it becomes obvious that scarcity is a human-made concept. Only unlimited possibilities can be manifested from the void.

Spirit is birthed into form within and through the void, and many people experience the void when they transfigure into their divine light. It is powerful to work with the void during dreaming work. If you would like to visit the void, you'll find instructions in the practices below.

It is important to keep up your spiritual work and hold a good vision no matter what you see happening in the world. We are living in a time when the fabric of reality is unraveling. As we continue to examine unhealthy behaviors in lifestyle and ways we mistreat other humans, nonhuman living beings, and the environment, our dreams can start to create the new healthy fabric of reality. Instead of imagining the worst outcomes, let us use our imaginations to embrace a positive vision.

The spiritual work we engage in supplies the power to create positive changes in the world. Let us join together as a global community to envision a healthy planet.

We can learn from nature how to join together from a place of cooperation and collaboration to thrive and to sustain life. Let us join together in the spirit of cooperation and collaboration with the power of focused intent to dream into being a beautiful and healthy world.

🌿 Practices

Take a walk in a park or in a rural area. Walk with "soft eyes" as you gaze into the beauty of the landscape around you. To walk with soft eyes means that you allow your gaze to drift—you are aware of your environment without looking intensely at your surroundings. You can also sit by a body of water and let your mind wander. Let your internal radar guide you toward something that catches your attention out of the corner of your eye, or be aware of an intuitive feeling that a nature being is calling to you. Notice if a nature being such as a bird, mammal, tree, plant, insect, reptile, fungi, rock, or mineral presents itself to you as an ally. If you are sitting by a body of water, notice if a nature being that lives in the water calls to you. Trust your intuitive knowing. Keep your heart open and engage in a state of true awe and wonder at the all exquisite beings who live on the earth, in the air, and in water. You might be pleasantly surprised at who presents itself to you as an ally.

Once you meet your ally, open up both your visible and invisible senses to begin communicating with it. Shamans learned from the trees, plants, animals, and other nature beings by sitting with them, observing their qualities, and communicating through deep listening. Learn what special qualities of life this nature being has to share with you. For example, a nature being might teach you about the power of stillness, how to connect in deeper ways to yourself and the Earth, or maybe how, with your invisible sense of sight, you can fly above your life to observe it from another vantage point, broadening your perspective. Learn which valuable lessons this ally has to teach you. Learn through your ongoing communication with it how it can be a support in your life and share its power and knowledge with you.

When you begin to experience your connection with the web of life, you will find yourself feeling more gratitude for your life and the life forms that coexist with you. Living from a state of gratitude is one of the most important elements you can bring into your daily practice.

Each morning as you wake up give thanks for your life. Give thanks to earth, air, water, and sun for providing what you need to thrive. Give thanks to your ancestors who gave you life as well as the gifts and strengths you inherited from them. Give thanks for the nature beings that live on the Earth with you.

As you continue to engage in spiritual work, your gratitude list will naturally keep growing. You will find that your life starts to move into a place of harmony as you do this. You will also feel better emotionally and physically, which will help you to ride out the challenging times from a place of strength and grace.

Listen to a meditative piece of music or a track of shamanic music. You can also find a nice peaceful place in nature where you can sit quietly without being disturbed. Imagine yourself traveling within to a hidden place that I call the Cave of Lost Dreams. Simply by setting an intention to do so, travel into this imaginal realm to discover and identify a dream or wish that you have forgotten. In the past you might not have felt confident about your ability to manifest this dream. Or you might have felt you did not deserve to receive the goodness in life that would come from dreaming this dream into being. In this place, discover a dream you would like to manifest. Retrieve this dream and bring it into the light. Find times in the day to perform your dreaming work as I described in this essay, to work on manifesting this dream. It is time for you to experience the goodness that life has to offer.

Continue to work with the dreams you feel inspired to manifest from spirit into form. Over time you will naturally weave this work more and more into your daily life. Right before falling asleep is a potent time to do your work of engaging all your senses to create the world in which you wish to live.

If you would like to travel to the void, it is easy to do. Start with some meditative music or listening to a drumming track.

I suggest that you set your intention to visit and experience your own inner void. What is without is also within you. Performing your dreaming and creation work from the inner void will fuel the power of your work.

Intention is the key to traveling into any spiritual territory you wish to explore. With your eyes closed, listen to the music and state your intention.

Travel within to your inner landscape. Experience the void—the place right before creation. Feel the pulsating of potential and possibilities that exist in that space.

Take a few minutes to experience the sensation of unpotentiated energy. And then begin to form your dream. Engage all your senses, feel the passion that fuels creation, put yourself into the dream, and experience the form birthing into the world. It is done!

Work with focus and full concentration as you continue your creation work. At the same time, surrender your outcome to spirit.

12

WILD WESTERN HEMLOCK TREE AND COTTONWOOD TREE

Wild Western Hemlock Tree

Llyn

When I was a child growing up in New Hampshire, my favorite tree was the Eastern hemlock, or hemlock fir tree. I loved this delicate tree with its miniature cones, soft needles, and limbs that sloped like draping shawls.

The Hemlock Tree of the Pacific Northwest where I now live is very much like its Eastern cousin in that this dainty tree is slow to grow, loves the shade, and can weather tough winters.

Western Hemlock was integral to early tribal life on the Olympic Peninsula. The wood of the Hemlock Tree was carved into utensils and everyday items, its bark was used to make dyes that colored baskets and wool, and the cambium inside the bark that black bears love to eat was also a favorite food of the native people of these lands.

🍂 *Imagine lying on your back on a cushiony bed of conifer needles in a lush temperate rain forest. Breathe in the cool, moist air, then expel a long steady breath. See the steam release with your breath and evaporate into the air.*

Gaze up at the grand Wild Western Hemlock Tree. Take all the time you like to open your heart and sense the spirit of this nature being.

When you feel ready, imagine yourself now lying on the earth in a different location—beneath a conifer sapling in a new forest that is growing up from clear-cut land.

Note how your body feels resting on the earth. Take in a smooth and steady breath. Smell fresh life all around you. Listen as little birds hop through the underbrush plucking thimbleberries.

The Hemlock branches above are feathery light. Imagine reaching up and touching supple green needles. Now, tug on a tiny limb. In your mind's eye watch

*the tree jiggle as if giggling from a tickle, as the thin, limber bough bounces right
back.*

Take a moment to open your heart to the baby Hemlock Tree.

I always notice that the young Wild Hemlock appears limp and
fragile next to its perky neighbor, the fir tree that people plant on
Northwest tree farms. Yet like the wild and wispy willow that digs
fast into the rocky soil of the Hoh River gravel bar, Hemlock is anything but frail.

Tenacious roots, pliable leaves, and flexible limbs anchor willow
through violent winds that sweep up the Hoh Valley from the Pacific
Ocean. Similarly, Western Hemlock endures savage weather from
the untamable Pacific. Like the tender-leafed willow, soft-needled
Hemlock is unsuspectingly tough, rooted, and supple so harsh weather
filters through.

I've never seen a willow or a Western Hemlock growing alone;
they are protected in community. However, when trees are cut the
forests are divided and high winds ravage the unnatural open spaces.
More trees fall. This blowdown happens all the time at the edge of
clear-cuts.

Like Hemlock we benefit in being with others. It helps us to
weather difficulties if we're not all alone. Hemlock encourages us to
stay grounded and flexible as life's gales blow, so turbulence can pass
through with less harm.

Being amenable on the surface yet unshakable and protected at
the core has helped indigenous groups hold on to their traditions during times of persecution. This is true among the beautiful people of
the small Republic of Tuva on the Asian steppe.

Tuvan folk ballads and the haunting whistling sound of its throat
singers are admired the world over, yet it wasn't long ago that Tuva's
shamans were shot to death or burned alive. Old traditions fostering
harmony with nature, community, and natural healing were outlawed.
Shamanism went underground, the sacred held secret until the Soviet

regime collapsed. Tuvans and other Eurasian indigenous groups, like so many of the world's first peoples, camouflaged or concealed ancient knowledge and banded together to weather painful change.

Few of us know what it's like to hide what we believe in and hold sacred, for fear of death. The closest we may come is in hiding who we are to avoid being judged.

As one instance it's not that unusual today for an allopathic physician to also do some form of energy or even shamanic healing, and psychics and mediums—living people who see and talk to the dead—draw thousands of followers. Just decades ago none of this was happening. What seems normal now was practiced in quiet by healers and spiritualists until society grew more accepting.

This is a good example of Hemlock medicine, which keeps the wisdom fire burning while surface winds are choppy. When used for firewood Hemlock burns strong and silent and its embers last a long time.

The Mayans and the Quechua people of Central and South America also shrouded their teachings to protect them when the Spanish invaded. In 1991 the Quechua finally began releasing long-held spiritual wisdom and acknowledged that a prophesied era is upon us; the world is at a precipice and humanity is ripe.

Winter gusts eventually smooth out along the Hoh River Valley. The seemingly never-ending rain gives way to summer's warmth, and Hemlock grows straight and tall toward the blazing sun. In this more conducive climate, Hemlock calls to us each in her divinely feminine voice: "Stand tall with me now. If your soul is still hiding, it is time to come out."

"But, but, but, oh dear Hemlock," we may stammer.

"Stand tall with me now," murmurs the gentle tree being with branches that dangle like soft wings.

Western Hemlock and sitka spruce are the trees we most often see in the Hoh Rain Forest. It takes hundreds of years for Hemlock to fully mature, towering to heights of three-hundred feet and spreading to widths of twenty-three feet. Standing in the presence of these trees inspires awe.

Like the Western Hemlock, it takes time for us and for our species to evolve, but we must all grow up sometime and the signs abound that now is the time.

In the global arena, and for many of us, the winds of uncertainty still toss. Bridging any new season or change is a letting go of one way to another, the dissolving of what was, just as winter snow and ice melt to warm and water the new life of spring. If we live in a four-season climate, we might easily imagine wanting to hold on to summer.

Imagine trying to hold on to winter. This may seem silly. Even before the end of a long, dark, cold winter, everyone is ready for spring. Yet imagine if winter were the only season you knew. If you lived in a winter world, as the snow receded on the mountains and in the valleys, and the ice melted in the rivers and lakes and ponds, you would feel that your world was literally falling apart. And it would be.

As the ideas that hold our reality structures in place give way, our world appears to fall apart. The old stories do not fit anymore, and new stories have not yet fully formed.

The Western Hemlock of the Hoh Rain Forest dies, yet never dies. This tree can stand deteriorated for decades while birds, insects, and small mammals make it their home. When the tree eventually falls, it opens up the space for the sun to nurture other plants and then it is host to microbes, insects, and fungi, such as bright yellow chanterelle mushrooms. These all eventually reduce the trunk to humus, which is seeded by forest animals. From the seeds grow new trees.

Imagine strolling through a richly scented Hemlock forest. Look at the Western Hemlock's narrow trunk columns. Some of these tree giants lift off the ground at their roots as if they're walking, like the race of tree beings called ents in J. R. R. Tolkien's fantasy world. These mammoth Hemlock beings sprouted from fallen nurser logs, which nourished the saplings that literally grew on top of the mother Hemlock while she receded back into the earth.

Hemlock advises: "Anchor now. At the same time be as flexible as my limber limbs and Mother Hemlock, who surrenders to new life. Let go and trust."

The life cycle of the Hemlock shows that beauty often grows from death; the dying times feed and inspire a surge of new life. Death and darkness have their own beauty and intelligence, and like the Hemlock, we are dying and growing all the time.

When I relocated to the Northwest six years ago, I was so drawn to the intriguing Western Hemlock with its fancy telltale tassel, dangling as if weighted by an invisible ornament from the tiptop of its tall growth. I had an amazing feeling of déjà vu in looking at Hemlock; this nature being and I were friends.

Was it the time I spent as a child lying on the earth under wispy hemlock branches during New England snowfalls—looking up through white-dusted needles and cones as snowflakes drifted down to melt on my cheeks—that induced such strong sentiment for this conifer? This is ever more poignant as Northeast hemlocks die of woolly blight.

The Celts have a beautiful phrase that describes unexplainable affinities—*anam cara,* meaning "soul friend."

Most of us have known someone we felt immediate kinship with upon first meeting. And everyone has heard the term "soul mate." We may even have asked ourselves: "Where is my soul mate? When will my other half find me so we can transport each other to unending bliss?"

If you've ever discovered a soul mate (there are many) and tried to live with that person in twin-soul rapture, your reality likely did not match your dreams. The true gift of special connections, which is to help each other evolve and grow so we can fulfill what we were born to do, is often lost to modern culture because we have too many superficial ideas and expectations for what a soul friend is and must be.

We also overlook the amazing anam cara, or soul kinship, people can have with nature.

Take a moment right now to think on your own favorite tree in childhood, an indoor plant that you speak with and listen to as it speaks back to you, a cat or dog that came to you serendipitously and whose spirit you recognize, a foreign landscape that is hauntingly familiar, or the uncanny feeling you get when sniffing an iris or other flowering plant—some aspect of the natural world with which you feel an unusually deep or unexplainable connection.

The striking sentiment that arises with certain nature beings is soul recognition, anam cara.

All indigenous shamans I have met revere the land they were born on; this is the source of their power. Years ago my friend and colleague Bill Pfeiffer and I traveled in Siberia with a fierce shaman woman named Ai-Tchourek who insisted we visit her homeland. This woman's connection to home moved me. Surprisingly, though I had never walked these lands, they felt familiar. I knew the river and lay of the *taiga* (tundra forest). Feeling so at home in these lands I had never known before was a beautiful experience.

When I was a child, my love for the Hemlock Spruce opened me to sacred kinship with nature. Hemlock and all nature beings invite us to explore special bonds with the land, water, wind, trees, stones, animals, and so forth. Through these relationships we open to magic and love, bridging the chasm between people and the natural world. Our reality expands.

Do we draw nature beings to us, or do they call us to them?

Did we live a past life on lands that speak to us?

If a child tracked her feet while riding a bicycle, the little feet would get caught up in the bike pedals or the child would be looking at the feet instead of where the bicycle was headed; either way the child would fall off the bike.

Hemlock Tree suggests: "To engage the mystery, become the mystery. Think or even care about it too much and you fall out of it."

I have found that the best way to understand soul kinships with nature, or with people, is to explore them with feet on the ground and an open heart. In tracking for animals among Western Hemlocks in the Hoh Rain Forest, I am learning to identify signs—prints, tree markings, dung, nipped twigs, items in an animal's scat (berries, hair), and so forth. I notice how fresh or old the prints appear and scan the area with my senses and intuition, seeking clues and tucking them away in memory. I find that tracking is an art of invisibility—blending into the environment, being precise in what I observe and sense, and staying open and not jumping to conclusions. It involves thoroughly enjoying a journey that may never fully reveal.

Track this way in the Olympic Mountains and you may bump into an elk. Regardless, you will walk the forest freshly, full of wonder.

As much as we sometimes think we know why animal, person, stone, tree, or land shows up in our life, magic increases when we let go of the search and immerse in the unfolding. This also opens us to know anam cara with everything and everyone, without judgment about how that expresses.

Sacred kinships stir the soul awake, reminding us that we are one source, never separate. They reconnect the collective spirit of people and nature.

Ripe to help us discover who we are, Hemlock tells us the hiding times are over; it is time for the soul force to shine. We simply have to trust that the world is headed there, too.

🌿 Practice

Hemlock Tree teaches about the internal wisdom fire and how to flow with difficulty, as well as into who we truly are. You will find below a way to embody these teachings and make them available in daily life. No special music or preparation is needed.

Wherever you are right now (ideally outside with bare feet, though anywhere is fine), stand tall like a healthy tree.

Imagine your roots extending deep into the earth. Feel the sun's warm caress. Sense your trunk, soft needles, sloping branches, and tiny conifer cones.

Take a nice deep breath. Then exhale.

Become Hemlock or a tree in your locale, or one with which you feel a special bond. Feel this tree's spirit. Sense your soul kinship with this nature being.

Take another refreshing inhalation, breathing in wonderful Hemlock (or other tree) qualities. Then exhale and relax.

For several moments simply breathe naturally while feeling the tree's goodness.

Take all the time you like.

When you are ready, let go of being a tree. Continue to sense goodness, yet just be you. Sense your essence, soul, or sacred center, whatever notions or words work for you.

Where in your body is this feeling strong? Where does the deepest part of you reside?

Take time to sense what you note.

When you have located this place where your essence feels strong, take a deep breath here and touch your sacred center. Allow this to be palpable.

Take another refreshing breath in, and then release a relaxing breath.

Now firmly place your feet at the same time onto the floor or on the earth. Or jump if you are able, landing both feet onto the earth at once. As you do feel your roots. Dig in fast, anchoring into the earth.

Take time to note how it feels to be secure and sturdy, your sacred center rooted deep in the earth.

How do you feel?

Still standing, let a light feeling come over you. Allow your body to feel loose and weightless as you gently move. Imagine you are a rag doll coming to life, stirring fluidly. Move and flow intuitively from your center. You may feel a ripple or buoyant quality to the air as you slowly move, as if in water. Move your feet, too, but don't lose that feeling of being rooted—centered in yourself and the earth with a light, limp body.

Follow your impulse, moving in whatever ways feel right. Try making arcs and circles with your arms and legs, allowing your torso and head to flow and bend and spiral, unfolding in a joyous dance. Just as spiraling winds and water cleanse, we can wash and spin away the tendency to be rigid and fearful in favor of flowing more from the heart.

Move for as long as you like or feels comfortable. Indulge slow movements first, and then you might like to explore how it feels to move a little faster as the wind howls through tree branches and leaves.

Then move slowly again.

Enjoy moving until you come to a natural place of rest.

To close, consider taking a leisurely stroll while feeling both anchored and fluid. As you walk, and at any time when you find yourself among them, study how the trees move. Watch them intently, and observe the fluttering of leaves and the sway of boughs and even trunks, which can bend dramatically in ways we barely detect.

What do you notice?

Let yourself go to mimic and express as the trees do and as you did in the movement practice above.

What do you feel?

Hemlock says, "Breathe with us and move with us until you move *as* us, soul friends. There's a world beyond words we are waiting to share."

Cottonwood Tree

Sandra

Some of my most magical meetings with nature beings have been with the trees I've met while walking in the arroyo. On my frequents walks I meet up with ponderosa pine, piñon pine, juniper, aspen, mountain oak, and cottonwood trees.

I have fallen in love with one very old Cottonwood Tree about a mile from my house. This Cottonwood has an immense trunk and branches that span over a large part of the surrounding landscape. No matter how intensely the sun is shining, any nature being can cool off in the shade created by this massive tree.

One of the great teachings we receive when we spend time in nature is that nature is intelligent. We recognize beauty and the Divine in nature, but nature recognizes us as well.

I have an unusual relationship with this magnificent Cottonwood Tree, and its behavior toward me exhibits this teaching. The Cottonwood has a prominent place in the arroyo. It grows beside a steep sandy cliff in an area that is so full of prickly desert bushes that I cannot continue walking on the path unless I walk through the expansive Cottonwood branches, which touch the ground in a wide circle around the trunk.

Frequently as I walk through the arroyo and approach the Cottonwood, the leaves on the tree stir, creating a gentle rustling sound. The rustling of the leaves is not dependent on the wind or breeze. The air can be perfectly still, yet as I walk toward this giant ancient Cottonwood, the leaves make a welcoming sound. During the dead of winter when the leaves are brown and dry, I still hear the rustling sound of leaves. As I walk away from the tree, the gentle rustle of the leaves always stops.

Due to my teaching schedule, there are weeks when I am away from home. There are also times of inclement weather or temperatures that are simply too high to support my walks. It could be weeks before I get back to visit the Cottonwood Tree.

Once I start to walk again, when I come upon the Cottonwood, I am met with complete silence. The silence is quite striking. Even if the wind is blowing, the leaves remain still. After a week or so of visiting the tree daily, the rustling sound starts again.

I feel that the Cottonwood Tree recognizes me and responds to me in the same way a cat treats its owner who has been away for too long. Some cats ignore their owners when they return home after a trip, but warm back up in their own time. And trust me, I know how strange this sounds to you, but this Cottonwood treats me in the same way. The Cottonwood's greeting behavior has been going on for the twenty years I have visited it. The pattern never changes.

Cottonwood trees are large deciduous trees with thick, deeply fissured bark. Graceful and solid, they know how to stand their ground against flooding and erosion. Their leaves are diamond shaped and the colors change with the seasons. Hawks use them for nesting, and their soft wood makes them a favorite medium for carvers.

It's worth noting that when the upper limb of a cottonwood is cut crosswise, it reveals a five-pointed star, which in some spiritual traditions represents the divine. When we stand with our arms raised to the sky and our legs straddle the earth, we stand in the shape of a five-pointed star.

As I shared in the essay on Juniper, trees are sacred as they bridge heaven and earth through the connections of their branches and deep roots.

Trees always grow toward the light. We also grow toward the light on a physical level as well as through our spiritual practices.

The Lakota Sioux have a sacred ceremony called the Sundance, for which the dancers fast for days and sometimes are pierced. They sacrifice themselves while they dance as a prayer for the benefit of their community. A cottonwood tree is used as the center pole of the prayer arbor in the Lakota Sundance ceremony.

Susanne Simard, a professor of forestry with the University of British Columbia, shares that trees in a forest ecosystem are interconnected, with the largest old mother tree serving as the hub. The fungi that grow on trees work together with the tree and help to transport carbon back and forth among trees. Dying trees will move resources into a new tree that is growing.

I can easily see this with the Cottonwood Tree I visit. Each year I watch as more and more branches on the tree die. The bark has been stripped off most of the branches by time, rain, snow, and wind. But a short distance away new cottonwood trees are growing. Their branches grow in a way that they overlap, allowing me to walk through a beautiful arbor.

When I visit the Cottonwood Tree, I always stop to place my hands on the bark and share my love with it. I can feel the love being returned to me. I feel a tingling sensation as I place my hands on the fissured bark. Then I feel warmth flooding my heart. I feel my heart beating in connection with the life force of the tree. I feel recognized and loved by this magnificent, graceful being.

I also feel deep sadness as I watch this tree dying, for it has lived a long life dealing with intense and dramatic climate changes. I run my fingers along the bare branches that are now light gray and smooth as the bark keeps falling to the ground. I grieve knowing that it is time for the spirit of this tree, who has become such a precious friend, to transcend to the world of spirit.

The Cottonwood has become a great friend for me to practice the teaching that giving and receiving is all part of one cycle. In our culture we often are taught that it is better to give than to receive. But as giving is only part of the cycle, we never really understand what it means to give if we do not also learn how to receive.

In most of the essays in *Speaking with Nature,* I've shared soulful experiences and teachings I have received by taking walks in the arroyo where I live.

Once I step out my door, I walk through a narrow path surrounded by piñon pine and juniper trees. I walk on the soft ground blanketed with needles, and I hear the crunching sound as I pass over the brittle needles and leaves. After walking around a dog pen, I gaze upon the marsh that is the home of an artesian spring. Depending on the time of year, I might be met by tall, lush marsh grass dancing in the wind. And much of the time the grass lies flat as a blanket covering the marsh. As I walk further, I cross an open gate and enter the arroyo.

I call this a "magic arroyo." As soon as I step onto the sand and walk over the red and crystalline rocks, a veil parts for me and I step into the hidden realms of nature and magic. I hear birds singing and scolding me as I disturb their sense of safety, lizards and snakes scurrying away from me through the bushes, bees buzzing, and other songs of nature. I delight in seeing the brilliant colors of the trees, the bushes, the blooming cholla, prickly pear, yucca plants, and the wealth of nature beings in the landscape. I feel a deep connection with the earth through my feet and feel her heartbeat as I walk. I smell the fragrances in the air and feel the dry desert air going through my nose, and I can taste it in my mouth.

I have been walking through this arroyo for the twenty years I have lived in my house. Sometimes I jog simply for exercise and allow my mind to wander. And there are times I walk slowly, truly connecting with the wealth of cacti, plants, and trees that grow here. I have gotten to know the juniper, piñon pine, pondersosa pine, cottonwood, oak, and aspen trees. Over the years I have felt so deeply connected with some of them that I can truly call them my friends. There is a very old piñon pine close to my house that I have developed a deep relationship with in the same way I describe my relationship with the Cottonwood Tree. Even when the air is silent and still as I approach, the leaves on certain trees will move as if greeting me.

I love walking through the small grove of aspen trees in the arroyo. The leaves quake making a melodic sound and sparkle and shimmer in the sunlight with different shades of green, to yellow, to deep gold, depending on the time of year.

Aspen leaves tremble even when there is no apparent or the slightest breeze, making a soft whispering sound. Some legends held that wind was the messenger of the goddess. Anything closely associated to the wind, such as aspen, was deemed sacred.

One magnificent, very old ponderosa pine in the arroyo seems to thrive during the most extreme climate changes, such as cold, heat, wind, and of course drought. This tree gets a lot of love and respect from local residents.

Some trees I worry about. I can see them struggling from a lack of water. I do my work to not project struggle and illness onto them. I see them in their divine light, and I often touch their trunks, deeply feeling their bark, and radiate love and light. And there are times when I walk through the arroyo in a very focused state and perceive all the trees in their divine light as I walk.

There are also times when I do not feel well emotionally or physically and ask that the trees recognize me in my divinity. This is a powerful practice that you can try. As you are outside engaging in your daily activities, set an intention asking nature to perceive you in your divine strength and perfection. Simply notice how you might feel nature connecting with you in a new and deeper way.

As I walk through the arroyo with questions or concerns, I find that nature continues to show me omens. I love working with omens, as this is a way to experience just how much support we are always being given by the universe. The universe, the helping spirits, and nature itself are always giving us signposts that light our path in life.

At the end of *Speaking with Nature,* you'll find an essay on "How to Work with Omens," which includes more ideas for ways you can recognize the signs the universe provides to light your way.

There are times I have walked through my arroyo praying and crying, asking for some help to guide me through particularly challenging times. And I always receive some kind of extraordinary sign showing that the universe is listening and sending help my way.

In my essay on Snake, I shared how she appeared to me during a challenging time. Snake continues to appear to me when I am in need of a sign. I had an amazing experience in which hawk and hummingbird appeared together when I was in need of some guidance. I have also watched a hawk or a group of ravens circle over me as I leave offerings on the land in honor of all of life. There have been some days when there was not a cloud in the sky yet a light rain fell, blessing me and letting me know I was being supported in a choice I had made and that I was walking on the right path.

While I was writing *Speaking with Nature,* I received a wealth of omens. I would like to share some stories with you.

In October of 2013 I was leaving to teach five different workshops on shamanism. I walked through the arroyo the day before my flight and asked for an omen that would inform me about my workshops. I had never seen a bear in the arroyo during any of my walks, but as I came to the spot where I always turn to head back home, I looked up and was surprised to see a large cinnamon bear walking slowly up a hill. The bear was very close but the wind must have been blowing in my direction so that the bear could not smell me. I stood very still and watched it meander up the hill. I assumed it was an old bear as I could see quite a lot of white strands in its fur.

As I wrote in my essay on Bear, many shamanic cultures consider Bear to be the sign of the shaman. I knew the universe was telling me that my workshops would go very well, and indeed, they were deep and powerful for all who attended.

Then in March of 2014 I was leaving to teach "Medicine for the Earth and Healing with Spiritual Light" to a very large group of participants. Before leaving to teach I could feel the excitement and energy of the group forming, and I was a bit nervous about being able to meet the high expectations of those attending.

I walked through the arroyo, and when I came to the Cottonwood Tree, I put my hands on its bark as I often do and told the tree I would miss it. The previous day it had snowed about five inches, and although the sun shone brightly on this day, there was still snow on the ground beneath the tree, as the shade of the branches prevented it from melting.

As I started away from the tree to go back home, I suddenly intuited a message telling me to go back to the tree. When I went back and again touched the bark of the tree, a small piece of bark fell to the ground. This had never happened in previous times when I'd placed my hands on the tree. It felt as if the tree were gifting me with a piece of its bark to take along on my trip.

As I bent down to pick up the piece of bark that had fallen, to my amazement I saw a mushroom growing in the snow. It was a type I had never seen before, with a dark brown cap and white dots in a circle around the outside of the cap.

I had just completed writing my essay on Mushroom, and as you read it is an ally for me. I could not help but get the clear message that this workshop would be filled with magic. And it was!

I was so amazed to see this mushroom growing by the Cottonwood Tree that I went home and got my camera so I could have a photo that would remind me of this scene. On my way back home after taking the photo, I realized I had never photographed some of the special rocks and trees that I love so well. Since I had my camera, it seemed a good time to do it.

Close to my home I went to the old piñon pine that has always felt like a protector spirit for me. Everyone I bring to meet this tree is struck by its obvious age and how hardy it has been to survive the harsh environment. The branches are tall and full and curve in a way that seems to represent feminine energy. The relationship I have with the Cottonwood has felt like my relationship with my father, and my relationship with this piñon pine carries the energy of my relationship with my mother.

I took a photo of the piñon pine, and to my surprise the photo shows a very wide bright purple band that looks like a shawl crossing the trunk of the tree. My mother's favorite color was purple. I showed the photo to many photographers and asked if there was a logical explanation for why this purple band would show up across the piñon tree in a photo, and no one could explain it.

I had to open my heart to another wonderful omen that was being given to me when I felt vulnerable about upcoming time away from home, for I felt the love and support from my mother shining through from the transcendent realms.

As I reflect on how many gifts I have received while walking in the arroyo, I feel strongly that it has been my regular ongoing relationship with the spirit of this place that has brought forth a wealth of signs to help me on my life's journey. I walk the same path on a regular basis, always with honor and respect for all that is alive in this area.

I believe the relationship I have built up with the nature beings here has created a deep and strong field that lifts the veils between the worlds. The help of the hidden realms can reach through to give me guidance and let me know how much I am loved and supported.

I did not always live in a place where I had the opportunity to go right outside my door and walk for miles in nature. I spent the first half of my life living in cities where there was a plethora of buildings and cement between me and nature. But due to my love of nature, I found ways to go beyond the cement covering the earth.

I grew up in Brooklyn, where I sang to a maple tree outside my house every day. I talked to it and felt the tree communicating back to me, bringing me comfort and a deep sense of peace. The tree was so tall I had to strain my neck to be able to see the leaves on the top branches, but when I went back and visited the tree as an adult, this tree that had seemed so enormous was certainly not as tall as I'd remembered.

I later lived in San Francisco, where I had favorite walking paths in nature and built up a strong relationship with the nature beings there. I felt a strong sense of mutual love and support with those nature beings.

The point I am making is that you can build a mutually supportive relationship with nature wherever you live—in a city or in a rural environment. There are probably parks you can walk in, and there is a tree or plant you can radiate love to every day. There is the sky above and the earth below that you can continue to honor. You can honor the living beings we call earth, air, water, and the sun as you go about your day. It does not matter where you live.

Nature will respond to you. Your life will change. Your relationship with the universe will change as you notice signs being given to you to light your path and let you know you are being recognized, supported, and loved by the spirit that lives in all things. Most importantly, your deep connection with nature will fill your soul.

There are a variety of animals, birds, and insects that appear to me on my walks in the arroyo, as well as in other places in nature when the universe is trying to give me a sign. Many times a heart-shaped rock will make itself visible to me as I am walking in a meditative state. The wind is another one of my spiritual allies, and I have come to rely on the messages that travel through the wind and breezes when I need guidance in my life.

As you spend time in nature, notice what nature beings appear to you.

All of life responds to love. As you express your love for nature, you will receive that love back exponentially.

🌿 Practices

Find a special place in nature where you can build up a relationship with the nature beings and the spirit of the land. Connect there with nature every day or a few times a week.

This special sacred place is a landscape you can visit to clear your mind, regenerate, heal, and find comfort. The trees, plants, rocks, and animal life get to know you as you walk through the land on a regular basis.

With intention, start to be more conscious of your energetic interactions with the spirits of nature. There are times when you might stop and say hello to the nature beings you have come to know. And there are times when you will walk the land sharing your energy, love, and light as you flow through that special space.

This place will become for you what my magic arroyo is for me, and as you deepen your relationship to this place, the omens and signs lighting your way will become more numerous and more obvious. As you build a relationship, notice how the universe responds to your questions, challenges, and prayers.

13

The Hidden Folk and the Spirit of the Land and the Star Beings and Starry Princess

The Hidden Folk and the Spirit of the Land

Sandra

In the 1990s I became devoted to creating a healthier garden. This sparked my interest in working with the Hidden Folk. I performed a series of shamanic journeys with the intention of meeting the Hidden Folk, hoping they would help me with my gardening efforts.

In my first journey I saw a vision of an elf—a very small being. He was dressed in blue work clothes, construction boots, and a hard hat, and he was smoking a cigar. He was short with a very solid, stocky

build, and seemed to be the foreman of a group of elves. The first thing he did was kick me in the shin. I was not physically hurt by his kick, but I certainly was surprised by his behavior.

He said to me, "You don't want me to help you with your garden. You want me to do all the work for you!"

Well, I had to laugh for I was caught. He was absolutely correct. I wanted some mystical being to magically create the most beautiful garden filled with flowers and strong, healthy vegetables.

Over time I learned how to work in partnership with "the foreman" and the group of elves he managed. They continued to test me to make sure I was committed to the work before they offered any assistance.

As I moved to different homes in Santa Fe, my team of elves moved with me and helped me to caretake the gardens where I lived. They now have been with me for many years.

The times we live in call for finding new ways of perceiving reality. In the collective we are caught up in the realities of scarcity, violence, and severe climate change. But this is only one perspective of our world.

We can lift the veils, see beyond the dense collective energies, and experience another level of life—its mystical and magical aspects. Yes, of course we must pay attention to what is happening in the visible world. But the subtler energies can assist in our efforts to cultivate a rich inner landscape. New ways of perceiving life and nature will lead to a more harmonious life filled with inner peace, health, and joy.

Indigenous cultures recognize that nature spirits appear in many forms. In modern-day cultures they are often visible to children, but most of us cut off our spiritual connections to nature beings as we move toward adulthood.

We call these nature spirits faeries, devas, elves, forest guardians, or forest angels. Some people refer to them as the "little people." The Hidden Folk, however, are much taller than humans. Stories told by most indigenous traditions reveal that the Hidden Folk are recognized by people all over the world.

Just as we are, they are caretakers of this great Earth. By calling in and working in partnership with these beings, our chances of healing the planet can improve exponentially. As I travel I hear about many communities where people work in partnership with the Hidden Folk to grow beautiful gardens filled with healthy vegetables and other plants of great beauty.

I first heard about working in partnership with plant spirits when I learned about the community at Findhorn, Scotland, founded in 1962. A small group of people living on barren, sandy land worked in partnership with helpers they referred to as plant "Devas" to grow astonishing vegetables in adverse conditions.

I've also read books by Machaelle Small Wright at Perelandra. Small Wright works with the Hidden Folk to grow healthy fruits and vegetables and control pestilence. She suggests that if we work with "nature intelligences" to give the spirits of insects and rodents the food they desire, they will leave the main garden to thrive.

As children we knew the Hidden Folk and they brought magic and joy into our lives. As we grew older we closed the veils between the invisible and visible worlds and lost our connection with our invisible friends. When we reopen the veils, a twinkle returns to our eyes.

The key is to work in partnership with the nature spirits. The Hidden Folk remain elusive until they feel they can trust humans and their commitment to caring for the Earth. They will not do the work for us, but they will work with us.

For the past twenty years, I have gotten to know and love the juniper, piñon pine, ponderosa pine, cottonwood, desert oak, and aspen trees that grow and inhabit the land where I live. You might say my husband and I are "tree people."

Many years ago, when Santa Fe was experiencing terrible drought, we became worried about the trees, because we could water our small garden but there was no way we could water all the trees on our land. Due to drought many of the piñon pines became infested with bark beetle, and millions of trees in New Mexico died.

As I shared in Cottonwood Tree, I started to engage in a variety of spiritual practices. I lifted the veil of reality so that I could see the trees thriving instead of perceiving them suffering in the drought. I used to walk around the land seeing the trees in their divine perfection radiating spiritual light.

To add to this practice, I called in forest guardians and angels to assist the trees. These forest guardians and angels, taller than the trees themselves, opened their arms and embraced them with love and light. Their loving presence helped to keep the trees thriving during the drought. We lost only a few piñon pines to the bark beetle. These nature spirits provide ongoing support as it continues to be dry in the high desert.

I have learned over my years of spiritual work that as climatic events keep creating changes in the landscape of our planet, there is spiritual work we can do to caretake the land. We can radiate love and light and perceive nature in its divine perfection. In this way nature reflects back to us a state of radiance and health. We can call in an abundance of helping and compassionate spirits to partner with us in our work on behalf of the planet and all in the web of life.

We came here to be caretakers of this great planet Earth, which is a garden. The Hidden Folk are also caretakers and live in urban areas as well as rural, so we can all connect to them. But we must be willing to show commitment to our love of the Earth before the Hidden Folk will show themselves to us.

They have observed the ways we have dishonored nature and the environment and so have a basic mistrust and are suspicious of humans. But when we show that we live each day with honor and respect for nature, all of life, and the Earth, they are eager to join us in an our efforts to be caretakers.

While I was writing a previous book, *Medicine for the Earth,* I read an article in *The New York Times* stating that the Icelandic people still believed so staunchly in the Hidden Folk that they had a representative in government fighting to protect their homes from encroaching road development. It was also known that if roads did threaten to displace the Hidden Folk, equipment would break down or some on construction crews would suffer from work accidents.

My curiosity was piqued by this, and my husband and I flew to Iceland to learn more. We stayed in a bed and breakfast in Reykjavik owned by a man who had been born and raised in Iceland. When I quizzed him about the Hidden Folk, he denied that everyone in Iceland still fully believes in them. But he did say statistics show the majority of people in Iceland will not say that the Hidden Folk do not exist. They might not wholeheartedly embrace the Hidden Folk, but they don't deny their existence out of fear that the Hidden Folk might create blocks and obstacles if they are not honored.

While in Iceland we had the opportunity to attend Elf School, where we learned about the Hidden Folk and took tours of some of the places they are said to live. We also learned about a race of humans called the Spirit People, who are believed to live within the Earth. The instructor of the course shared research on a race of beings who wear pioneer clothes, live a simple life, and occasionally come up through rocks to rescue people who have suffered a hiking accident in the wilderness. They are said to have very advanced healing methods and can quickly mend broken bones. The research our instructor collected came from stories shared throughout the Northern Hemisphere—across Africa, Europe, and the United States.

In the West we have closed the veils between the worlds and have forgotten races of beings that coexist with us and offer their assistance. As we learn to sharpen our perception and enliven our senses, we can perceive the Hidden Folk all around us. When you look deeply into many of the beautiful flowers growing on the earth, you can see a face of the Hidden Folk.

When I moved to Santa Fe in the early 1980s, the locals and people who came to visit talked about "the magic of Santa Fe," but I was unable to lift the veil of reality to experience this magic.

Life was hard for me here. No matter how much I worked, I could not financially support myself. I did not feel at home in the high desert. At first I did not appreciate the look of the adobe structures or the way they blend in with the land. And the adobe walls around the houses felt like the walls around the people, as I had a difficult time creating deep and meaningful friendships.

I never really felt that I had moved to Santa Fe by choice, but rather that some spiritual force or destiny had drawn me here to learn certain lessons. I was in true resistance to any gifts and teachings that were being presented to me. Life for me in Santa Fe was simply hard and devoid of joy.

Since I use shamanic journeying as a way to connect with helping spirits, I decided to journey to the Spirit of Santa Fe. The helping spirits are spiritual energy and formless, but they tend to take on a form that can engage with us on a personal level. The form might change with each person who journeys to a helping spirit. The Spirit of Santa Fe presented herself to me as a striking and radiant goddess.

Once I met the goddess energy of Santa Fe in a journey, she became my teacher for many years. She shared with me why I had been spiritually called to Santa Fe to live and what she had to teach me. I learned many valuable lessons from her that helped me to grow and evolve into who I am today.

I asked the Spirit of Santa Fe why I was having such a difficult time here and how I could turn my life around. She shared a wealth of information and gave me instructions for five actions to take to improve my life.

I followed her instructions, and after taking action on all five pieces of advice, my life completely turned around. Then one afternoon I was drinking coffee with some friends at an outdoor café. I looked up at the Sangre de Cristo Mountains, and I experienced a veil lift open, and I felt Cupid's arrow strike my heart. I instantly felt the excitement and magic of Santa Fe and could feel my heart and energy align with that of the land. Colors seemed brighter, and I could hear a gentle hum in the land. I felt excitement surging through my body, and I could feel the light return to my eyes. The plants, trees, and land sparkled with vitality and radiance.

My life here changed dramatically, and for the past thirty years, Santa Fe has been my spiritual, emotional, and physical home. I love living here and cannot imagine leaving.

As I started to travel and teach around the world, I found myself journeying before each trip to meet the spirit of the land or city that I would be visiting. I asked if I had permission to come, and I told the spirit of the land/city that a group would be joining me to explore how to live a life of honor and respect toward the Earth and the web of life. I shared that those traveling to attend my workshops were openhearted people who wished to embrace spiritual practices that would improve the quality of their lives. I asked for support for the group and that the group be welcomed and held in love by the spirit of the land.

I continually found that my journeys to the spirit of the land and the city I was visiting helped to shape my experience into a beautiful adventure. My travels went smoothly, my workshops took place with grace and ease, and I experienced many levels of support with my groups. That did not mean we never experienced challenges, but we could feel the spiritual support around us, guiding us through all our experiences.

When I started to teach my Medicine for the Earth trainings, I incorporated journeys to meet the Hidden Folk and the spirit of the land and or city. I would ask participants to journey over the course of the workshop to these nature spirits and spirits of the land to ask for guidance on how they could help caretake the land or city where they lived. The other intention was to ask how to improve the quality of their lives by living in harmony with the energy.

The results reported back to me have consistently been extremely positive. After performing these journeys participants leave the workshops with a feeling of excitement about going home. When they arrive home they report feeling a deeper and sacred connection to the land and cities where they reside. They feel welcomed in a way they had not experienced before by the spirit of the land and also by the Hidden Folk, whether they live in urban areas or outside of cities.

With continued journeys over time, people have shared with me that the quality of their lives has improved dramatically, and their mood has improved as they've begun to experience living on sacred ground. They felt an aliveness to the land or city they had not experienced in the past. The wildlife, plants, and trees seemed to communicate messages of love and support. For those who planted, their gardens flourished. A greater state of harmony was achieved. Most importantly, people report that they feel at home on the land and in the cities where they live.

ᘉ

As I end my writing of *Speaking with Nature,* I reflect on the hills I gaze upon as I leave the arroyo to return to my home. The hills are curved in such a way that I feel deeply loved and embraced by the feminine energy of the spirit of the land. There are different aspects of the feminine that Llyn and I have written about throughout this book, but ultimately all aspects of the feminine weave together a beautiful tapestry of love. Earth is our home and she loves us.

Love is the greatest healer. Do we really understand love? I think we all have a basic understanding of love, but our destiny is to learn about the power of true unconditional love. This is love that goes beyond the personal to mirror the love that went into our creation. Universal love is not a concept that can be understood or rationalized. Universal love is a formless energy that has no bounds. The universe and the helping spirits in the transcendent realms only see us in our beauty and light, and they love us unconditionally.

If we experienced true unconditional love of Source, the feminine, and the Earth, would we be facing the illnesses and planetary challenges we face today? And if love heals, how do we move our rational minds out of the way and surrender to this pure power? This love is in our cellular memory, as we were created from unconditional love. Universal and unconditional love transcends and is beyond our egoic understanding.

What will happen if we ask the Source, the goddess, the Divine to help us? If we say, "Thank you for helping me open to your love," what would change? What is possible if we stop trying to understand how to experience a luminous state of being and just open and give thanks for the experience of love?

It is time for all of us to open and surrender to the creative force of life and experience the power of true unconditional love. As we do this we become a channel for that love to flow through us healing all of life.

We all know how love feeds both new growth and mature flowers, plants, blossoms, and garden vegetables. We all have witnessed the difference of a garden tended with love. The same is true for tending our inner gardens.

We do not try to give love to a baby, a family member, or loved one. True love effortlessly flows through us. Each day give thanks to Source, the Divine, and the feminine to help you to open to the unconditional love that created you. When you love yourself you can share love with others.

As we reconnect to ourselves and to the Earth, we remember how to honor and respect all in the web of life with each breath and each step we take. It is our responsibility to love ourselves, others, all the nature beings, and the Earth through our behavior. As we open together as a global community, love can once again flow through each and every one of us and create healing and transformation for all in the web of life.

🌿 Practices

Are you ready to meet the Hidden Folk? Turn on some expansive music or a drumming track and hold the intention that you would like to introduce yourself to the Hidden Folk who live in your city. Remember, the Hidden Folk live in both urban and rural areas.

You can also go outside and sit quietly and close your eyes with your intention to meet the Hidden Folk.

Tell them that you love the Earth and the land. Let them know you wish to work in partnership with them to caretake the Earth.

Be persistent; it might take some time for them to communicate with you while they test your commitment.

Once you start communicating with the Hidden Folk, ask for their guidance on how you can be a caretaker of the land. Be aware they might give you tasks that are time consuming. Be sure you are ready to do some work once you initiate a relationship with them.

You might invite some friends or others in your community to clean up trash in an area of the city or land where you live. This is an activity that the Hidden Folk will take as a sign of your commitment to be a caretaker of the land.

If you are a gardener, call in the Hidden Folk to help advise you about caring for your garden. Once they see how much work you are willing to put in, they will join you in your efforts. You will feel yourself working with them in the spirit of cooperation and collaboration.

Leave offerings for them. You can leave some food or a drink in gratitude for their help and partnership, but not just remnants. One time I left an offering of some cake that had gone stale. As I left the stale cake on the earth, I heard a message, "You always leave us things you don't want to eat or drink. Leave us the good stuff!"

In the same way you performed a meditation to meet the Hidden Folk, you can also meet the spirit of the city or land where you live.

Start by introducing yourself to the spirit of the land, and when you feel you have a good connection, ask for advice on how you can live in spiritual harmony with the land. You can also ask for advice on how to improve the quality of your life and move through challenges you might be experiencing.

Look at yourself in the mirror in the morning and reflect on the shine in your eyes and the brightness you radiate. Even if you do not perceive yourself as bright, acknowledge that you are. Your perception creates your reality. When you feed your light, it shines through you.

When you carry on conversations with others during the day, comment on how their eyes are shining or how bright and beautiful they look. Breathe through your heart and be a vessel of universal love. Watch what happens as you do this. I can guarantee you that you will start a chain reaction of bright smiles wherever you are willing to bring through love and acknowledge the light in all you meet.

Go outside and feel your connection with the spirit of the land and the Earth. Feel the energy of love for life emerging through you. This love feeds you, all of life, and the Earth and the elements. Write the word *love* in the ground. Share your love with the Earth.

By shifting your perception you will find yourself stepping into a new dimension of nature that shimmers with a vitality and radiance you have not previously experienced.

By doing all these practices, you will notice that you feel more at home in your body and in the city where you live.

Together, as a global community, let us join our hearts in love as we work in partnership with the Hidden Folk and the helping and compassionate spirits to create a healthy planet. All the nature beings are alive and share this planet with us. Earth is our home. Together let us commit to its care. Together let us dream into being a world that embraces joy, love, light, harmony, abundance, peace, and equality for all in the web of life.

Star Beings and Starry Princess

Llyn

Sandra writes beautifully about the spirit of the land and the Hidden Folk. I laughed when I read about her mischievous garden helper. Through Sandra's writings I could see her New Mexico garden, desert, mountains, and all of our lands come alive with playful beings that invite us to co-create with them.

Tales of the land's hidden forces are found in all cultures. For instance, I traveled with a group recently to a humble village at the shores of Lake Atitlan in Guatemala. The elder we work with who lives there, Tata Pedro Cruz Garcia, spoke about diminutive nonhuman people. The individuals I was with assumed the grandfather saw beings we didn't because the man lived simply and sacredly in a place where the veils that separate the spiritual from material reality are thin. Lake Atitlan is a portal to other dimensions.

Certainly we all felt the power at Atitlan. After a few days many of us felt our bodies slightly rock as if to a secret pulse. The sway made me dizzy. Given that volcanoes surround the lake, whose depths are unknown, I was convinced the earth was moving beneath our feet. Yet there was no tangible movement. The wobble was not physical. Had we stayed longer we would perhaps have started to see little people.

It's exciting to be in exotic parts of the world having such experiences, but we don't have to travel to part the veils. Sandra mentions that nature spirits were visible to us when we were children; we've all heard of children in contemporary settings who have invisible friends.

When I was young I spoke with beings from a far part of the universe. Though I couldn't see the beings, I felt them. A soft charge in the air, a cared-for feeling, and sometimes, musical tones in my ear or telepathic words told me the Star Beings were near. They were from a world I couldn't remember, a home beyond Earth. The sense of belonging I felt with my stellar family told me it was real.

There were times when I pressed the people of the stars with questions:

"How can you be so far away, yet with me at the same time?"

"Does the universe really go on forever?"

"Why can't I see you, and why am I on Earth without you?"

I wanted to figure it all out.

My star friends' responses were simple: "You cannot know everything with your mind."

I would sigh and come back to the wonder of stars and my love for my invisible family.

Sandra writes that opening to hidden parts of reality helps us develop a rich inner landscape and enhances how we perceive. Likewise, Star Beings invite us to feel our way to expanded reality. There are countless ways to cultivate this; one is to be with night as it turns to day—at dawn.

On Guatemalan journeys our group rises before dawn to join our Mayan elder Tata Pedro and his shaman wife, Nana Shumatla Fenix. We stand together silently in the chilly air, listening to the water lap and to other natural sounds in the darkness. Night gradually thins as dark births light; dogs bark and roosters crow, sun rays paint the sky in violet streaks, the air gets warmer, fish leap from the water, hummingbirds flit and dip long beaks into fragile white blossoms. The liquid abyss before us is illuminated, and glowing mists swoon over Lake Atitlan. The sunrise ignites us. Gradually human sounds—voices, cars, radios, and clatter—break the day and our reverie. In our opened state we embrace it all.

The threshold time of sunset is equally potent.

Recall being outside, sniffing dusk scents and watching stars come out. Take time to really remember this.

Scientists say there is an unending expanse of galaxies in an infinite world of universes, that Earth is a tiny planet amidst vast realities. How could we be all alone?

Star People invite us to ponder this and to boldly feel our way to truth, not merely intellectualize about the true nature of our reality or take someone else's word for it.

"Dare to let go," they seem to say. "As a guileless child, sense the life all around, including us; we share with you in a multidimensional expanse of universes."

Just as Sandra encourages us to create with the Hidden Folk and the spirits of the land, star families coax us to explore a fresh reality design during changing times on planet Earth.

Stars provide a looking glass for where we came from and who we are. The Eldar Wood Elf, Tauriel, a character in the film *The Hobbit: The Desolation of Smaug* based on J. R. R. Tolkien's book, expresses it beautifully: "All light is sacred to the Eldar, but Wood Elves love best the light of the stars."

Tauriel's admirer, the Dwarf Kili, responds, "I always thought it is a cold light, remote and far away."

Her look shows her surprise as Tauriel replies: "It is memory, precious and pure."

Many of the contemporary myths being brought to film reflect what we are now trying to remember. Perhaps Star Beings are the light in us we've forgotten or projected out, just as angels, avatars, saints, and ascended masters are light-filled figures who feel separate from us and distant. Nature spirits, also nonmaterial, reflect the magic and possibility we have forgotten, yet which is inherent to all life on Earth, including us.

As we go deeply into nature, we will remember who we really are. We will bridge the gap between us and the transcendent. Star wisdom tells us we don't have to be feral to love the Earth, and we don't need to act like angels to be light.

In fact, you may have noticed that the more you seek light, the more your wounds and blocks seem to trip you up and get in your face. They want you to know that they are light, too.

All of it—what we perceive as light and the light in us, and also the hidden shadow of ourselves and our societies—comes home to us now. All is one with the light of Source. It's blissful to rejoin with the light of joy, harmony, connection, and love. It's usually more difficult to welcome the light of fear, grief, suffering, loss, separation, and anger, as these bring a different ecstasy. Yet it is in wholeness that we shine.

Don't ever think that you or your circumstances are not worthy. Always look for that light and feel it—just as you are. Starry sisters and brothers remind us, "If the dark is intense, illumined it will be truly powerful." As we nourish our wounded aspects, we reclaim the life force they protect.

This helps me so much as I grapple with my own shortcomings and what I feel forlorn about in the world. Mayan teachings say we have to know the dark to know the light; we must descend to the lower world before we can rise to the upper world. Similarly, my artist son Eben explains to me that the role of a "dark artist" is to reflect to society aspects of life we don't want to look at, such as poverty and suffering. What is difficult for us, we often ignore. All indigenous cultures I have worked with include the darker, more challenging aspects of the human journey as one with the luminous whole. Rugs woven by Navajo peoples include a flaw in the weave as a reminder that humans are not perfect. Just as in nature it's impossible to mark the line between night and day, as we find ways to love our wounded aspects, we blur the separation between ourselves and the other, transforming our views of and our relationship to suffering around us. From this some good may come.

What do stars have to do with Earth?

Stars and space are also nature, and everything on Earth is made of stardust. Organic particles and moisture from a distant part of the universe may have seeded life on our planet. Perhaps we migrated here from other galactic homes.

The idea that we came from elsewhere reflects the cosmologies of diverse indigenous groups.

Many say we have exchanged with sky beings since people started showing up on this planet.

Among those is an almost-extinct tribe from the Amazon Rain Forest known as the *Uru-eu-wau-wau,* "People of the Stars," who claim the Pleiades as their home. My Brazilian friend Ipupiara was one of these remaining tribal members.

Ipupiara shared with me the *Uru-eu-wau-wau* legend, which says their Princess had visions of a small planet named Earth whose people were doomed unless they changed their ways. The compassionate star nation sent a convoy to help the wayward species.

John Perkins writes in his book *Shapeshifting* that the chosen emissaries—including the Princess—were transformed into spheres of pure energy and sent into the darkness of space. The light orbs were drawn to the dense forests of the Amazon.

I visited a remote Amazon tribe over a period of many years with John. Shuar members spoke to us about spheres of light that frequented their night skies.

Curiously, when I gifted a cherub faced shaman woman named Anga in Hakassia, Siberia, with a Shuar seed necklace from a world away in the Amazon Basin, tears brimmed the rugged woman's eyes. I was stunned to hear Anga say, "I travel through the rain forest all the time as a ball of light. I have never been there in this physical body, but I know the rain forest is my true home."

Orbs often appear in photographs participants take at shamanic events. Many globes contain elaborate patterns. Several years ago orbs with fantastic designs showed up in a night photo taken of my son, Eben. Are the light patterns inside these spheres a sort of communication, an energy language? Are the balls of light actually us, or perhaps beings from other worlds?

A lot of orbs are being seen and documented these days, far from the Amazon. They have appeared to me in broad daylight. Many photographer aficionados feel the glowing spheres *want* us to see them.

We are not who we've been conditioned to think we are, and we are not alone. It's time to know about life beyond our own. Yet I don't feel as some do that humanity is ready to dissolve into formlessness or that "higher" beings can save us from ourselves. Star friends reflect who we are and inspire us to embody the starlight that is within us. They unleash the quantum potential hidden within us and within the Earth from our starry inception. Opening to them will help us understand our role in the cosmic scheme of things and see a healthy planet synonymous to life.

Why did the Pleiadian Princess and her light emissaries aim for the jungle when they came to Earth? Forests, the breath of our planet, also breathe water. Trees absorb and release water, and rain forests are amazing water engineers. For example, in the Hoh River Valley in the largest temperate rain forest in the world, up to fourteen feet of water a year tap dances on evergreens and trickles down their grooved bark. Thick mosses and other alive and decaying plants soak up the deluge like sponges. Riverbanks swell to handle heavy downfalls, just as our watery lungs expand with air. The river also breathes through its gravel bars—moving rivers of rock that sift water through stone and sand. The Hoh Forest and its river canyon breathe and manage water so efficiently that I can nap under trees when it's pouring, and the river can gush to torrents one day, then dramatically recede the next.

Watershed ecosystems have an astonishing intelligence. Just as fluids facilitate electrical brain impulse, imagine that water breathing through rivers, forests, and trees carrying natural electrical forces.

Foresters will tell you that the majority of a tree is dead; only the outer cambium layer, which bears love to eat, is alive.

Have you ever felt a sense of loss after cutting your hair, as if a part of you had gone missing? It's interesting that our hair grows, yet we also regard it as dead. Something in us knows our tresses are more than dead cells. Shamanic belief is that hair channels energy, life force. Indigenous tribes associate hair with spiritual power, strength, even tracking skills; individual hairs are spiritual antennae.

Trees respond in the same way. Every bit of a tree is part of a vibrant physical and spiritual system. Its branches and the tree itself are spiritual antenna; light and information from Earth and the cosmos course through it. These forces pour out with the tons of water trees release and through rivers and other water bodies.

We humans are also composed of water, and we are conduits for the informational light passing between Earth and the cosmos.

Star People encourage: "The light in the sun and stars is one with the conscious light of Earth and you. With toes and fingers luxuriate in the Earth's luminous mud and soil. Lie belly to your Mother, and sniff starlight—her sweet scent. Never again will you wonder who you are."

As we remember the whole of us, just as trees release cosmic light through watering, we release spiritual light through our own watering—by being and offering to life all that we are.

🍃 Practice

Star Beings tell us there is no need to look elsewhere or aim for the stars, because starry influence is here and now. Listening to music you love, doing what deeply moves you, and being in nature musing with light orbs, faeries, stars, trees, and elves, or other little people brings the glow back into life. This meditation can invite the Starry Princess to help us remember the light—our own and that of the Earth.

Choose a space inside or outside where you will not be disturbed. Do some gentle stretching; unwind. Then settle into either a lying or sitting position and close your eyes.

Take a deep, cleansing breath.

Take another long, refreshing breath.

In your mind's eye picture glowing balls of light, emissaries from a starry world floating through the night sky toward earthly folks who have forgotten their own starry relations.

Take a few moments to really see or sense the radiant orbs.

Envision the Starry Princess among these light emissaries, a magical glowing sphere.

Imagine looking at the designs in the sphere that is the Pleiadian Princess. What do you see? What do you feel?

Take some time to tune in to her language of light; listen to the Princess with your whole being. Open your heart.

You may hear or see something, or nothing.

Most importantly—feel. The Princess is a light vibration your wisdom body knows.

Sense the luminous feminine. What does she share?

Settle your heart, feel her presence. Relax as the Princess reflects your essence to you.

Hold your hands out in front of you, palms open and level to your face as if gazing into a mirror. See your face reflected in the looking glass of your hands. Gaze at your palms, at your reflection. Now allow the image of you to transform into the golden sun, your solar system's star. Take your time and make this real for you. Sense the sunlight and warmth on your palms and face. Then when you are ready, feel or say the following, guided by the Princess:

"No matter how I see myself, or how others view me, or what beautiful or tragic life stories play out on this Earth walk, I am pure light, like our golden sun."

Continue to see your image in your palm mirror as a radiant sun. Breathe in the warm life glow of you, your light. You are an ego persona, and there is no problem with that. You are also so much more.

Take all the time you like.

When ready, gently let the sun's image fade, still gazing at your palms.

The Princess continues, "Now look into your palm mirror to watch the events of daily life. Notice what you see."

Then consider the following, guided by the Princess: "No matter what plays out in life or how I feel about it, everything is light—a compassionate brilliance that has long been forgotten but now wills itself to be seen and experienced."

Take your time to gain a sense of the radiant weave that is always there, and see life's reflection become less solid. See that the dream we know as "daily life" can change at any time.

The mundane world we engage every day as we relate with our families, jobs, and communities is fine, just as it is, and we can also awaken to see it as a vivid and fluid dream that invites us to go more deeply into each moment to unravel who we really are.

Take all the time you like with these experiences and reflections.

When you eventually want to transition from your time with the Starry Princess, simply allow the focus to fade, but stay with the feeling of being with the Princess, a living force of love. Relax fully with these sensations and breathe with what you feel.

Continue to simply breathe and feel.

Now imagine balls of light from the Pleiades, a Princess among them, disappearing into the canopy of dense forest and blending with the living force of trees.

As the last glowing sphere dissolves among the treetops, you sense and hear a voice. The melodic whisper warms your heart like liquid gold.

"Just as your old-growth trees carry the genetic memory of old forests, trees carry the original memory of your species, seeded from stars."

The Star Princess concludes, "Take from the Earth no more than you need and give back to her all that you can. Respect, love, and journey deeply with nature for there you will find me—radiant feminine, stars, and nature spirits—in the Earth, in your trees, in you."

Nature is calling you home.

How to Work with Omens

Sandra

Native traditions hold that everything in nature is alive and interacts with us. Nature communicates with us by showing us omens and signs.

Physics uses the term "unified field" to describe a state of oneness. In indigenous cultures the term for this is the "web of life." We are connected to one universal force, and we are part of nature. The universe shows us signposts that lead us to make healthy and wise decisions so we can flow gracefully with the river of life. These signposts are offered to us in nature and in urban areas. The key is raising our awareness to the daily messages we are being given.

In *Speaking with Nature* we have included practices for you to do in nature. A wonderful practice to add is working with the omens and signposts that nature shares with you.

As you work with the practices, you might find yourself holding questions about what your next step in life should be. If you pay attention, you will see signs to light your path as you take your next steps. In spiritual traditions these signs are also called omens. You might say the

universe is laying down breadcrumbs for you to follow. You are being led to receive guidance in ways that are beyond your logical understanding.

As you walk in nature or even travel to work, you might see the appearance of an animal whose qualities provide an answer to a question you have been pondering. You might notice the forms of the clouds in the sky presenting a metaphorical response.

After meeting a complete stranger or having had a random conversation, you may realize you have received an answer to a question or problem that has been troubling you.

Sometimes you'll receive a sign while listening to the words of a song playing on the radio while you are pondering a question. While focusing on an issue in life, a bus may drive by with an advertisement posted on the side featuring words that hold a solution or share an inspirational phrase you needed to read in that moment. You might be skimming the pages of a book and gaze upon the perfect sentence or paragraph that provides you with an answer or the inspiration you need.

You might wonder if the omens you receive are an answer to a question or a coincidence. Albert Einstein is quoted as having said, "Coincidence is God's way of remaining anonymous."

In the 1980s I found myself going through a challenging time. One day I spoke a prayer out loud to the universe. I said, "Please show me obvious signs I can follow." I felt that I'd made a series of bad choices, and I was looking for a more graceful way to live my life.

From that day forth I have found that as long as I pay attention, life gives me all the omens and signs I need to make healthy choices. Of course the key is to heighten my senses, look around me, and listen deeply to the messages I receive.

We can all reflect on a past event when we realized we ignored signs we were given. We might have decided to ignore the information we were shown, or we just were not aware enough to see or hear the guidance given. Many of us go through life asleep, living in a collective trance created by so much outer stimulation in our lives.

We don't always realize that the help and guidance we need is being shown to us. We are not awake to the signs appearing throughout the day. Our minds are often too busy and distracted to notice what the universe is revealing to us for our highest good.

A good way to start your practice of watching and listening for omens and signs is by walking in nature. Before your walk think about a question you have where you could use some guidance. You might be considering making a decision that will have a big impact on your life. Think about this and hold the intention that you wish to be shown a sign that will lead you forward to your next steps.

As you walk allow the beauty of nature to quiet your mind. Just be observant. Or you might find a beautiful place to sit and be still while opening up your sensory awareness. Take some deep breaths. Notice if there are cloud formations in the sky that might provide insight for you. Observe the animals, birds, insects, or other nature beings whose qualities or behavior might provide an answer you are seeking. A bird or an insect might land on or by you, or an animal such as a squirrel, fox, or deer might come close and stand or sit by you for an unusual amount of time. If you are sitting by the ocean, you might notice a school of dolphins jumping or a group of whales breaching in the distance. Their appearance might be a sign. An eagle or a hawk might circle overhead, or ravens might caw in respect as you perform a ceremony, pray, and leave offerings to honor nature and the land, signifying that your prayers have been heard. Notice if the shape of a rock in the landscape reveals an answer or guidance. You might even hear a message carried to you by running water or the wind. Use your imagination, and heighten your level of awareness. Open your heart, and feel the message a nature being is sharing with you.

When you come to a decision about a change you are planning to make, take a walk and ask for a sign of confirmation. As you focus on your new decision, a breeze might come out of nowhere that feels like it is whispering "yes" to you. A beautiful butterfly might come along and land on your hand as you imagine making a change. You might notice that the sky is thick with clouds, and when you think about a new life choice, the clouds part and beams of sunlight shine on you. Suddenly a rainbow might appear in the distance, affirming a decision you have made. A light rain that falls for just a minute might bless you. As you pass a tree while considering a life change, the leaves might rustle in a way that feels like an affirmation. You might look down and find a rock in the shape of a heart at your feet. With this way of working, you must trust your intuition as nature responds to you.

Be persistent and be willing to practice. At first you might not be aware of any omens. Have patience and take time to awaken to the signposts nature provides. Keep holding your intention while you continue to walk and spend time in nature. Hold your intention as you travel to and from work or while doing errands.

At home, work, or school, let your intuition lead you to a book on a bookshelf. Simply open to a page. Read the page, and reflect on a message it might contain.

Notice if you end up having synchronistic meetings with old friends or strangers where what seems like a random conversation holds great wisdom that inspires and assists you in some way.

As you do this more and more, you will notice that your path ahead is being lit to show you the way. When you open your awareness to how the universe participates in your healing, growth, and evolution, life takes on a deeper meaning. You might find yourself desiring to spend more time focusing on signs being shown to you. As you do this you will experience a new sense of joy and magical connection with life.

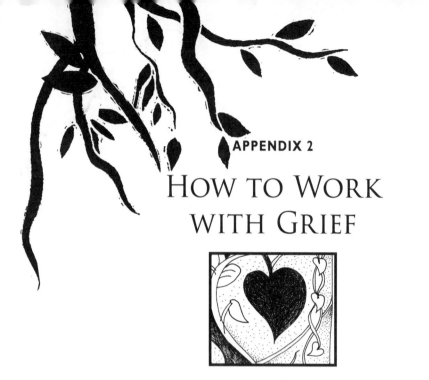

HOW TO WORK WITH GRIEF

Sandra

As you connect with the natural world, you will notice that all creatures grieve. Elephants, gorillas, dolphins, and other animals show grief when they lose a parent, mate, or baby. When a bird loses its mate, you will hear it cry. A squirrel will cry for days when a raven takes her baby. When a house plant dies, the plant sitting right next to it might deteriorate.

When we spend a lot of time in nature and connect back to the beauty this life has to offer us, we get attached to our favorite places, trees, plants, animals, birds, insects, and other nature beings. When we watch the changes occurring in nature through human destruction, weather changes, and environmental disasters, we may experience a state of grief.

We are familiar with the grief process when we lose a friend or loved one, but some of us are in unfamiliar territory as we deal with the loss of nature beings we have grown to love. And just as we do when we grieve loved ones, we must allow the process of grief to be expressed.

Death is not an end; rather it is a transition into another realm of being. The experience of grief is important for our growth and evolution. Grief helps us to develop a deep inner well that will help us to expand.

When you feel your heart breaking, your heart is actually expanding. The expansion helps you to be a greater vessel of love, which is the greatest healing force. There is nothing like grief to assist you in opening to a greater state of love. When your heart expands you feel more compassion for the suffering of others. And with compassion you hold the space for others to heal.

When you try to stop grief you attempt to stop growth. In nature life that is not growing is dying. The state of grief, no matter how bad it feels, is so filled with life. Grief helps to create more expansion in our inner world and a greater flow of life force. Grief creates a fertile state in which new relationships and opportunities can be created.

The issue to look at and reflect on is how you can support yourself while you are grieving. It is not beneficial to repress grief altogether.

First you must acknowledge your feelings. Acknowledging your sadness and emotional pain creates energetic movement that leads to transformation. When you repress a feeling, it continues to build inside, where the energy of the feeling creates emotional and/or physical stress, possibly seeding a future illness. It is important to express the full range of your emotions.

You have to return to your job and your daily routines, but it is important to create time to grieve. Find friends and community with whom you can share your feelings. Spend some alone time when you can be with your feelings.

For many people it is important to have a loving community that can just be there to listen. It's our tendency to want to fix those we love when they are in need, but with grief there is nothing to fix and no way to take grief away from someone else. Just being present, listening, and being a loving support helps tremendously.

It is important not to pity someone in a state of grief. Energetically pity is a heavy energy to carry. Imagine thousands of people pitying you if you are in a state of grief. Do you want to experience that kind of energy being sent to you?

Find ways to pamper yourself. You may want to relax in a bath. Water is a healing element. Release your pain into the water while asking the water to transmute your pain into energy that radiates love and light.

Physically lie on the earth or imagine yourself lying on the earth. Let your pain drain from you into the earth. Give thanks to Mother Earth for taking your pain and composting it into fertile organic matter that will create new growth. Reflect on how the earth composts the leaves that have died and fallen to the ground in autumn to create rich and fertile soil.

You can also write down feelings you wish to release and burn them in the flames of a fire. In indigenous cultures fire is seen to be the element of transmutation and transformation.

Go outside and allow the wind to carry away your feelings of pain while you stay open to loving messages that you hear from the breezes.

Giving thanks to the element you are working with is a way to honor the elements that sustain your life. Decree that the energy you are releasing be transformed into love and light. In this way you feed the energy in the world with blessings that heal all in the web of life.

Most of all give yourself time to grieve. There is no time frame when you "should" feel better. As you allow yourself to fully embrace your feelings, time itself will bring you to a place of regeneration. Everything in life changes, including grief. It may not end, but it changes.

You can also perform a simple ceremony to honor the life that has moved on to the transcendent realms—the realm of spirit.

You can leave an offering by a tree that has died, giving thanks for the beauty it shared on this great Earth and wishing it a good journey home. When you see an animal that has died, you can lift your arms up giving thanks for this being's life and wishing it a good journey home. You can do this after the death of any nature being you wish to honor. All living beings deserve to be honored when they die. You can also do this long distance as you hear about the death of many living beings in destructive environmental events.

You may feel deep grief when your favorite place in nature is destroyed through a climatic event, if the land is sold, if you move, or if a building project will prevent future visits. The spirit of the land is always available to you in your memory and through your meditations. You can still visit this place through your spiritual work. The spirit of this place is eternal.

There is also the grief we feel as we observe the unconscious behavior of humans who act in abusive ways toward other life forms. It is important to acknowledge the feelings that arise as we watch graphic images and read stories provided by the media of animal abuse. We need to speak out against abuse, but at the same time we create healing for all of life when we can embody a state of peace. As you continue to honor the Earth and all that is alive, you will find peace in the spiritual practices in which you engage.

About the Authors and Illustrator and Their Work

SANDRA INGERMAN

Sandra Ingerman, M.A., is the author of ten books and seven audio programs. She has been teaching workshops internationally for more than thirty years on shamanic journeying, healing, and reversing environmental pollution using spiritual methods.

Sandra is devoted to teaching people how we can work together as a global community to bring about positive change for the planet. To that end she founded an international alliance of shamanic teachers and practitioners (see "Finding a Shamanic Practitioner" on page 275). She is passionate about helping people to reconnect with nature and is recognized for bridging ancient cross-cultural healing methods into our modern culture to address the needs of our times.

Through her monthly column Sandra inspires the spiritual global community to keep working with spiritual practices even if we do not see immediate results from the work we are doing. She has been writing her "Transmutation News" column since 1998, and it is translated by volunteers into thirteen languages and available on her website **www.sandraingerman.com**. Column readers are invited to engage in a variety of spiritual practices and ceremonies such as a full moon ceremony, "Creating a Human Web of Light."

A licensed Marriage and Family Therapist and Professional Mental Health Counselor, Sandra is also a board-certified expert on traumatic stress and certified in acute traumatic stress management. She was awarded the 2007 Peace Award from the Global Foundation for Integrative Medicine and chosen as one of the Top Ten Spiritual Leaders of 2013 in the November/December issue of *Spirituality and Health*.

To read more about Sandra's work, read articles and blogs written by her—including her "Transmutation News" column—listen to interviews, and purchase selected books and CDs, please visit **www.sandraingerman.com**.

Books by Sandra Ingerman

Soul Retrieval: Mending the Fragmented Self (HarperOne, 1991)

Welcome Home: Following Your Soul's Journey Home (HarperOne, 1993)

A Fall to Grace, fiction (Moon Tree Rising Productions, 1997)

Medicine for the Earth: How to Transform Personal and Environmental Toxins (Three Rivers Press, 2001)

Shamanic Journeying: A Beginner's Guide, book and drumming CD (Sounds True, 2004)

How to Heal Toxic Thoughts: Simple Tools for Personal Transformation (Sterling, 2007)

Awakening to the Spirit World: The Shamanic Path of Direct Revelation, book and drumming CD cowritten with Hank Wesselman, winner of the Independent Publishers Award in 2011 and a COVR award (Sounds True, 2010)

*The Shaman's Toolkit: Ancient Tools for Shaping the Life and World
You Want to Live In* (Weiser, 2010)

Walking in Light: The Everyday Empowerment of a Shamanic Life
(Sounds True, 2014)

Audio Programs

The Soul Retrieval Journey (Sounds True, 1997)

The Beginner's Guide to Shamanic Journeying (Sounds True, 2003)

Miracles for the Earth (Sounds True, 2004)

*Shamanic Meditations: Guided Journeys for Insight, Vision, and
Healing* (Sounds True, 2010)

Soul Journeys: Music for Shamanic Practice (Sounds True, 2010)

*Shamanic Visioning: Connecting with Spirit to Transform Your Inner
and Outer Worlds,* 6-CD audio program (Sounds True, 2013)

Shamanic Visioning Music: Taiko Drum Journeys (Sounds True, 2014)

"Transmutation" App

Visit the App Store on your mobile device to purchase the "Transmutation" app Sandra created. Designed to help you shift negative thoughts to those that lead to your desired outcome, the mobile app allows you to set an alert that asks you to reflect on what you are thinking about throughout the day and inspires you to shift your thoughts by viewing words, phrases, blessings, and photos that are provided in the app library.

Finding a Shamanic Practitioner

To find a local shamanic practitioner and/or shamanic teacher, please also visit **www.shamanicteachers.com**. This website includes an international alliance of dedicated shamanic teachers trained by Sandra Ingerman and based on the feminine principle of cooperation and collaboration. These teachers offer workshops on shamanic journeying and healing, planetary healing, and how we can live our lives in a more creative and conscious way. The site also lists hundreds of shamanic practitioners from around the world.

LLYN ROBERTS

Llyn Roberts, M.A., is an award-winning author and prominent teacher of healing and shamanism. Her teaching and writing incorporates her diverse background in contemplative psychotherapy, Tibetan Buddhism, work in remote locations with diverse indigenous shamanic groups, Shamanic Reiki, and Western body-mind approaches to healing.

Llyn holds a Master of Arts degree in Tibetan Buddhist and Western Psychology from Naropa University and was initiated by shamans in South America and Siberia. She has trained extensively with Ecuadorian Quechua healers and facilitated sacred journeys to indigenous peoples living in remote regions of the Amazon, the Asian steppes, high Andes, and on ancient Mayan lands. She translates ancient techniques into modern-day practices to transform personal imbalances, help us open to our higher purpose, deepen our relationship to spirit and nature, and reclaim our power to make a positive difference in the world.

Former director of the nonprofit organization Dream Change, founded by John Perkins, Llyn is the cofounder and president of the Olympic Mountain EarthWisdom Circle (OMEC), dedicated to inspiring a sacred and responsible relationship with the Earth. She serves as adjunct faculty for Union Graduate School and the Graduate Institute, and was consultant to the University of Massachusetts Sustainability Institute and the Panama-based nonprofit organization Earth Train. For twenty years she has taught at the Omega Institute, the largest holistic educational institute in the world.

Llyn lived for two years at the edge of the wilderness in the Hoh Rain Forest, Pacific Northwest, while writing her portion of *Speaking with Nature*. In conjunction with OMEC she facilitated the relationship between *National Geographic* and Mick Dodge for the prime-time television series *The Legend of Mick Dodge*.

A modern-day mystic and spiritual ecologist, Llyn inspires through her work a deep sense of belonging with the natural world.

To find out more about Llyn Roberts and her work, visit **www.llynroberts.com.**

Books by Llyn Roberts

Shapeshifting into Higher Consciousness: Heal and Transform Yourself and Our World with Ancient Shamanic and Modern Methods, winner of the Independent Publishers Award (Moon Books, 2011)

Shamanic Reiki: Expanded Universal Ways of Working with Universal Life Force Energy, cowritten with Robert Levy (Moon Books, 2007)

The Good Remembering: A Message for Our Times (John Hunt Publishing, 2007)

Audio Program

Pathways to Inner Peace, with Robert Y. Southward (Creston Press, 2006)

SUSAN COHEN THOMPSON

Illustrator Susan Cohen Thompson has focused on Earth wisdom for three decades. Susan's art appears on shamanic book covers, in "green" art books, and in environmental articles. Her paintings are shown in galleries, nature sanctuaries, and museums. She lives on Camano Island, Washington.

You can view more of Susan's work at her website, **www.thompsonartstudio.com.**

ACKNOWLEDGMENTS

FROM LLYN

I thank Sandra Ingerman for her openness and insights as we wrote *Speaking with Nature*. I have felt such ease and joy in working with Sandra, just as I did in the dream that prompted us to write this book together. I am changed by the experience.

My gratitude to Mick Dodge who shared his homelands with me. Mick gave me the gift of living in the Hoh, a profound time that inspired these writings.

Thanks to all those at Inner Traditions who dedicated themselves to helping make this book a reality.

My deepest appreciation for the inspired musings of shamanic artist Susan Cohen Thompson, who created the beautiful artwork for this book.

My gratitude goes to our agent, Barbara Moulton, whose expertise has allowed me to stay focused on the Hoh nature beings and on my writing.

My thanks to Marilyn Dexter and Patti Chiburis for their unwavering support. I also thank Mira Steinbrecher, Hope Fay, Jeanann Yarosz, Gisela Timmermann, Carol Donohoe, Bob Southard, Bill Pfeiffer, Lance Rosen, Monty and Marlene Davis, Renee Martin-Nagle, and Ryanne Hoogeboom for encouragement.

Thanks to my children, Eben Herrick and Sayre Herrick, who believe in me and inspire me.

Thanks to my mother, Dorothy Roberts, for her love and enthusiasm; and appreciation to my father, Edgar Roberts, for his special relationship with trees and nature.

I appreciate the indigenous elders I have worked with—Siberian, Mayan, Tibetan, and Central and South American, as well as Olympic Peninsula tribes, all of whose wisdom ways enrich this book.

I offer deepest gratitude to the lands, waters, trees, nature beings, nature, and ancestral spirits of the Hoh, a beautiful and powerful force. Thank you—and thanks to the amazing voices that spoke through Sandra's locales—for inspiring us to love ourselves and revere all lands, nature, and spirit beings.

I thank Gabu San for teaching me so much and for sweet canine company during lonely and all times, and the lovely Katie-kitty, now one with the Hoh.

FROM SANDRA

Llyn Roberts was such a delight to work with on *Speaking with Nature,* and I thank her for the depth of her vision in inviting me to join her in creating this beautiful book. It was a joy to write this book with her.

I honor and give gratitude to Susan Cohen Thompson for sharing her brilliant artwork.

Llyn and I both give special thanks to Laura Schlivek for her editing expertise; she was wonderful to work with. We also give thanks to Abigail Lewis for her careful line edit. And we give gratitude to Jon Graham, Jeanie Levitan, and Jessie Wimett for their support of our book. We give thanks to Peri Swan for designing such a beautiful cover. And we give thanks to all of the wonderful staff at Inner Traditions for helping to birth *Speaking with Nature* into the world.

Thanks to our agent, Barbara Moulton, for her continual support and friendship!

I am in deep gratitude to my husband, Woods Shoemaker, for all his continued love, support, and amazing patience as I worked long hours on this creative project. I give thanks to Jai Cross, Ann Drucker, and Mary McCormick, with whom I consulted on some of the nature beings in my writings.

I give thanks to my helping spirits for their continual love and guidance on how to live a life filled with joy and meaning and how to help others do the same. I also give thanks to the spirits of earth, air, water, and fire, who teach me how to live a life filled with honor, respect, harmony, and balance. I am in deep gratitude to the Spirit of Santa Fe, the helping ancestors of the land, the Hidden Folk, all the nature beings, and the spirits of the artesian spring, marsh, and arroyo where I live.

I give thanks and honor to my parents, Aaron and Lee Ingerman. I could certainly feel my mom's presence while I was writing this book. I honor my ancestors, and I give thanks for my life.